T0401236

Arctic state identity

Manchester University Press

Arctic state identity

Geography, history, and geopolitical relations

Ingrid A. Medby

Manchester University Press

The right of Ingrid A. Medby to be identified as the
author of this work has been asserted in accordance
with the Copyright, Designs and Patents Act 1988.

Published by Manchester University Press
Oxford Road, Manchester, M13 9PL

www.manchesteruniversitypress.co.uk

British Library Cataloguing-in-Publication Data
A catalogue record for this book is available from
the British Library

ISBN 978 1 5261 5390 6 hardback

First published 2025

The publisher has no responsibility for the
persistence or accuracy of URLs for any external or
third-party internet websites referred to in this book,
and does not guarantee that any content on such
websites is, or will remain, accurate or appropriate.

Typeset
by Cheshire Typesetting Ltd, Cuddington, Cheshire

Contents

Figures

List of figures

Foreword

On the evening of 23 February 2022, as Russian troops were entering Ukraine, the United Nations Security Council was in the midst of a special session that was attempting (unsuccessfully) to prevent that very invasion. With the war unfolding in real time, ambassadors' phones began buzzing with the news. The staid and constrained diplomacy of the United Nations was put on hold as tempers flared.

Recalling the situation for a BBC News documentary two years later, Ukraine's Ambassador, Sergiy Kyslytsya, noted that his Russian counterpart, Vassily Nebenzia, was 'clearly lost' when news of the invasion broke. Indeed, Nebenzia confirmed to the BBC that he had no advance notice that the invasion was to occur that evening.

Forty-eight minutes after news of the invasion broke, when Ukraine was scheduled to address the special session, Kyslytsya put aside his prepared statement, noting that his plan to call for de-escalation was no longer relevant. Instead, he waved his phone at Nebenzia: 'You have a smartphone; you can call [Russian Foreign Minister Sergei] Lavrov right now. We can make a pause to let you go out and call him.'

After a bit of testy interchange between the two, Nebenzia responded: 'I must say that I thank the representative of Ukraine for his statement and questions. I wasn't planning to answer them, because I've already said all I know at this point. Waking up Minister Lavrov at this time is not something I plan to do. He said the information that we have will be something we provide.' Later on, Nebenzia reflected on the exchange: 'He was telling me to call

Lavrov, but I wondered: "Who is he to give me instructions? I have my own bosses".'

The meeting concluded with a final exchange between the two. 'Call Putin,' Kyslytsya prodded. 'Call Lavrov to stop [the] aggression ... There is no purgatory for war criminals. They go straight to hell, Ambassador.' Nebnezia responded by noting: 'I wanted to say in conclusion that we aren't being aggressive against the Ukrainian people, but against the junta that is in power in Kyiv.'[1]

Although the conflict between Russia and Ukraine is taking place far from the Arctic region, the diplomatic exchange between Ambassadors Kyslytsya and Nebenzia exemplifies many of the themes about state identity that Ingrid Medby develops in this book.

At a surface level, the exchange at the Security Council was a dialogue between states, articulated by these states' designated representatives. However, a close reading of the dialogue reveals a much richer set of dynamics regarding state identity, and of those who constituted their respective states. The veneer of diplomacy was shattered by the palpable animosity between the two men. At one point in the BBC documentary, Kyslytsya reflects, 'I was thinking about all the statements, all the pathetic statements [Nebenzia] made in the weeks before the invasion. And then you find yourself right in front of him and the invasion is ongoing.' At the meeting itself, the two had an almost childish squabble over procedure. After Kyslytsya rhetorically asked Nebenzia whether he should play the video of Putin's speech on his phone, Nebenzia began to respond. However, Kyslytsya interjected, 'Do not interrupt me please. Thank you.' Nebenzia shot back with: 'Then don't ask me questions when you are speaking. Proceed with your statement.' Both men were attempting to align one portion of their identities – as professional ambassadors bound by the decorum of a high-level forum like the United Nations Security Council – with their identities as aggrieved individuals who were feeling personally insulted by their counterpart and by the government that their counterpart represented.

But the identities of Kyslytsya and Nebenzia had further dimensions. Not only were they individuals and state representatives; they also were individuals within bureaucratic institutions. Nebenzia, in particular, reflected on his position as just one person within a vast Russian state hierarchy: he had his boss, Lavrov, from whom he took orders. There was clearly an uneven power relationship between the two: Lavrov had kept Nebenzia in the dark about the planned invasion, and Nebenzia dared not wake up Lavrov in the midst of the Security Council meeting. Even if this was just an excuse for not escalating the matter to the Foreign Minister (was Lavrov really sleeping through the first night of the invasion?), it was a rhetorical move that reaffirmed the ambassadors' shared identity as subordinate employees with busy superiors who did not always appreciate off-hours communications from their representatives in the field.

The connections between the two states, and their ambassadors, went deeper still as, they also had a shared, post-Soviet identity. To this day, Russia points to the two states' linked history and a common identity as justification for the invasion. As citizens of their respective states, this shared identity presumably filtered down to the two ambassadors, not just in their cultures but in their personal histories and professional trajectories. Born in 1962 and 1969 respectively, Nebenzia and Kyslytsya likely had both undertaken some of their higher education in Soviet institutions, preparing for careers in the Soviet foreign service. One cannot help wonder if the sharp words that they directed at each other that evening in 2022 reflected not just their current differences but also the shared histories (at so many levels) against which the two ambassadors were now identifying their differences.

And finally, Nebenzia attempted to unravel the components of state identity by pointing to the differentiation between the Ukrainian nation ('the Ukrainian people') and the Ukrainian state ('the junta that is in power in Kyiv'). Although this distinction between nation and state is crucial to state theory, it, like the distinction between the state and the individuals who constitute the government, rests on invisible borders. The identity of the nation, its citizens, the government's personnel, and its place in broader regional constellations influence each other while drawing on real and imagined histories, geographies, and futures. The *state identity* that results – the subject of this book – is dynamic, relational, contested, entangled, and forever provisional, even as it is referenced to justify state policies as well as the actions of officials who implement those policies.

In short, the state is much more than the entity represented by the nameplate or flag in front of an ambassador at the Security Council or, for that matter, at the Arctic Council. It is a constellation of people and histories, and these persist within further stories about shared community, common experiences, and linked futures. The Arctic, where Ingrid Medby takes us in this book, is not unique in this respect. However, as a relatively 'new' region (at least from the perspective of southerners who have recently been drawn to circumpolar connections and differences and states that have recently been drawn to their Arctic frontiers), it is one where identities are continually being reasserted and, in the process, renegotiated and remade. By shedding light on the ways in which Arctic state identities are articulated and operationalised, Medby does much more than explain the politics of the Arctic. She also brings some clarity to our understanding of the state, an institution that, as Philip Abrams notes, is notoriously 'difficult' to study.

Philip Steinberg
Durham (UK), 2024

Note

1 For a transcript of the exchange at the United Nations Security Council on 23 February 2022 see the website of National Public Radio (Alex Leff, 'Read the impassioned plea from Ukraine's U.N. ambassador to Russia to stop the war', https://www.npr.org/2022/02/24/1082806285/ ukraine-ambassador-russia-security-council, 24 February 2022). A promotional trailer for the BBC documentary 'Putin vs the West: At War' can be viewed on the website of BBC News ('Watch: Diplomats recall moment war broke out at peace council', https://www.bbc.co.uk/news/ av/world-68113443, 29 January 2024).

Preface

What does it mean to be from the Arctic; what does it mean to be an Arctic state? How do you feel about this title, if anything at all, and what does it mean?

Personally, I 'became' Arctic only when I left the region. Growing up in North Norway, I identified as northern – both among fellow nationals and internationally – but can't remember thinking much about the Arctic at all. Trying to think back, I don't think I would have associated the noun with much else than the North Pole and the adjective with polar bears and the icebergs I'd seen on TV. I don't think I was unusual in that way – the Arctic did not feel *present* in my day-to-day life then. It took me moving almost as geographically far away as I could, to the southern hemisphere, to realise that others saw my small hometown as 'Arctic'. When no one had heard of Tromsø, Bodø, or Kirkenes, it was easier to say, 'just above the Arctic Circle'.

Fast forward some decades and the Arctic is, I would argue, very much *there* also in the north. It is a term that people are more familiar with, even one that some may identify with. The term is now present as labels for events, organisations, and even everyday objects such as bottled water. And of course, the Arctic is now also frequently talked about as a region where climate change, economic opportunities, and geopolitical competition are 'heating up' a previously frozen part of the world … Looking back home from overseas, I have therefore become increasingly interested in how the Arctic is felt and identified with (or not).

This book is not about my own or other northerners' sense of identity, however, nor is it about Arctic geopolitics as it is usually framed: a competition between abstract powers responding to economic and climatic forces from elsewhere. Instead, it is about countries – or more accurately states – and how they are given an identity as Arctic states, a title with roots in circumpolar geopolitics and Arctic Council membership. But I don't believe in states 'doing' anything as actors in and of themselves; states are a constellation of peoples, institutions, and territories, and their actions performed by a number of state personnel. This book therefore turns to these personnel to ask them about their views on state identity, and here specifically Arctic state identity.

Writing this book, I am hoping to bring the stories and insights that were shared with me during my research to a wider readership. As the book betrays, I'm hoping this will be useful both to those interested in the Arctic and to those interested in statecraft and identity more generally. For this reason, you will find first theoretical and then empirical introductions in the next chapters that you might feel are unnecessary for yourself – in that case I would encourage you to skip forward a few pages to the parts that are more relevant. However, I have chosen to include this extra material in order for all readers of all starting points to potentially engage fully with the generous reflections shared by state personnel from three states. Through listening to the views of the many people of the state, the many diverse voices of those who 'represent' us, I believe that we may learn more about the Arctic, more about the state, and perhaps even more about our own geopolitical realities in the process.

Ingrid Agnete Medby
Newcastle upon Tyne (UK), 2024

Acknowledgements

This book is the result of many years of not only my own work but also the generous, kind, and constructive support of others.

First and foremost, I wish to thank the state personnel who gave me the time to share their views and stories that have eventually led to this book. Although it has taken me far longer than I had thought, I hope that seeing these presented together in print will do justice to this generosity.

I also want to thank the fantastic scholars who supported this research from the start: Philip Steinberg, Angharad Closs Stephens, and Andrew Baldwin; and later in moving it forward, Fiona McConnell and Joe Painter.

I have been lucky to be surrounded by brilliant friends, peers, mentors, and colleagues over the years, some of whom have read versions of this work along the way. Thank you to Sarah Hughes, Peter Forman, Johanne Bruun, Alice Cree, Olivia Mason, Mark Griffiths, Matt Benwell, Doerthe Rosenow, Tom Chambers, Rico Isaacs, John H. Morris, Jason Dittmer, Klaus Dodds, and many others.

I am grateful to the anonymous reviewers of the proposal and manuscript, who provided encouraging and helpful feedback that has made the final book a much better one. And to the editorial team at Manchester University Press, who have been supportive and, importantly, patient through the process. Admittedly, I did not follow all of the reviewers' suggestions, so please note that all errors and potentially poor structural choices are wholly my own.

Acknowledgements

Finally, a personal *tusen takk* to my parents who let me move away from the Arctic to realise that's where my passion lies, to Lagatha for the many ball-chasing breaks from writing, and of course to Phil for the patience, support, and love.

Abbreviations

AMAP	Arctic Monitoring and Assessment Programme (WG)
CAFF	Conservation of Arctic Flora and Fauna (WG)
C.i–xxi	Canadian interviewee 1–21
C.AAND	Canadian Aboriginal Affairs and Northern Development
C. DIAND	Canadian Department of Indian Affairs and Northern Development [at the time of the interviews, C.AAND; since 2015, C.INAC]
C.FATD	Canadian Foreign Affairs, Trade and Development [since 2015, Global Affairs Canada]
C.INAC	Canadian Indigenous and Northern Affairs [previously C.AAND and C.DIAND]
EU	European Union
I.i–xii	Icelandic interviewee 1–12
I.MFA	Icelandic Ministry of Foreign Affairs
NATO	North Atlantic Treaty Organisation
N.MFA	Norwegian Ministry of Foreign Affairs
N.MTIF	Norwegian Ministry of Trade, Industry, and Fisheries
N.i–xvi	Norwegian interviewee 1–16
PAME	Protection of the Arctic Marine Environment (WG)
RAIPON	Russian Association of Indigenous Peoples of the North
UNCLOS	United Nations Convention on the Law of the Sea
USSR	Union of Soviet Socialist Republics [Soviet Union]
WG	Working Group (of the Arctic Council)

Introduction: a conceptual framework of state identities

There are only Arctic states and non-Arctic states. No third category exists. And claiming otherwise entitles China to exactly nothing. (Pompeo, 2019)

It was May 2019, and Finland's two-year chairmanship of the Arctic Council had come to an end, transferring to Iceland by the end of the ministerial meeting in the Arctic town of Rovaniemi. On the stage was Mike Pompeo, the US secretary of state for the Trump administration. His speech 'stunned' the audience with what was referred to as a 'tongue-lashing' of other states' activities in the Arctic (Quinn, 2019). The speech made international news, as Pompeo criticised China's geographical description of itself as a 'Near-Arctic State' in its 2018 Arctic Policy (Chinese Government, 2018). In so doing, he inadvertently seemed to affirm that it is only the eight so-called Arctic states – the United States of America,[1] Canada, the Russian Federation, Norway, Sweden, Finland, Iceland, and Denmark with Greenland – that are 'entitled' in the region, and that no suggestion of relative proximity or interest may challenge that (see Figure 0.1).

Five years later, no other state had dared suggest it is anything but 'non-Arctic'.[2] And no one has challenged the eight Arctic states' title as such: a title that has given these a primary role in Arctic matters. But what has happened in the meantime can perhaps be described as fracturing within the circumpolar region, as one of the Arctic states, Russia, invaded its neighbour Ukraine. Its military posturing and oceanic claims in the Arctic are increasing as well, to the concern of other Arctic states (see Reuters, 2023) – which in turn has brought the remaining seven closer together, not least through

Figure 0.1 The Arctic states and the Arctic Circle

NATO. Following the full-scale invasion, ministerial meetings of the Arctic Council have been put on hold, and most of its activities have been affected. In short, the Arctic region is deeply affected by geopolitical events elsewhere, and experts have questioned what the future of Arctic governance will look like. And yet, all eight Arctic states continue to express their commitment to the Arctic Council – for what would the alternative be? – which gives them the exclusive title as its only members.

It is of course not only the geopolitical tensions of recent years that have led to increasing attention to the Arctic, but also record-low sea-ice, potential natural resource extraction, starving polar bears, and dramatic climate change statistics to mention but a few examples. And with ever more media headlines about *them* – about northern peoples and governments – local attention has also been directed to their particular geographical denomination, gradually transforming the 'North' to the 'Arctic'. However, the formalised title of Arctic states is of far more recent nature than it might seem: It was actually not until the post-Cold War 1990s that a circumpolar Arctic, made up of the above eight states, really became an indisput-able political region of the significance it has today. And enshrined in the 'Declaration on the Establishment of the Arctic Council' (1996), these states became the Arctic states, all of which have territories north of the Arctic Circle (approximately 66° 33′ N).

In this way, an 'Arctic' title came to hold particular weight from the end of the last millennium, only to increase further in the decades to follow. And as the world expresses a growing interest in the Arctic region, so too have its inhabitants taken note of this attention. What might have historically been considered national peripheries – sparsely populated areas at the edges of countries' territories – have suddenly become central to both political and popular discussion. And there, from a new image reflecting back from screens and a new name from speakers, the Arctic gradually becomes more than an externally imposed label, more than just a marketable brand: it is received, interpreted, and – as is the focus of this book – adopted, adapted, and identified with. For the countries just mentioned, this has meant that their northernness gives them exclusive circumpolar membership, Arctic statehood, and a global position with rights and responsibilities. But a formal title is one thing, geopolitical practice and feelings of attachment are another. This book therefore asks what an 'Arctic state identity' might be. Specifically, it asks those tasked with representing formally titled Arctic states – namely, state personnel – what meanings they ascribe to Arctic identity and statehood; and, if anything at all, how this may influence the professional practice of statecraft and geopolitics. It does so in the context of the above changes that are already under way in the region – not just the most recent geopolitical changes, but also environmental, cultural, and economic changes that have made the Arctic a region of global importance. Who has a voice and who does not, how power and authority are legitimised and communicated, are all tied to these questions of state identity.

This book deliberately takes three of the Arctic states as its focus – Norway, Iceland, and Canada – due to their political leaders' rhetoric of Arctic identities, yet different relations with the region. As will become clear throughout the book, the three states' commonalities may also be what sets them apart, depending on context and interest. In global terms, they are all relatively small-medium countries (although comparatively the range is wide) with population numbers of approximately 5.5 million, 382,000, and 38.9 million in Norway, Iceland, and Canada, respectively (World Bank Open Data, 2022). Territorially, however, this description fits less well, with surface areas covering 624,500 sq km, 103,000 sq km, and 15,634,410 sq km, respectively (World Bank Open Data, 2021). They are all closely tied to the oceans, as coasts, islands, and archipelagos characterise their geographies. Yet, the nature of these related features ranges from permafrost to the more temperate and urban. And while their political leaders have all talked about Arctic identities, histories, and characteristics, the way in which these are articulated are far from the same. In one setting, a state's role may be that of steward, leader, focus of affective attachment, or voice of neoliberal reasoning; and a historical narrative may shift from that of pioneers and explorers to colonial settlers and Indigenous peoples. These parallel stories can be heard in and from all of the Arctic states, but the ways and contexts in which they do so differ in significant ways.

These are some of the themes that will be explored in the rest of the book, but suffice it here to say that: yes, we can talk of 'Arctic state identities', but no, these cannot be singularised or generalised. There is no essence or clear-cut definition of 'Arcticness' that any study or book can reveal for all to see. Instead, there are innumerable, contextual articulations of what it might mean to be in, from, and of a region with fluid boundaries. However indeterminate as this may sound, this irreducibility is important in and of itself. It shows us that the region is not 'defined', and therefore bounded, once and for all. Who, what, where, when, and how the Arctic *becomes* is something that happens through relations that are both social and political. And with that follows a profound question of responsibility and ethics: how, why, when, and by whom an Arctic identity is claimed, and to what effect, is part of shaping the region's future. It is this insight that has guided my studies of the topic over the years, and which now guides the present book.

In what follows, the book's conceptual starting points are introduced, and in particular the main concept of 'state identity'. This includes a brief review of the literatures that I draw on, with the aim of allowing readers from varied backgrounds to engage more fully with the remaining book. These include literatures on discourses, the state, and national identities in particular. This is followed by an elaboration on the research that it is based on – though more on the empirical context, namely Arctic geopolitics, is offered in Chapter 1. In closing, the chapter provides an overview of the book's structure, which mirrors the conceptual framework that is presented here.

Discourses and a critical account of geopolitics

The starting points for the book, and concept of state identity, can be found in political geography, but from there it extends outwards towards other disciplines and scholarly traditions that also seek to critically understand our present moment in time. As alluded to above, the guiding insight is that identity, both how it is viewed and how it is represented really *matters*. It matters because it is an idea that can structure people's experiences of themselves, their communities, and the actions available to them. And the focus here is on states and statecraft, and how identity plays part of this, which is a focus that can be found across political and social sciences. My approach to these questions is also based on this broader foundation in critical scholarship, starting with an understanding of state identities as 'discourses'.

As it is a concept we will encounter throughout the book, let me spend a few paragraphs here at the start to clarify how the concept of 'discourses' are used. Despite not being easily defined, Campbell (2009: 166) describes discourses as 'specific series of representations and practices through which meanings are produced, identities constituted, social relations established, and political and ethical outcomes made more or less possible'. And although precise definitions differ, they tend to be rooted in philosophical debates about representations and their relationship to 'reality', generally agreeing that the former plays an active part in producing the latter (Howarth, 2000; Campbell, 2009). So, if we think of state identities as discourses, that means that we acknowledge their power to influence how we come to see the world – and, thereby, they shape how relations and politics play out. In other words, discourses of state identity are ideas, tales, and behaviours that have a real effect in the world and how we come to understand it – and ourselves.

The way discourses are used here draws in particular on the early work of Michel Foucault (1972, 1981), who describes a discourse as 'a group of statements in so far as they belong to the same discursive formation; [...] it is made up of a limited number of statements for which a group of conditions of existence can be defined' (1972: 117). A statement refers to an expression or representation – here including both linguistic and non-linguistic articulations and practices – within a 'formation' such as that of (Arctic) geopolitics (see e.g. Schiffrin et al., 2003; Potter and Wetherell, 1994). What are here of particular interest are these 'conditions' that serve to govern what *can* be expressed, i.e. 'the rules that determine which statements are accepted as meaningful and true in a particular historical epoch' (Jørgensen and Phillips, 2002: 12). In other words, discourses of state identity delimit what can and cannot be said and done. The implication is that through discourse, 'reality', a certain view of the world, is naturalised at the expense of other ways of seeing. And, as in the case of Arctic relations, they may then foreclose alternative ways of being and seeing the world.

Here it is also worth noting that practices and statements are understood in the broadest sense, recognising the 'performative' nature of discourses – another term we will encounter again in later chapters. This means that through naming, enactment, and so on, discourses produce what they 'speak' of (Butler, 1999, 2011; also Bialasiewicz et al., 2007; Campbell, 1992). In this particular context, that means that the Arctic state and its identity do not actually exist in and of themselves, but that it comes about through these actions. These practices and statements, the Arctic state's performance, are therefore products but also 'citations' of discourses: iteratively, by invoking statements past and future, each works to reify and stabilise it as 'truth'. This does not mean that there is no reality outside of discourse, or that all is representation, but rather that it should call attention to our own position as always within discourses – and, with that, the impossibility of a so-called objective view.

Also just to be clear, 'performance' is meant not in a theatrical sense as deliberate acts for an audience but rather as the actions and practices that produce the actor, the subject itself (see Gregson and Rose, 2000). Rephrased in this context, the numerous ways that discourses of Arctic state identity are performed are that which *constitutes* the Arctic state and its many state 'performers', in this case state personnel. These discourses are neither externally imposed on individuals nor internally dictating their thought, but they condition what can be meaningfully thought (or enacted, expressed, and so on) (Foucault, 1972: 209). And this means that power does not lie in any deliberate construction of discourse(s) – i.e. there is no 'mastermind' plotting what an Arctic state identity should be – but rather lies in the specific ways in which enactments are done and statements made in each specific context. Also worth noting here, each subject will always inhabit numerous discourses and relations at once – a person is always more than 'just' Arctic – which means that there is always a potential for change too (Gregson and Rose, 2000). Again, there is not just one way of being, even if we do recognise that there are guidelines along which we act. It is this interplay of ideas and materiality, and the relationship between and across discourses, that is of particular interest (Foucault, 1972: 209; see also O'Farrell, 2005: 81). As the book will go on to do, critically questioning discourses means questioning the foundational premises of what has come to be seen as 'natural' or 'true' – not only what an Arctic state identity may *be* but how and why it *becomes* so.

Although more will be said about specifically Arctic geopolitics in the following chapter, It is worth noting here that a discursive approach to 'spatialised' political relations places the book among political geography and related critical geopolitics scholarship (see e.g. Murphy et al., 2004; Sparke, 2009). As critical geography more broadly, these subfields seek to expose some of the assumptions underlying seemingly common-sense categories of political-spatial analysis, such as here 'the state' (see Campbell, 2009; Agnew, 2013; Atkinson and Dodds, 2000; Dalby and Ó Tuathail, 1998; Agnew and Muscarà, 2012). In this way, attention is directed to how political geographies, such as territories and borders, are produced through discourses, and how they tend to favour the worldviews and knowledge of those in power. By asking how geopolitical narratives become normalised, or how discursive practice spatialises politics (Ó Tuathail, 1996; Ó Tuathail and Agnew, 1992), critical geopolitics has provided a disciplinary bridge to international relations. That is, while 'classical' geopolitics was concerned with 'power over geography', this more critical aim is in contrast to interrogate 'geographies of power' (Knecht and Keil, 2013: 186). And it is also for this reason that the book's subtitle refers to geopolitical relations, highlighting that those we will go on to explore in Part II of the book are all part of Arctic geopolitics, even those that some might think of as 'personal'. In this way, this book too is driven by a critical and emancipatory ideal of disrupting dominant and prescriptive ways of seeing the world to ask how it may be otherwise.

Even more specifically, the book is situated in critical *polar* geopolitics: a field that has emerged in recent decades with the 're-politicisation' of the region, largely as a result of climate change (e.g. Powell and Dodds, 2014; Bruun and Medby, 2014; Steinberg et al., 2015; Dittmer et al., 2011). In particular, the subfield examines how states come to hold the privilege as the key Arctic 'players', how the Arctic has come to be seen as a region of states, and how alternative modes of politics, governance, and *being* become discursively foreclosed.[3] Questioning how and why Arctic space comes to be seen the way that it does today therefore matters: In short, 'the way actors re-imagine Arctic territory [...] shapes their foreign policy behaviour and responsiveness to new risks and opportunities' (Knecht and Keil, 2013: 186).

However, more than this, the implications reach beyond the Arctic and beyond the state. Critically *destabilising* that which through discursive practices seems to have taken on solidity (Butler, 2011) allows a glimpse into the production rather than product, its material*isation* and spatial*isation*, Arctic or not, and a glimpse of our own continuous process of becoming: political subject and 'self' in and through discourses.

The state and statehood

This book focuses on Arctic states and their personnel. Yet, we know that the state, both as institution and as ideal, is undergoing change, leading some to consider it less relevant in a time of globalisation and neoliberalisation (see e.g. Brenner, 2004; Brenner et al., 2003). However, states do still remain the primary political unit, bearing tangible and material consequences for billions of lives around the world – as news headlines of diplomatic disputes, migration movements, and trade agreements all remind us. This also means that the state persists as a key category of political analysis, motivating research to understand how and why it remains so – in this case, the how and why of 'Arctic statehood'.

Attempting to define our focus, 'the state', is less straightforward than it may seem, though. A common place to start (if, for no other reason than to critique it) is Max Weber's assertion that a state is 'a human community that (successfully) claims the monopoly of the legitimate use of force within a given territory' (1946: 46). However, the state – and scholarly conceptualisations of it – is continually changing, and so the definition first presented by Weber in 1918, with its emphasis on 'force', is potentially less useful today. Accepting that states are both spatially and temporally contingent, Michael Mann (1984, 1993) expands on Weber's definition by suggesting four characteristics in common among states: a set of institutions and personnel; some political centrality; boundaries that define the territorial limits of it; and a monopoly of coercive power and law-making ability. Again though, as pointed out by Joe Painter (2006), these kinds of classical state theories tend to characterise the state in one of three ways: functions, mechanisms, or spatiality – all of which are problematic and disputable. In practice, there are no functions that belong exclusively to the state, no mechanisms that cannot be questioned (such as their 'monopoly' or legitimacy), and no bordered territory that is either fixed or incontestable (Painter, 2006: 756–757). Additionally, each of these characteristics will inevitably vary both inter- and intra-state. And yet, despite the many reasons for scepticism of seemingly clear-cut definitions, such ideas about what the state 'is' persist with a high level of both social and political potency. So again, understanding how and why this is so – not least in a rapidly changing Arctic context – is the point of departure in what follows.

Trying to define any elusive 'core' of the state, it becomes clear that it may actually be the numerous *layers* of interacting individuals, institutions, ideologies, imaginaries that defines it, makes it, and invests it with power (see e.g. Pierson, 2011: 2). However, the key point here is that we tend to think that it holds importance, which then *gives* it importance and gives this 'abstraction' materiality through the practices attributed to it. Following Philip Abrams (1988), it is therefore the *idea* of the state as an ideological power that should be the object of analysis. Here there is a distinction to be made between the system of institutional practice, the 'state system', and the reification of this system, 'the state-idea'. In Abrams's words:

> The state is not the reality which stands behind the mask of political practice. It is itself the mask which prevents our seeing political practice as it is [...] The state comes into being as a structuration within political practice; it starts its life as an implicit construct; it is then reified – as the *res publica*, the public reification, no less – and acquires an overt symbolic identity progressively divorced from practice as an illusory account of practice. (1988: 82)

In a related vein, Timothy Mitchell (1991: 94) adds that the state should be studied as 'the powerful, metaphysical effect of practices that make such structures appear to exist'. As such, he differentiates himself from Abrams by arguing that seeing the state as an 'ideological construct' obfuscates its very 'real' and very material 'structural effects', including institutions such as bureaucracies, schools, armies; and moreover, seeming to provide an external framework for the social world (Mitchell, 1991).

Building on the above, Painter (2006: 758) provides us with the following useful definition of the state: 'an imagined collective actor in whose name individuals are interpellated (implicitly or explicitly) as citizens or subjects, aliens or foreigners, and which is imagined as the source of central political authority for a national territory'. He discusses how everyday life becomes 'statized' in prosaic ways, concluding that, though '[t]he state is not a structurally coherent object or even a rational abstraction', it is *actualised* through 'countless mundane social and material practices within and outside the institutions conventionally referred to as the state apparatus' (Painter, 2006: 771). Among these countless practices that actively make, unmake, and remake statehood[4] are those of the personnel tasked with its everyday running, as they in their work within the institution contribute to its 'actualisation'. That is not to say that theirs are the only practices that bring the state into being, but is rather a recognition that, if state and society are *not* to be seen as totally separate 'spheres', *not* to be understood in binary terms, then the ways that state personnel come to be named as such influences how the state comes to be performed. And following this, recalling the performativity of discourses, the way in which Arctic statehood comes into being is in the end an effect of the numerous performances of it, the numerous times it is invoked through practice (Dunn, 2010; Weber, 1998). And so, the question of 'how' it is performed is also a 'why' it is performed in this manner. Or, in other words, what is really at stake when examining how state personnel perceive discourses of Arctic state identity is the delimitation of what it means to 'be' and 'represent' an Arctic state, and how this in turn conditions what it possibly *can* be.

State personnel

If we think of the Arctic state as an outcome of the many practices enacted in its name, focus shifts towards the many actors performing it as such. That is, the political practices that produce the Arctic state as 'real' are those of numerous people: politicians, bureaucrats, civil servants, diplomats, advisers, and so on – all of whom may (or may not) also imagine themselves as part of a national community. Of course, a formal, political title of Arctic statehood may not necessarily mean a felt sense of Arctic nationhood (see Medby, 2014). However, the point here is that notions of identity may matter not just to an electorate but also to the elected, not just the 'represented' but also the representative. Far too often, references to 'people' are made solely to a population defined in seeming opposition to a state or government. In other words, 'people' comes to be seen as a near-apolitical (or even populist) mass, who never really interact with what seems a mechanistic state – except through pencils on ballot papers once every four years or so. Even when the role of state personnel *is* acknowledged in political commentaries, they are often cast as separate and autonomous from society, as a demarcated, near-homogeneous group with specific interests based on their sole characteristic as 'elites', such as upholding a specific class system.

Given the impossibility of any clear-cut definition of the state, attempting to draw a line between where 'it' ends and so-called 'society' begins may be both arbitrary (see Jones, 2012) and potentially part of reinforcing a problematic state idea (see e.g. Agnew and Corbridge, 1995) – one based on discursive binaries of state/society, politics/people, which may potentially generate deference, disengagement, and even disenchantment. Some scholarly analysts have therefore made a concerted effort to move away from an excessive preoccupation with 'the top echelons of the state apparatus', and give attention to all the important political practices that happen outside these imaginary boundaries (Dodds et al., 2013: 7). And to be sure, 'power in its exercise goes much further, passes through much finer channels, and is much more ambiguous' (Foucault, 1980: 72) than only the obviously state-led politics. However, acknowledging the importance of those beyond the 'apparatus' should not mean dismissing the state altogether. Following Mitchell (2006: 170), 'we must take seriously the elusiveness of the boundary between state and society, not as a problem of conceptual precision but as a clue to the nature of the phenomenon'. In other words, it is not a matter of moving across the discursive borderline – analysing *either* the state or society – but, rather, there is a need to examine the line itself: how and why it has become so, persists as such, and what it *does*. Merely shifting the analytical balance to privilege non-state actors risks reifying the very same binaries. Instead, for a fuller understanding of the state and its practices, a reconceptualisation of social entanglement is arguably needed: one that recognises the multitudes of relations in which all subjects find themselves (and *define* themselves and gain their subjectivities), which all bear influence on the way in which the state comes to be seen, felt, and also enacted.

Acknowledging that state practices are inherently social, relational, enacted by practitioners means that there is a need for 'peopling' conceptualisations of the state (Jones, 2007; Kuus, 2008). Indeed this is one of the contributions that I hope that this book will make to wider scholarship: bringing people back into analyses of geopolitics. While defining state personnel is far from straightforward, using a working definition of those identifying as professionals at the state or federal level is one step away from an unhelpful categorisation of 'elites' seemingly above or beyond society (see e.g. Woods, 1998; Smith, 2006). And although at least political geographers tend to accept states and territories as produced rather than pre-given (though the finer details of how and why remain debated), limited attention has been given to its most obvious 'producers' (with the exception of studies of particularly high-profile leaders). Hopefully this may be changing as 'state insides' are increasingly recognised as diverse and influential in its external enactment – including the myriad of bureaucrats, civil servants, and politicians who will *not* have their names written in history books (e.g. Herzfeld, 1992; Kuus, 2008, 2013, 2014, 2015; Le Grand, 2003; Peck, 2001).

Influential in arguing for a 'peopling' of the state, Rhys Jones (2007: 4) directs attention to 'a state apparatus and territory that is continually negotiated and translated by those individuals working within its organizations and boundaries'. He notes three interrelated themes for such a 'peopled' understanding of the state: firstly, the importance of the identities of state personnel; secondly, the relationship between these and organisational aspects of the state apparatus; and, thirdly, the link between the state as a peopled organisation and its territorial form (Jones, 2007: 15). Key here is their *interrelatedness* in that people, organisation, and space all co-constitute each other in mutually reinforcing ways. In this sense, the composite idea of the Arctic 'nation-state' may matter not only for its instrumentalism in reifying the 'state system' but also for providing state personnel with meaning and purpose as they go about their work. On the one hand, the mundane and prosaic ways in which the state comes to be *felt* may affect them too as they go about their everyday life (see e.g. Jones and Merriman, 2009); while, on the other, a professional position may also influence their understanding of own identity (Neumann, 2005, 2007; Dittmer and McConnell, 2015). Either way, as 'representatives', the question of state personnel's conceptualisations of own state – what and whom they are representing – is undoubtedly important to the ways in which it comes to be actualised. To appreciate the state as performed through a range of practices, to appreciate that state power flows through relations at all scales, it is also necessary to appreciate its performers, practitioners, and how they relate to themselves, their state, and their 'others' – how they see the state's identity.

National communities and identities

Although frequently conflated, state and nation are not synonyms – which indeed is why we arguably need a concept of 'state identity' at all, given the extensive literature on national identities. However, while we should not confuse the two, they are also closely related and even constitutive of each other. Recalling Weber's formulation above, the people – the state's 'human community' – was his first component. And ever since the 1648 Treaty of Westphalia, the 'nation' has been an integral component to statehood. In fact, it is so fundamental that the two – state and nation – *are* frequently merged and hyphenated as 'nation-states', a linguistic symptom of an idea of political consequence (Sparke, 2005: xii; see also Antonsich, 2009). For this reason, it is worth spending some words here to clarify what is meant by nations and national identities – paradoxically both as intrinsic to and distinct from state identities.

To borrow Benedict Anderson's famous proposition, a nation may be defined as 'an imagined political community'. He explains that it is 'imagined' not because it is 'false' but 'because the members of even the smallest nation will never know most of their fellow-members, meet them, or even hear of them, yet in the minds of each lives the image of their communion' (Anderson, 1983: 5). Through their imagining, and through the acts that may follow such deep-felt 'communion', nations serve as 'key elements in the creating and sustaining of a world of states' (Storey, 2001: 50); the two become seemingly inextricably linked, instrumentalised, in an ideology of 'nation-states' (see e.g. Barth, 1969; Breuilly, 1996). It is this insight that leads some scholars to see nations as an invention of the sovereign state (see Painter and Jeffrey, 2009: 148–152), a 'tool' in a nationalist quest for congruence between people, territory, and governance (Gellner, 1983; see also Penrose, 2002; Hechter, 2000; Hobsbawm and Ranger, 1983). And no doubt, the sense of community *is* politically powerful, potentially generating strong sentiments linked to national belonging (Guibernau, 2004). However, while scholarly debates have centred on whether states beget nations or vice versa, in practical terms the temporal boundaries of self-identified community and governing institution or territory tend to blur – often, each reinforce the other. There is no denying that several practitioners of statecraft have sought to construct (and homogenise) national 'communities' through the ages; but, equally so, several collectives have actively sought to gain statehood. Hence, emphasis here is less on the question of states for nations *or* nations for states, and more on how they are *both* part of the discursive reinforcement of the other. In other words, what is at stake is how ideas of Arctic nations reinforce that of the state, and how notions of the Arctic state reinforce that of the nation.

Given our conceptual focus on states and identity, it is worth noting, not least in the Arctic context, that not all nations hold national*ist* aspirations. That is, not all self-identifying peoples seek sovereign statehood with the governing institutions and bordered territories that this involves. In fact, within the boundaries of any one state there are in most, if not *all*, cases more than one nation. In the Arctic region this is relevant not least for Indigenous peoples[5] who may identify within, across, and wholly separate from state borders. However, it is Arctic *statehood* that has become synonymous with membership in the Arctic Council: 'an organisation sui generis in that the body is not purely intergovernmental, but also authorises a number of non-state [actors], particularly indigenous groups' (Knecht, 2013: 167). As the distinction between 'member' and 'participant' of the Council implies, the state retains the privilege of decision-making through voting (Graczyk and Koivurova, 2014). The Permanent Participants are to be 'consulted', but otherwise the onus is on state representatives to listen and, as their title suggests, *represent* nations. Similarly, non- and sub-state collectives – regions, municipalities, and so on – are all expected to have their views represented by the state, their identifications seemingly ancillary. In other words, a level of diversity is accepted, even expected, within the state, but only in so far as its many heterogeneous elements serve to constitute the whole. Much as the illusion of a 'nation-state' provides an ideological foundation for a world of states, Arctic statehood too is premised on its people, including their diversity. Performing the Arctic state means consulting and representing – paradoxically, the *inclusion* of non-state actors strengthens state claims to legitimacy and authority. This is something we will explore further in later chapters, and especially Chapter 6.

By wedding formal Arctic statehood to cultural Arctic nationhood, territory is wedded to population, and 'an almost transcendental entity, the nation-state' is manufactured (Mitchell, 2006: 180) – the 'Arctic nation-state' – 'appearing as a structure containing and giving order and meaning to people's lives' (Mitchell, 2006: 180). As noted, this ideological construct is politically powerful, and may aid in generating support for what could otherwise be considered controversial. And importantly, *also* 'giving order and meaning' to the lives of state officials: The conviction that you represent not just a space but a people likely alters your approach to a given political question. Although large parts of the Arctic region are uninhabited oceanic spaces, the imaginary scripting of it as inherently part of the 'homeland' opens up and closes down possible actions and policies. Moreover, as noted, it works to position the state – at least in the eyes and minds of its practitioners – within relations of power both with other states and with other spaces, institutions, and people. In other words, these identity discourses naturalise a certain, seemingly stable order. This order in turn implies and conditions conduct. For example, an Arctic state is expected to hold not only rights but also important responsibilities to act when relevant issues arise; which action is deemed the most appropriate one is limited by, *inter alia*, perceptions of 'who' and 'what' said state inherently 'is' and should 'be'. These perceptions are of course highly dynamic and contested, but, nevertheless, the state is often considered to hold certain stable characteristics and values, many of which form the foundations for patriotic pride or identity.

Identity and identities

The focus of this book, 'identity', in the most basic sense refers to individual or unique characteristics, and to 'sameness' across time, selfhood, and 'who you are' (Dubow, 2009). It is a concept that has attracted much scholarly attention and has seen shifting conceptualisations of the human subject. Today, social scientists tend to agree that any individual will always represent a multitude of different social groups and individual characteristics at any given time, making identity both contextual and multifaceted (e.g. Yaeger, 1996). Influential to and contemporary with many poststructuralist thinkers in the twentieth century, psychoanalytic theory has contributed to furthering conceptualisations of identity, recognising it as an inherently social and continuous process: identity more as *identification*, never achieved but always ongoing. And, moreover, if identity is understood as 'our sense of ourselves as individuals and social beings' (Bondi, 1993: 86; see also Fearon, 1999), and our sense of belonging to social groups (Tajfel, 1978: 63), then it follows that identity is also deeply political (see Pile and Thrift, 1995).

Although there may never in reality be a singular and stable way in which 'the self' or identity is defined, what matters more is that there is often a *belief* in such. Its social and political contingencies matter little if the 'essence' of who we are (or believe ourselves to be) is perceived as under threat. More than just a belief or myth, however, we can understand identity as a discourse as discussed above. It comes about through a set of 'acts' (or statements, citations, practices) that all condition the meaningful production of new ones. As such, identity is an iterative process through which the subject gains 'subjectivity' through the innumerable relations in which they are temporarily positioned, namely the performance of identity discourses (Butler, 1999). And rather than what subjects or collectives 'are' in and of themselves, identity is defined by its discursive boundaries. That is, negatively defined not as much as 'being' what it is *not*. The Arctic is always defined by whatever is not, the north always by the existence of a south. But this constitutive outside, negative excess, or 'other' of the self is never wholly external (Connolly, 1991). It is intrinsic to the performance of any identity – and may thereby also be what disrupts, unsettles, and changes the self and changes discourse. In other words, talking about 'Arctic identity' always already implies a non-Arctic identity, and through this co-constitutive relationship change might take place too.

Defining state identity

While much has been written on both (national) identity, on the one hand, and the state, on the other, there have been fewer attempts to bring these into conversation with each other. With the concept of 'state identity', the aim here is to bring together the above concepts of discourses, identity, and statehood in order to understand how identity discourses may feature *within* the so-called state – among those effecting the state abstraction into material being on a daily basis.

A use of the term state identity can be found in certain scholarship of international relations (see e.g. Biersteker and Weber, 1996; Mitzen, 2006; Wendt, 1992, 1999; Steele, 2008; Larsen, 2014; Ashizawa, 2008; Alexandrov, 2003; Biswas, 2002), however, often referring to an identity of an anthromorphised state seemingly with agency in its own right (e.g. Wendt, 2004; however, see Lomas, 2005). And often, the focus remains at the level of how states interact and relate at the scale of the international – often as thinking, speaking, opining actors in and of themselves (see Murray, 2018). And although the construction of a seemingly coherently acting state is often recognised, the level of analysis often remains at that of the 'system of states' and foreign policy behaviour (e.g. Kassianova, 2001; Campbell, 1992). Reviewing a growing body of political scientific work on identity, Fearon (1999) makes a useful distinction between literatures on group and individual identity: the former referring to membership in various groupings of states (e.g. middle powers, Western, NATO, the Arctic Council, etc.) (see also Wendt, 1994); whereas the latter referring to the distinguishing features of a specific state or its 'type'. Adding to this, a state's 'identity can refer also to that package of attributes the possession of which makes something a state and not some other kind of thing' (Fearon, 1999: 34) – in other words the believed essence of statehood. And finally, the seemingly constant properties that make a state remain 'itself' even after a complete turnover of population and staff (Fearon, 1999: 34). Notably, however, studies tend to adopt one of the given perspectives, thereby missing their interrelatedness: how memberships, 'types', statehood, and continuities all intertwine in mutually constitutive ways. And, while the ways in which identity has featured in political analyses are varied, they seldom deal with identities among the individuals 'inside', enacting the state – namely, its broadly defined personnel, as is here the focus.

In the field of political geography and elsewhere, there is growing attention to identity, relationality, and the political power of the affective. Inspired by insights from anthropology, some have contributed to more nuanced views of the production of not only geopolitical knowledge and policy but also subjectivities – seeing politics as 'lived' through the mundane and everyday, and indeed, seeing it as 'peopled' (see e.g. Clark and Jones, 2011; Jones, 2012; Kuus, 2014; Peck, 2001; Woon, 2015). This extends also to methodologies, drawing on ethnographic work that turns attention to the wider realities of human lived experiences that all play into the state and statehood (e.g. Hansen and Stepputat, 2001; Krohn-Hansen and Nustad, 2005; Sharma and Gupta, 2006). Insights from feminist geopolitics have been particularly influential in this regard, as it 'challenges the scales of geopolitics and refocuses on the mundane, everyday reproductions of geopolitical power' (Massaro and Williams, 2013: 567; see Dowler and Sharp, 2001; Hyndman, 2004; Mountz, 2004; Dixon and Marston, 2011). So, both indebted to and building on this work, this book explores how the performance of the state idea – through discourses of state identity – bears traces of the state's people, who, importantly, are always more than personnel, *more* than elites.

It is this irreducibility of identity that the concept of 'state identity' discourses directs attention to. As the concept is used here, it refers to how those *within* the state institution (personnel at the state or federal level) articulate discourses of their state's identity: Articulations that are, importantly, always relational, always excessive to conceptual boundaries of the state, but nevertheless, internal to it through its many articulators. In what follows, the book explores how these articulations (broadly defined) are geographical, temporal, and inherently relational; and, in turn, how the insights gained may contribute to a fuller understanding of Arctic statehood and identity – and, more generally, to understandings of geopolitics.

Studying state identities in the Arctic

Bringing the concept of state identity to Arctic geopolitics, this book focuses on how state personnel from Arctic states – specifically Norway, Iceland, and Canada – come to understand the identity of own state and self as a 'representative' of it. The remainder of the book is based on reviewing key policy documents related to each state's Arctic policies between 2009 and 2024; and, most importantly, interviews with 49 state personnel from Norway, Iceland, and Canada conducted in 2014–15; as well as attendance and participation at numerous Arctic policy-meetings, fora, and conferences between 2014 and 2024. The interviewees cited in the book include 16 Norwegian, 12 Icelandic, and 21 Canadian state personnel, representing 20 different ministries or departments, the Norwegian and Icelandic parliaments (*Stortinget* and *Alþingi*), and the Canadian Senate. They represent a wide range of positions, from advisers to ministers, and include both Indigenous and non-Indigenous people. The interviews were conducted primarily in person in each of the countries' capitals – Oslo, Reykjavík, and Ottawa – and a handful on the phone. Those in Norway, and one in Iceland, were conducted in Norwegian, and all translations are my own; as are those from Norwegian policy documents. The remaining interviews were conducted in English, but note that, for most of the Icelandic and some of the Canadian participants, this was a second language (as it is also for me) or possibly even a third. Each conversation was recorded and subsequently transcribed by myself – and so again, any errors are my own.

As noted above, the related terms state personnel, representatives, officials, employees, etc. are used more-or-less interchangeably throughout the book, as the focus is deliberately not on specific titles or positions. That is of course not to deny that there are significant variations between these – not least in terms of professional autonomy – but the point is rather to explore how discourses of state identity are shared *across* such variations. The aim is to look across the widest range possible of agencies, institutions, ranks, and positions, in order to gain a broad view of how such Arctic state identities are articulated by personnel. So, the primary criterion for inclusion is employment at the state or federal level, irrespective of particular policy responsibilities. And as will be clear in later chapters, even though all spoke as personnel of Arctic states, they nevertheless reflect on views and share stories that are *theirs* under the strict promise of confidentiality. It is also for this reason that you will not find any identifying information about each quote's source – and indeed, the differences in influence and position are also not the point here. Instead, inviting state personnel to reflect and narrate the story they wished to tell, the aim has always been to open up a space for subjective articulations of meaning and sense of identity as 'Arctic'. Articulations, however, are never made in isolation but are the result of co-actors' interaction and the relations between them (including with me, as researcher and author). In the end, and as will become clear, it is the entanglement, overlap, and overspill of innumerable subject-positions and relations that together speak the state into being.

Overview of the book

Following the key terms and concepts so far discussed, the book is structured thematically. In all chapters insights from all three states will be included rather than presented as separate case studies. This decision was made in order to show what are ultimately shared dynamics across specific contexts – perhaps also beyond the three discussed here – while also paying homage to what is unique, singular, and sometimes even personal.

To this end, Chapter 1 introduces the empirical background of the Arctic region, geopolitics, and the three Arctic states Norway, Iceland, and Canada. This is by no means an exhaustive overview but aims to offer non-expert readers an entry-point to a contested region – not a region of geopolitical contest but one of competing geographical imaginaries. How and where the Arctic is defined is wholly context-dependent, which is part of why it is such a fascinating (yet slippery) region to work with. This chapter situates the present study among a rich body of work on Arctic geopolitics past and present, and identifies the particular gap it seeks to fill.

Part I of the book focuses on what I refer to as the structure of Arctic state identities: space, and time. Chapter 2 offers the first axis of these: geographies. That is, it elaborates on state personnel's views of Arctic spatialities: territories, definitions, boundaries, materialities, and climes. This takes us from paper maps, lines, and latitudes, to climates, weather phenomena, and embodied experiences. As will be clear, Arctic space can *simultaneously* be Euclidean co-ordinates and a familiar sitting room where the hockey is watched on TV – what we may think of as contradictions can all play out at once in and through social relations.

The second axis, temporality, is elaborated on in Chapter 3. Temporality in the context of Arctic identity suggests historical narratives, such as tales of explorers, settlers, Indigenous peoples, or Vikings. These narratives are important in all three states, each with its own stories of its Arctic past. Yet, temporality is also about the present: about the present moment of *inter alia* climate change, fossil fuels, election campaigns, and everyday neoliberal restructuring. And, perhaps more than both past and present, Arctic temporality refers to futures, plural and open still. Arctic geopolitics is undeniably about anticipation – about optimism and pessimism of opportunities and threats yet-to-come. The point here is that, even while firmly planted in day-to-day politics, the temporal horizons of Arctic geopolitics always extend outwards. And, in particular for state personnel, it is an explicit duty to look ahead: to plan, prepare, and pre-empt.

With the underlying structure in place, Part II of the book charts the relational articulations of Arctic state identities through political scales. Chapter 4 starts this, centring on the international: how 'being' Arctic is a membership, privilege, and position for a state among states. For all of these relatively small- to medium-sized states, it is clear that Arctic statehood is considered an advantageous status, but how, exactly, this attaches to other understandings of international roles differs across them. Interestingly, all three states' personnel describe a position of Arctic leadership, but in different ways and settings.

Chapter 5 moves to the national context of each, whereby state identities become intertwined with national such: perceptions of self that are ostensibly shared, or at least known, across the state's citizenry. National identity is undeniably tied to the previously discussed notions of geography and history, but what this chapter highlights are the particularly social and human characteristics that tend to get framed in these spatio-temporalities. This includes national characteristics or stereotypes, inclusion and exclusion, and how Arctic statehood is flagged in the everyday.

Following directly from this, Chapter 6 continues by exploring the differences and heterogeneities inevitably produced as part of any such national project. Not least considering that, according to formal latitudinal lines, the Arctic is only part of these states' territories, namely the north. The focus in this chapter is therefore on how northern and Arctic identities intersect or differ at different moments; and how domestic relations feature in understandings of identity. Moreover, in particular in the Arctic context, this also centres on the role of indigeneity within these articulations of identity: how Indigenous peoples, politics, and perspectives are variously included or excluded in state identity discourses.

The final step on the scale of relationality is the individual – both professional and personal. Chapter 7 focuses on how state personnel see themselves and their own Arctic identities (or lack thereof), and more generally, the role of the person within and among the people. This includes particularly vocal personalities and their potential influence on the development of Arctic political relations, as well as the anonymous politicians and civil servants who offered their perspectives on the topic. Although any personal articulation of self is both highly contingent and socially adaptable, not to mention rather elusive to subjective grasp, what this chapter does is highlight the more anthropological side of the state. The Arctic state, as any other, is made up of a myriad of diverse peoples and practices, mundane and improvised, emotional and embodied, all at once. While what emerges as the effect of these practices may be 'the state', the only way in which to engage with it is via these many minor 'causes', its people.

The final chapter offers a conclusion, drawing together these spatio-temporal relationalities to constitute, once more, an outline of meanings and implications of state identities. It summarises the preceding discussions and their implications both for the Arctic and for geopolitical understandings of statehood and identity more broadly. And, not dissimilar to Arctic visions too, the chapter looks to futures, plural and open. As should be clear by now, the book is not merely diagnostic, not descriptive of an identity 'out there' (or 'in here', for that matter): it is, most of all, a deliberation of commonalities and differences, of unities and divisions, driven by a conviction that these things *matter*. Who we are – who 'we' are – shapes what we all become.

Notes

1 Hereafter Russia and USA/the US.
2 Although it is interesting to note that for example Scotland has referred to itself as a 'close sub-Arctic neighbour' and 'the world's most northernly non-Arctic nation' (e.g. Robertson, 2023) to little if any criticism, suggesting this is an issue of states and of wider geopolitical relations.
3 One example of an alternative governance arrangement that is sometimes suggested, and which is always categorically rejected for being 'wrong' on the basis of dominant knowledges (e.g. international law) is the potential for an 'Arctic treaty' (as with the Antarctic Treaty). In this case, those with the power to reject it point to knowledges of cartography, oceanography, geology, which in turn produce the Arctic as a certain type of space (ostensibly) requiring a certain type of politics (see

e.g. Young, 2012, 2011; also Powell, 2008 for discussion of the notion of an 'Arctic commons').

4 Joe Painter uses the word 'stateness' as a translation of the French '*étaticité*' ['state-icity'], explaining that the perhaps more obvious 'statehood': 'refers almost exclusively to the recognition of a state in international law' (Painter, 2006, p. 755). For the purposes here, however, 'statehood' is used, pointing to 'Arctic statehood' largely being a title with its root in international law (as conferred by e.g. latitudes and territory). Indeed, the focus here is how 'legal' statehood may or may not interweave with notions of identity among those working *within* the formal institution of the state – how one discourse may reify or rupture another.

5 In Canada, one of the state's three recognised Indigenous groups is indeed the 'First *Nations*'. In Norway, the former President of the Sámi Parliament, in contrast, had to defend and define the use of the term 'nation' (and specifically 'national day' celebrations) to stress the non-nationalist, non-separatist nature of it (Keskitalo, 2015).

1

The Arctic: a contested region

Much has been written, said, speculated, and forecast about the Arctic in recent years. Yet, defining the region is not as straightforward as it might seem – no more so than disentangling truth from fiction, or reality from inflated rhetoric, in a region undergoing rapid change. Thankfully, a rich body of scholarship and literature has kept pace with regional developments – and this book contributes a piece to that continually evolving picture.

This chapter provides background on the region and Arctic geopolitics, as well as on the particular focus of the three Arctic states. It is meant not to be an exhaustive review but to introduce some useful background and topics that will feature throughout later chapters. It also provides the context for later articulations of state identities: the wider geographies in which the states are situated, and the longer timelines of which this book is a slice. The chapter proceeds by discussing the various definitions of the Arctic region and its history of regionalisation, before introducing some of the main governance mechanisms. These include in particular the Arctic Council and the UN Convention on the Law of the Sea (UNCLOS), but also an array of other fora and venues for states and stakeholders to meet. Before the chapter ends and we turn to the space and time inherent to state identities, it offers a further discussion of the choice of case studies, Norway, Iceland, and Canada.

For those unfamiliar with the region, the chapter will hopefully provide the necessary background. And for those already well versed with the Arctic, it will situate the book in a wider set of literatures that may or may not already be familiar. Either way, the chapter communicates one key message that will be important for the remainder of the book: the Arctic, however defined, is undergoing rapid and profound change, but while this means that it is a *contested* region it is not necessarily one of conflict. The most immediate competitions at hand are not resource races, scrambles, or a 'New Cold War' in the region, but rather about imaginaries. Before we ask 'whose', we need to ask 'how', 'where', and perhaps even 'which'. By now a cliché in Arctic fora, one of the few things experts *do* agree on is that there is not just one, but 'many Arctics'.

Defining the Arctic

Prior to opening any atlas, if you were to look up 'Arctic' in a dictionary, you would find that it is a name of distant etymological origin. From ancient Greek, *arktikos*, the name refers to 'of the bear' – that is, the constellation the Great Bear or *Ursa Major*, which came to signify 'northern' (*OED Online*, 2019). According to Greek myth, 'Zeus placed the nymph Callisto in the northern hemisphere in the shape of a bear and thus this particular star constellation was named by the Greeks *Ursa Major* "Great Bear". Close by is *Ursa Minor* "Little Bear", which includes Polaris, the pole star, which marks the approximate position of the north celestial pole' (Everett-Heath, 2018). As will be a theme throughout, this already hints at two Arctic truths: it is a region largely defined from and by the 'outside', and it is a region steeped in myth.

Bears aside, the Arctic region is contextually defined according to specialist field and purpose. Perhaps most commonly known, and mentioned in the introduction, it refers to the geographical region north of the Arctic Circle, approximately 66° 33' N. This is the latitude at which the sun does not set on the summer solstice or rise on the winter solstice (Mayhew, 2015). In other words, it is the region of midnight sun and polar night. This is the definition most frequently used in political contexts, with the Arctic Council member states – the 'Arctic states' that this book centres on – comprising the eight states whose territories and oceanic areas extend north of this invisible line of sunlight and darkness.

Even this seemingly simple definition becomes blurry, however, when mountain tops and planetary tilts are taken into account.

And more importantly, neither flora and fauna nor culture respects gridlines imposed by Euclidian logics, of course. For climatologists, meteorologists, biologists, and other scientists, more useful definitions have been those of the treeline or the ten-degree July isotherm. The former refers to areas of tundra and permafrost, where no trees but shrubs and lichens grow; and the latter to areas where the average daily temperature in July does not exceed 10° Celsius (50° Fahrenheit) (Mayhew, 2015). By these accounts, the seemingly sensationalist 'shrinking' Arctic is not so far from the truth, with trees and new species creeping northwards alongside upwards-creeping temperatures. Figure 1.1 shows some of the definitions adopted by different Arctic Council Working Groups,[1] beautifully braiding the multivalent 'Arctic' around the Pole.

Defining what we mean when we talk about the Arctic is important for a number of reasons, of course – including political decisions and delimitations of policy, for scientific purposes, and for cultural expressions. However, there are also reasons to keep definitions multiple if not necessarily malleable: different regionalisations serve different purposes, none of which is more 'true' than the other. This is particularly clear when we consider social, political, and cultural questions. When the first Arctic Human Development Report (2004) was published, it deliberately employed a wider understanding of 'being' Arctic. This allowed researchers to consider peoples across the boundaries drawn both by cartographers in the south and by scientists with an aim to quantify and measure. What matters more in this context – as it does for the later discussion of Arctic identities too – are practices, ideas, narratives, and feelings of belonging. In this way, we are starting to see the contours of an Arctic defined from within rather than externally imposed.

That being said, Arctic communities – however defined – have historically not named themselves after Greek myths or celestial bears. More often than not, the 'Arctic' has been known quite simply as 'the north' – or, locally, by its numerous constituent places, towns, and regions. (Unlike a relationally defined 'north', in this book the capitalised 'the North' is used more specifically in the Canadian context. This is further discussed in Chapter 2.) Talking about a circumpolar north makes more sense when gazing at a globe than when looking out of your kitchen window. Nevertheless,

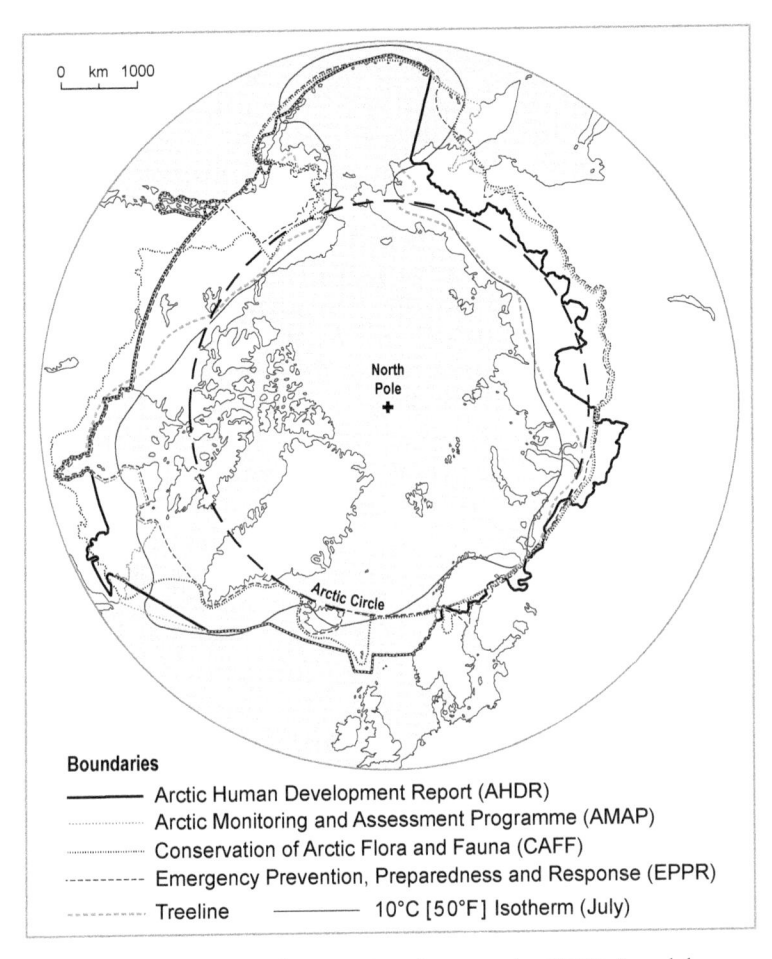

Figure 1.1 Arctic definitions. Based on map by GRID-Arendal, 2013: www.grida.no/resources/8387

it *is* a name and a label that has arguably come to take increasing hold also within the region in recent decades, no doubt as a result of international attention. And, no doubt, there is far more recognition of 'the Arctic' than names of specific northern towns or counties.

'Recognition' of the Arctic does not necessarily mean understanding or knowledge of it, however. Among the many competing visions of the Arctic, some of which we will see state personnel reflect on in later chapters, that of a romanticised north 'frozen in time' is particularly pervasive in more southern representations. This includes both the imaginary of an empty wilderness – to be variously overcome through hardship or protected from incursions – and that of Indigenous peoples living 'traditional' lives of centuries ago. Because of such misunderstandings and misrepresentations, Indigenous peoples have invested much effort in turning this narrative, emphasising the need for not just recognition and 'consultation' but full rights and participation. For example, Inuit organisations have successfully intervened in museum exhibitions to communicate the Arctic as a space of rich vitality and abundance (see Medby and Dittmer, 2021). This is a topic that features throughout later chapters' discussions of Arctic statehood too, but in particular Chapter 6 focuses on dynamics within as much as across state borders, pertaining in particular to Indigenous peoples' role in Arctic geopolitics and identities. Suffice it here to say that the many Indigenous peoples of the Arctic – represented by six organisations in the Arctic Council – are increasingly making their voices heard, defining the Arctic on their own terms. While there is still a long way to go before we can talk about full self-determination or even self-definition, what is already clear is that externally and imperially imposed boundaries are far from final.

A region comes into view

In considering the regionalisation, statisation, and identity discourses of the Arctic, it is useful to recognise how past narratives and trajectories have led to those prevalent today. This is also a topic that resurfaces in Chapter 3, which focuses specifically on ideas of Arctic temporalities – that is, Arctic histories as well as understandings of the present and anticipations of futures – which permeate political discourse (see also Wormbs, 2018). However, when it comes to Arctic history and historiography, as opposed to perceptions *about* this history and historiography, this book provides only an entry-point, necessarily having to leave out some of the finer details and knowledges it is indebted to.

Returning briefly to ancient Greece, one of the first representations often associated with the Arctic in Europe is 'Thule', referenced to the explorer Pytheas (around 380–300 BC). It is not clear exactly where he had ventured, but it was supposedly about six days' sailing from the British Isles and a place 'where the sea became solid and the sun never set', yet the story goes he was not believed (Jacobsen, 2015: 122). Another ambiguous, and more utopian, northern region beyond the reaches of most was 'Hyperborea' (beyond the north wind), also a term used by the Greeks and Romans (Jacobsen, 2015). And in a book pivoting not just on the far but the *furthest* north, Michael Bravo (2019) adds that also Arab and Hindu ancient texts detail a utopian North Polar region. While northerners themselves would certainly tell a very different story of their lands, these tales matter due to their persistence in the narrativisation of the Arctic. For example, Elana Wilson Rowe's (2018) book on present-day Arctic governance opens with reference to Ultimate Thule, drawing also on Edgar Allan Poe's 1844 poem 'Dream-Land'. In this way, a narrative thread runs from ancient Greece, through nineteenth-century America to current politics in the Arctic.

Following this often hidden thread of explorers' diaries, literature, poetry, and art is also what Sámi Professor Britt Kramvig does in the film *Dreamland*. Using Poe's poem as an aural structuring device, the film traces how Arctic pasts shape the present – including Kramvig's own identity as Indigenous Sámi, as an anthropologist, as a woman, and so much more (Kramvig and Andersen, 2019). With the seams of 'the sublime' in plain sight, the Arctic is rendered 'banal'. Yet, the act of tracing these stories can itself become a transcendent process of making new connections and new threads elsewhere – to, for example, Indigenous struggles on the other 'side' of the world. It is this pursuit of uncovering how the present Arctic is stitched together that also motivates the present book, whereby tales of the past matter for their current presence and impact.

Beyond the textual, other visual representations, and in particular maps, are notable in any discussion of the Arctic. There are, like historical nodes, certain maps that tend to feature prominently, not least when discussing the Arctic past. For example, Olaus Magnus'

Figure 1.2 The 'Carta Marina', by Olaus Magnus in 1527–39, showing Nordic countries with place names (Source: Wikimedia Commons)

'Carta Marina' from 1539 is one such cartographic rendering, where sea monsters and whales variably occupy the tumultuous seas of what we today know as Scandinavia (see Figure 1.2). Cartography was an important tool of empire, exploration, and power in what Felix Driver (drawing on Joseph Conrad) calls the period of 'Geography Militant' (Driver, 2001). In the 1800s, numerous Arctic expeditions took place, some more immediately disastrous than others, but all arguably playing their part in the history of colonisation and domination to follow. Among the most famous, and fatal, Arctic expeditions was Sir John Franklin's 1845 quest for the Northwest Passage – and this is one we will encounter again in later chapters, as state personnel from Canada talked about it as part of their country's identity. Both of the expedition's ships disappeared and all 129 men perished, but the story has persisted in the public imagination. No doubt the mysterious disappearance – the ships remained lost until 2014 and 2016 respectively – and speculations about the crew's fate was part of this. And moreover, Lady Jane Franklin in her time invested energy and money into keeping the story alive. While the numerous searches were fruitless in their primary goal, their secondary search for knowledge and data about the Arctic region proved highly valuable in years to come. In addition, the ongoing mystery was part of a wider Victorian imaginary of the Arctic region: one that was empty, inhospitable, and frozen – to be conquered by brave, white men (McCorristine, 2018). Numerous songs, paintings, poems, and books have been inspired by Franklin's demise and others' – and today, tales of explorers resurface in political rhetoric, as is indeed a topic throughout this book.

From Victorian Britain's 'filling in' of maps, the next maps by now familiar throughout Arctic policy spheres are Polar projections from the Cold War period. Unlike the literally Euro-centric Mercator projection, these maps tend to show the globe 'from above', centring on the North Pole. These maps, like all maps do, tell a story – in this case, usually of geographical proximity, and thus threat, between the USSR and North America. For many scholars, it was this period that really brought the Arctic into public (or rather, southern) consciousness. But unlike the utopia of the Greeks and the sublime of Poe, this was a space representing mortal danger – also for those far south of its latitudes. Arguably, this is an Arctic imaginary that has not been fully erased; as a palimpsest, southern discourses of the north should be considered as layered over rather than erased.

Governing an international region: The Arctic Council

The Arctic has been referred to as a 'Cold War theatre' that, to borrow Oran Young's (2005) term, transformed into a 'mosaic of cooperation'. As the USSR disintegrated, the space previously measured in missile-ranges could be reconceptualised as proximities inviting peace. Although the order of events and weight of certain words are always rendered impossibly neat in historical-causational narratives, the USSR President Mikhail Gorbachev's 1987 speech is often highlighted in retellings of the development of the Arctic region as such. In a time when *glasnost* was gaining momentum, he famously declared the Soviet Union's interest in seeing the Arctic become 'a genuine zone of peace and fruitful cooperation' (Gorbachev, 1987: 31). Irrespective of whether or not this indeed was a real watershed moment at the time, it has undeniably become a yardstick in the telling of Arctic governance stories. His speech is said to have sown the seeds of what would eventually become the Arctic Council, preceded by the Finnish government's establishment of the Arctic Environmental Protection Strategy in 1991 (Rottem, 2020).

The Arctic Council was formally established in 1996 as a 'high level forum', described in the Ottawa Declaration as purposed to 'provide a means for promoting cooperation, coordination and interaction among the Arctic States, with the involvement of the Arctic Indigenous communities and other Arctic inhabitants on common Arctic issues, in particular issues of sustainable development and environmental protection in the Arctic' (Arctic Council, 1996). And again, these so-called Arctic states are the Council's eight members and founding governments: Finland, Sweden, Norway, Denmark/Greenland, Iceland, Canada, the USA, and Russia (see Figure 1.3). As such, it is an intergovernmental forum, with no decision-making powers in its own right, nor does it have an internal budget for projects (Arctic Council, 2018). Another important exclusion from the Council's remits of consideration – footnoted under the above 'common Arctic issues' – is 'matters related to military security' (Arctic Council, 1996). In addition to the eight state members, six Indigenous peoples' organisations hold status as Permanent Participants: the Aleut International Association, Arctic Athabaskan Council, Gwich'in Council International, Inuit Circumpolar Council, Russian Association of Indigenous Peoples of the North (RAIPON), and the Saami Council. These are to be fully consulted with and involved in all matters, although voting is the privilege of states. As all decisions in the Council require unanimous consent, this means that in effect the eight states hold veto rights (Graczyk and Koivurova, 2014; Keskitalo, 2004; Knecht, 2013).

Since its inception in the mid-1990s, the Arctic Council has developed and expanded to consider a wider range of issues, while remaining committed to science via its six Working Groups[2] (Axworthy et al., 2012; Young, 2010). Increasingly, the Working

Groups' efforts and outputs also include Indigenous and traditional knowledges alongside scientific data, although this has been a slower process than many would have liked. There are likely a number of practical as well as ideological obstacles, but, perhaps most significantly, the lack of Council funding mechanisms has meant that full Indigenous participation in all matters below ministerial levels remains challenging. Another important aspect of the Working Groups is their inclusion of, and indeed encouraged contributions by, non-Arctic actors. Hence, this is an avenue through which international scientists and organisations can take an active part in Arctic issues. At the ministerial level, in contrast, so-called non-Arctic states and organisations can participate only as 'observers'. In 2024, there were 13 states, as well as a number of intergovernmental, inter-parliamentary, and non-governmental organisations, that have achieved observer status (Arctic Council, 2023). However, this count has been rising steadily in recent years, in tandem with increasing attention to the region (see Woon and Dodds, 2020). A number of other non-Arctic states have also expressed their interest in applying, and as long as they fulfil the formal criteria there is no reason to believe they will not be admitted in future ministerial meeting rounds. At the time of writing, however, the more pressing question is when ministerial meetings and other Arctic Council activities may fully recommence, following a pause and limitations posed by Russia's full-scale invasion of Ukraine in 2022.

In addition to growing non-Arctic interest, another significant development is the signing of three legally binding agreements by the Council's eight members. These relate to cooperation on search and rescue efforts (2011), potential marine oil pollution (2013), and scientific cooperation (2016) (Arctic Council, 2018). Not only are these important instruments in their own right but they have also represented a shift towards a more assertive tone of the ministers' collaborations, prior to the present situation. Despite this, however, many argue that the Arctic Council should do more to keep pace with a rapidly changing geophysical and geopolitical world. Calls for reform often point to the mentioned exclusion of any military matters as well as the need to strengthen efforts in relation to social and health-related matters

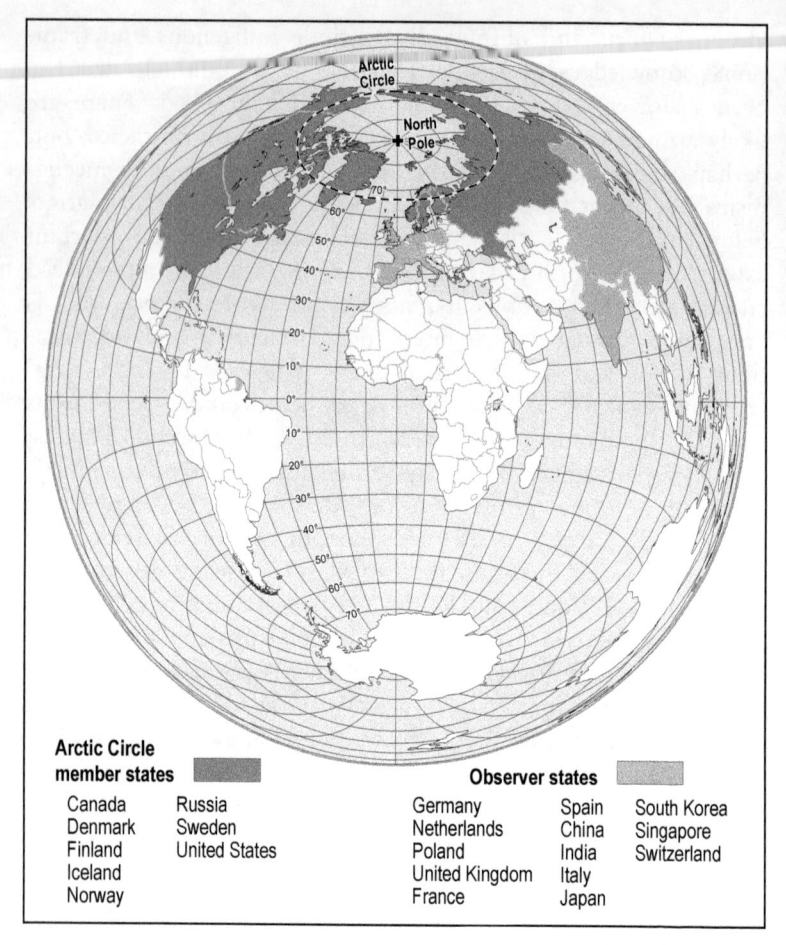

Arctic Circle member states

Canada	Russia
Denmark	Sweden
Finland	United States
Iceland	
Norway	

Observer states

Germany	Spain	South Korea
Netherlands	China	Singapore
Poland	India	Switzerland
United Kingdom	Italy	
France	Japan	

Figure 1.3 Members and observer states of the Arctic Council

(see Koivurova, 2010; Wilson, 2016). Perhaps in particular its 'soft' character, lacking enforcement mechanisms in its own right, has led some to question the Arctic Council's purpose (Koivurova and VanderZwaag, 2007). Nevertheless, while some may want to see less talk and more walk, we may consider the 'talk' – or, more accurately, the negotiation and interaction – as important practices of interaction and integration in and of themselves. Although it is hard to measure, the diplomatic contact facilitated by the Council has likely been a factor in creating that zone of peace Gorbachev famously called for at the time. And considering the number of actors confined to observing, the (right to) 'talk' is of high currency in the region (Dodds, 2013a). Who may talk, when, and who may listen, are integral to the ways in which decisions and their adherence come to be enacted – as we will also see in the articulations of Arctic state personnel in chapters to follow. Without this forum, actors from across the circumpolar region have been without a meeting space to discuss common concerns, scientists from around the world have one less venue to collaborate on crucial issues, and Indigenous peoples of the Arctic have one less opportunity have their voices heard. If the pause of 2022 has made one thing very clear it is the value, even arguably the necessity, of the Arctic Council.

Beyond the Arctic and beyond the Council

Important as it clearly is, the Arctic Council is not the only organisation or governance arrangement in the Arctic. While it may be the 'pre-eminent forum', according to then US Secretary of State Hillary Clinton, Depledge and Dodds's (2017) metaphor of the Arctic as a 'bazaar' might be more illustrative: a range of mechanisms and fora overlap and interrelate – not all of which happens in an entirely orchestrated order. Recent decades have seen a proliferation of Arctic-themed conferences, events, festivals, and meetings of various kinds. All of these are part of the 'spatialisation' of the Arctic, constructing it as a distinct region geographically, politically, culturally, and environmentally (see Knecht, 2013; Knecht and Keil, 2013; Steinveg, 2023). Some of these were set up with the explicit aim of contesting the exclusivity of Arctic discussions between not just the eight Arctic states, but the even more narrowly defined five coastal states (see the Ilulissat Declaration (2008)). Perhaps most famous among these alternative meeting arenas, and mentioned again by state personnel in Chapter 7, is the Arctic Circle Assembly, initiated by the former Icelandic President Ólafur Ragnar Grímsson (Depledge and Dodds, 2017; Dodds, 2013b; Steinveg, 2021a, 2021b). Although some say it was established as a reaction to Iceland's exclusion from Arctic Ocean discussions in 2008, it has by now come to be one of the annual events on the Arctic policy calendar. In contrast to the Arctic Council, the Assembly is a broadly inclusive event, where a wide range of states, companies, academics, and non-governmental organisations share the Harpa Concert Hall in Reykjavík for a few days. This means that although Arctic politics is often presented as confined to the Arctic Council – and while this book centres on Arctic states – its arrangements are in practice both complex and globally enmeshed. Arctic politics can be considered made up of constellations of actors and institutions from both within and beyond Arctic latitudes, which temporarily come together, morph, merge, or disperse (see Young, 2009). As the naming of a 'global Arctic' suggests, the region has come to serve as a focus-point around which diverse interactions happen, both drawing in global while also extending out far beyond topographical boundaries.

Also worth mentioning here is the importance of the UN Convention on the Law of the Sea (UNCLOS), despite not 'governing' in and of itself. Rather, this is a convention that state personnel frequently refer to – in interviews here and elsewhere – as the primary mechanism through which Arctic Ocean boundaries are agreed, and so power is distributed and decisions made. In very brief, UNCLOS was adopted in 1982 and provides the international rules for ocean use and resources. A state's varying rights – for example to manage shipping transit, fishery, and subsea resources – are determined by distance from the shore, and bilateral agreements with neighbouring states. What is particularly relevant for discussions of Arctic statehood is not only designated territorial waters (out to 12 nautical miles) or Exclusive Economic Zones (out to 200 nautical miles) but the extended continental shelf claims they can make beyond this (see Figure 1.4). While the rights of the state decrease the further out you go, it will retain rights to the seabed of the continental shelf – including, for example, potential oil, gas, minerals, and rare earth metals. And so, considering that much of the Arctic region is oceanic, decisions about continental shelf extents and boundaries are crucial to statecraft – and in fact to imaginations of a state's identity. While submissions are sent to the UN's Commission on the Limits of the Continental Shelf, where there is overlap or disagreement between states' claims, they will

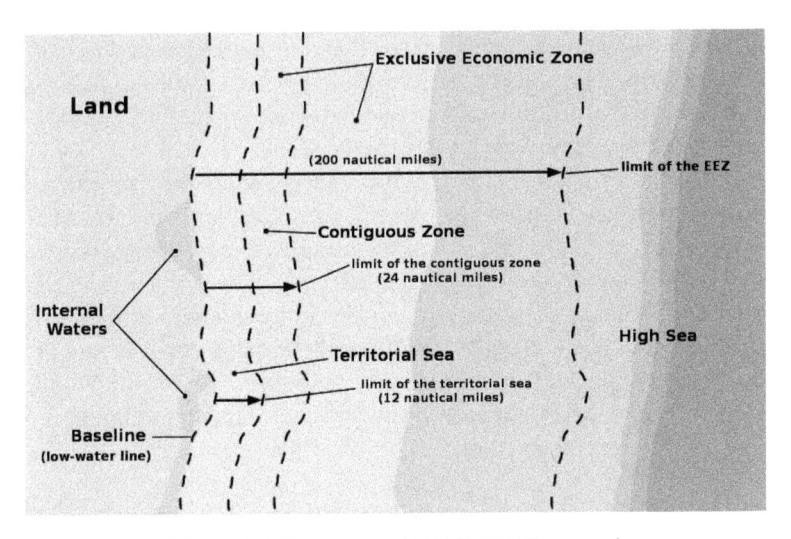

Figure 1.4 Key terms of UNCLOS illustrated
(Source: Antonioptg, CC BY-SA 4.0)

need to negotiate bilaterally. Reaching an agreement on the Barents Sea delimitation between Russia and Norway in 2010 has been seen as a major achievement in Arctic geopolitics (Jensen, 2011), and one that is still talked about more than a decade later (see Figure 2.1 in the next chapter for a map). As such, UNCLOS is important for Arctic statehood in at least two notable ways: it is the mechanism through which states determine their delimitations from others and associated rights in the region; and it is an agreement that all Arctic states agree should lie at the heart of Arctic geopolitical decision-making, and as such brings them together for negotiations and scientific research to determine continental shelves. It is, in short, a convention that is a key part of the performance of Arctic statehood.

As increasing numbers of voices are making themselves heard through various channels and fora, it is clear that issues of the Arctic are no less ambiguously demarcated than its geographies. It is the recognition that Arctic developments – whether melting ice-sheets, warming ocean currents, or geopolitical changes – cannot and do not stay in the north that has formed the basis for many of the aforementioned new observer admissions to the Arctic Council and more general growing interest in the region. In particular, climate change has highlighted the global influences of the planet's north, as well as leading to the ongoing reassessment and questioning of its current regimes of governance (Solli et al., 2013; Stokke and Hønneland, 2007). For some, the growing involvement of non-Arctic actors represents a threat, for example to the influence and agency of Arctic states and peoples; whereas, for others, this involvement does not yet go far enough considering the extra-territorial sources of pollution and greenhouse gases. Either way, there is no doubt that the Arctic is changing both environmentally and socio-politically, and it is this that has also prompted the questioning of Arctic identity in the present moment and book.

The age of the Arctic

Already in the 1980s, the 'Age of the Arctic' was heralded (Osherenko and Young, 2005; Young, 1985). As should be clear by now, the present is a time in which the Arctic has come to hold a particular place in popular media and imaginaries. Its position in the public spotlight has been due to all of the above, including the end of the Cold War, global warming, and its globalisation. Running beneath all of these developments however is environmental change, which is what has led to the possibility of even asking questions about potential resources, shipping routes, and new industries. While this is hopefully something most readers will be familiar with, what is here of interest is how this comes to shape not just the Arctic today but also how its futures can possibly be articulated. That is, how a narrative of an 'age of the Arctic' becomes a discourse, as laid out in the previous chapter, with material effects in the present.

An important aspect of current discourses about the Arctic is the prominence of science, and, specifically, sets of often repeated scientific numbers: firstly, that the Arctic is warming at four times the average global rate or more. And secondly, that the region is believed to potentially hold thirty per cent of the world's undiscovered gas and thirteen per cent of the world's undiscovered oil (Gautier et al., 2009). Sat next to each other, the two statements highlight the Arctic paradox well: the same reasons some people worry about the Arctic provide others with hope. While few (if any) would say that environmental change is a positive thing, its outcomes can look very different depending on the scale and standpoint from which they are viewed. To take one example, Arctic investment, employment opportunities, and even expanded education and healthcare services are often wanted – and needed much more immediately than the damages that may follow from the same investment. Seen from the south, 'saving' the Arctic might seem a laudable aim; in the north, however, that is often translated to mean the opposite, namely exclusion and cordoning-off from prosperity. For those most affected by that intense warming, it is often not clear how the science and data actually benefit or help them. In other words, the recent attention given to the Arctic may well be welcomed by the region's inhabitants, but until the 'age of the Arctic' means that the region is actually *heard* – on its own terms, rather than in numbers and percentages – there is still a way to go.

Different and divergent discourses demonstrate once again the contestation around Arctic imaginations, especially when it comes to Arctic futures. This contestation extends also to Arctic identities, as might be expected. Environmental change, and in particular the climate crisis, lies at the heart of almost any discussion about the Arctic, including articulations of identity and belonging to a space undergoing transformation. One of the things that the next chapter shows is how geographies and environments matter for people's sense of identity – so what happens when those spaces dramatically change is an open question. Also part of these discussions are often issues of resources, whether renewable or non-renewable. These include not only the above 'undiscovered' oil and gas repositories but also a range of minerals and rare earth materials, as well as marine resources (fishery, aquaculture, and even biopharmaceuticals) and agriculture (Bruun and Medby, 2014). Moreover, this book would quickly become outdated by not mentioning that there is continually cutting-edge innovation taking place also in the north. For example, the cold climate has proved useful for instance for Internet servers, and renewable energy sources such as wind, wave, hydro, and geothermal power production are all currently being explored and expanded. Also worth mentioning, hopes for new shipping and transport routes through the Arctic are frequently highlighted in such forecasting discussions. In particular, the Northwest Passage, the Northern Sea Route, and the transpolar route are the three most often mentioned – and, equally, most often explained as over-hyped (see Humpert, 2013).

The final topic that cannot be evaded is the frequent speculations about conflict in the military sense. There is no denying that the Arctic region – Young's 'mosaic of cooperation' (2005) – has seen re-armament since the 2010s. This has paralleled increasing hostility between NATO and Russia elsewhere (first with the 'Crimea crisis' of 2014 and then the full-scale invasion of Ukraine in 2022), leading to some of those aforementioned critiques of the Arctic Council's reluctance to allow these issues to enter its (now temporarily closed) meeting rooms. However, despite growing numbers of military exercises and investments in the Arctic, there seems to be a publicly expressed consensus from policy-makers involved in the region that military conflict remains unlikely in the Arctic. What is likely, however, is the performance of force and capability, including recent GPS 'jamming', highly visible flights, and equipment testing. The point here therefore remains that what is currently contested is less about territory and traditional security concerns, and more about the construction of a region and human security. While the above couple of paragraphs are a very brief summary of some of the most commonly cited topics under the Arctic headline, what they jointly do is underscore that, even with only selective awareness, most people *will* have a view on what this 'age' might mean. And it is this plurality of issues, concerns, hopes, and knowledges that together form the basis for discussing Arctic geopolitics and identity.

Arctic geopolitics

If the chapter so far has offered a potted summary of some key topics that tend to arise when talking it, we have yet to unpack the concept of Arctic geopolitics itself, familiar as it might be to some readers. Whereas the previous introductory chapter presents the book's conceptual framework, the notion of 'geopolitics' brings these more directly to this chapter's more empirically focused elaboration on context.

In popular vernacular, geopolitics tends to refer to international relations between states – often relating to borders, territories, or resources. That is, it suggests a geographical politics, which is also how it was traditionally used. When the term was first coined at the turn of the twentieth century, scholars were particularly interested in how environments influenced, or even determined, politics (as well as peoples and societies). Fast forward to the present, however: the academic use of 'geopolitics' has come to mean precisely how such connections between environments and politics are constructed and performed. At least when preceded by 'critical', geopolitics refers to the ways in which worldviews and world orders come into being as a result of these ideas of geographical causation, as was also mentioned in the introduction. Beyond the academy, however, the term in its classical sense is still used, for example 'explaining' how certain geographical features 'cause' this or that political outcome. This means that a magazine's take on 'Arctic geopolitics' might offer striking maps that draw neat lines of causation between oil fields, militarism, and climatic changes; whereas an academic article's take might deconstruct and critique those same neat lines.

This book takes an approach that is founded on that academic understanding of the performativity of these discourses – that is, they produce the Arctic as a certain kind of space and a certain reality – but recognises the popular understanding and interest in the Arctic as shaping how that identity is articulated. In other words, if we want to explore how people identify with the Arctic, the starting point has to be their own conceptualisation of the region and its geopolitics. On the one hand, this requires caution against presuming the views of interconnectedness between geography and politics; while, on the other, it also works on the premise that, whatever this view might be, it will have implications for the ways the region is engaged with. When these people happen to be policy-makers and state personnel, those implications might well extend to the enactment of 'geopolitics' itself, leading to a circular relationship between identity and practice. It is with this recognition – that identity *matters* in a highly material and political sense in the Arctic – that the book hones in on three of the Arctic states to explore this further.

Three Arctic states

The reason for choosing to focus on these three Arctic states – Norway, Iceland, and Canada – among the eight was their state personnel's shared political rhetoric of Arctic identity. Politicians and diplomats from all three have frequently stood on podia, expressing their country's inherent northernness – increasingly retold as Arcticness. As the broader turn towards 'the Arctic' both in language and in media, identity seemed to become political legitimacy from the early 2000s onwards. The ways that these identities were and are articulated are very different, however. In other words, the specific ways in which Arctic identities are articulated differ – not just between states but also individuals – but they all converge around how certain characteristics and aspects of identity are ostensibly connected to political practices, rights, and responsibilities in the region. And as the introduction explained, coupling the state's practices with ideas of the nation is politically powerful. However, due to the Arctic being largely oceanic, it does not readily fit imaginations of traditional 'national homelands'; and, so, some re-narration and re-imagination of self, state, and space have taken place in interesting ways.

Admittedly my own interest in this topic was initially piqued by how 'Arctic identity' and related geographical imaginaries were used instrumentally in order to construct a political platform, for example potentially generating emotive ideas and patriotic sentiments among the public. However, my own research over the years led to the realisation that such a 'top-down' construction of identity was too crude an explanation. A similar ambivalence and contextual relativity as I experienced myself and witnessed among other young citizens in one Arctic state, Norway (see Medby, 2014), was apparent also among those professionally representing the Arctic state. In these three states then, identity is not just a 'tool' to be wielded for a specific political outcome but is instead implicated in the process and practice of that politics. Again, it is with this in mind that the book refers to 'state personnel' rather than 'the state' doing something, in this way highlighting the people behind, within, and as part of politics.

Although this book does not *compare* the three states, it does offer three cases that may be contrasted on the basis of their surface-level similar articulations of Arctic identities, which in practice turn out to manifest in different ways. These differences are in part due to their geographical and historical relationships with the Arctic. However, for all three the title as an Arctic state provides a privileged status for otherwise small- or medium-power states, and an opportunity to be internationally heard (see de Carvalho and Neumann, 2015). These differences and similarities are explored throughout the remainder of the book, but a brief introduction to each starts to shed light on why the topic of Arctic identity is not only fascinating but also of analytical and political importance.

So, to start where I did, Norway has both land and sea areas above the Arctic Circle. This means that not only is it one of the Arctic states, it also one of the more 'exclusive' five Arctic Ocean coastal states. Although only a portion of the Norwegian mainland lies above the Arctic Circle, not to mention its Gulf Stream-influenced climate, discussions about the country's involvement in the 'High North' tend to be framed in international terms. That is, the emphasis is often on the international or even global, rather than the regional, North Norwegian. Tellingly, past years' Norwegian Arctic policies have been co-ordinated by the Ministry of Foreign Affairs (N.MFA), albeit this work has become increasingly inter-ministerial. Moreover, with an Indigenous Sámi population, the 'Norwegianisation' of the region has a problematic legacy linked to historical assimilation processes at the behest of the state (e.g. Hønneland, 2011; see also Sannhet- og forsoningskommisjonen, 2023). That being said, the Norwegian Sámi Parliament is today an active political player – also in the Arctic Council with the transnational Saami Council as Permanent Participants. It is also worth noting that in addition to the Sámi people (who span four states), there are also several hundred thousand non-Indigenous northerners to whom the question of level of governance is also pertinent – about nine per cent of the Norwegian population live in the north. Furthermore, the Norwegian government's Arctic involvement is inevitably bound together with, on the one hand, strategic concerns relating to bordering Russia (with memories of the Cold War and new tensions arising);[3] and, on the other, commercial interests relating to potential petroleum and mineral resources in the north (Norway's economy being, first and foremost, hydrocarbon-based). From the early 2000s Norwegian governments have stood by the assertion that the Arctic is their 'number one strategic priority' (N.MFA, 2014b). Indeed, today the Arctic has become regarded as both the country's 'source of future wealth and claim to historical greatness' (Emmerson, 2010: 7; see also Burgess, 2001; Eriksen and Neumann, 2011) – however that may or may not be felt among its Arctic residents (Gjerde and Fjæstad, 2013; Østhagen, 2023).

Moving to the west and out to sea, Iceland provides a different example of an Arctic state. Despite being the only Arctic island state, it does not hold claims to an extended continental shelf in the Arctic Ocean, meaning that it is actually not considered an Arctic coastal state. In fact, in terms of latitude, only a small island off the north of the main island is even north of the Arctic Circle, leading some to cast doubt on Iceland's authority to speak on questions of the Arctic whatsoever. However, this is a critique the Icelandic government has repeatedly, publicly refuted (and which indeed might have played a part in the aforementioned launch of the Arctic Circle Assembly). As they argue, they are in the middle of oceanic streams going to and from the Arctic Ocean, and therefore arguably *more* implicated in Arctic matters. And, with a historical fishery-based economy (and related identity), any exclusion from ocean-related discussions is inevitably wrapped in controversy (I.MFA, 2011: 1; Dodds and Ingimundarson, 2012; Ingimundarson, 2011). For the Icelanders, the impetus to assert their Arctic statehood and identity has therefore become tied to wider discourses of independence. Furthermore, the (very) small nation – with no Indigenous population and fewer than half a million inhabitants – was arguably faced with a sense of identity crisis in the wake of the severe financial one (Bennett, 2012). Perhaps unsurprisingly, the Arctic has here become imbued with economic significance – including the way in which identity in relation to it tends to be framed – and a stronger sense of an Arctic future than a past. This renewed focus may, then, offer an interstice in the Icelandic narrative where the Arctic may gain salience (e.g. Oslund, 2011; Loftsdóttir, 2014).

Finally, charting further to the west again, Canada offers a third case of Arctic state identity. Like Norway, it holds claims to both land and sea areas above the Arctic Circle, but here it has historically tended to be framed as a 'frontier' and wilderness, both geographically and culturally removed from the nation at large. By the majority, southern-residing population, the (capitalised) Canadian North was – and to an extent still *is* – distant and exotic, a place of dreams and imaginaries, mythical and dangerous, accessible only to heroic explorers and local Inuit (Grace, 2001; see also Hillmer and Chapnick, 2007a; Baldwin et al., 2012b). In contrast to Norway again, distances are much wider, the climate much harsher (with no Gulf Stream), and infrastructures between the North and south less developed. The country's colonial past still runs through Canadian relations today, undeniably influential to articulations of identity too. Still, the 'frozen' North holds an important symbolic value for the nation's distinctiveness – as defined both against the former empire, Great Britain, and now the southern-lying USA (see e.g. Bone, 2009; Cairns et al., 1999; Keskitalo, 2004). While historically and symbolically important, the Arctic has today, once more, gained increasing material and strategic value to the country – in particular, as a stage upon which to perform sovereignty, rhetorically linked to the protection of homelands and people.

The geopolitics of Arctic state identities

Thinking about the Arctic in the present moment raises important questions of geopolitical rights and responsibilities. The eight Arctic states clearly hold a particular role here – as their representatives would be quick to point out – and yet it remains an open question how this region and space are related to. Having introduced the three 'case study' countries above, the following chapters of the book start doing just that, asking those whose job it is to represent the Arctic state what their sense of Arctic identity might be. As explained in the previous chapter, the framework for exploring state identities is based on understandings of geography and time, and their relational and contextual articulations. And so, to start understanding how Arctic state personnel view statehood and identity, the book turns to the 'geo' of geopolitics, namely Arctic geographies.

Notes

1 The six Arctic Council Working Groups are the following: ACAP: Arctic Contaminants Action Program; AMAP: Arctic Monitoring and Assessment Programme; CAFF: Conservation of Arctic Flora and Fauna; EPPR: Emergency Prevention, Preparedness and Response; PAME: Protection of the Arctic Marine Environment; SDWG: Sustainable Development Working Group. The map shows the Arctic boundaries used by AMAP, CAFF, and EPPR; and the boundaries of the Arctic Human Development Reports (AHDR), which were adapted from AMAP's (see GRID-Arendal, 2013).
2 See note 1.
3 Norway is an active member of NATO, and a previous Norwegian Prime Minister, Jens Stoltenberg, served as the organisation's Secretary General during 2014–24.

Part I

Space and time

2

State geographies: the spatiality of Arctic state identities

The topic of statehood and that of state identities are often about geographies: territories, borders that define 'us' and 'them', homelands, and feelings of belonging. In our particular context the question of 'who' is Arctic is also clearly a matter of 'where'. And geography lies at the heart of many if not most discussions about the Arctic. The previous chapter introduced some of the purpose-specific definitions of this geography, and so this chapter picks up where that left off: asking what geographies, cartographies, and spatialities might mean for state personnel's sense of Arctic identity. Not only is this a seemingly obvious place to start thinking about Arctic state identities, but it was also one of the first things many of the interviewed state personnel brought up: Arctic statehood is, first and foremost, about geography.

When probing further, 'Arctic geographies' might bring up topics such as regional definitions, latitudes, and borders on the one hand; and on the other it might bring up climates, environments, ice-cover, and topography. The word 'geography' is of Greek etymology – like 'the Arctic' itself – and means 'earth-writing'. Perhaps not surprisingly then, thought may first go to land and landscapes, as opposed to oceanscapes, ice, air, and other materialities in and through which we live. Yet the Arctic is a region that is far more, and far more dynamic, than mere lines on maps. This is why the term 'spatiality' is useful, highlighting that space is not just a sum of certain characteristics and features, but that the way in which the region comes into being is as much about how we decide on those characteristics and features in the first place.

This imagination of relation to and with spaces is something geographers and other scholars have become increasingly interested in. For example, approaching the Arctic as territory, terrain, a place, or indeed homeland all imply different behaviours and even feelings. And when it comes to Arctic geopolitics, the 'geo' takes on added meaning when recognising that not only is it changing rapidly in a physical sense, but also in social and cultural ways: What might have been seen as wilderness might be recast as a resource-space, or a space of environmental protection might be recognised as reindeer-herding land. These imaginaries and spatial designations clearly matter – politically, economically, culturally, and indeed to identities.

Spatiality and sense of belonging are arguably inherent to identities, based on a sense of relative position in the world, Arctic or not. This might be most obvious in notions of national identity with a defined 'national homeland', but is arguably the case in most if not all contextual identities – also those encompassing primarily an abstract social space. Identities are not only produced in and by space, however, but perceptions of space are also influenced by identities in the first place (Massey, 1993). This, in turn, has implications for how spaces such as the Arctic are understood, used, and inhabited, and what practices are rendered possible or impossible – in short, how the world is ordered (see Said, 1979). And in particular in a time marked by so-called identity politics, it is only appropriate to ask how people are both influencing and influenced by space, including the changing Arctic.

Recognising the geography inherent to articulations of state identities is not the same as saying that it determines it, however. Any book on geopolitics also needs to acknowledge the problematic legacy of the term and discipline, with a historical foundation in imperial and racist projects. In 'classical' geopolitical reasoning, the relationship between geography and people was historically seen as causal, where geography 'determines' collective character and in turn nations' position in the world (Dijink, 2002: 11). This, then, was used as an argument to justify colonialism, racism, and imperial violations around the world – many of which remain to be fully acknowledged in the present.

Even today, stories of harsh climates ostensibly 'shaping' strong people, for example, can still be seen in romantic(ised) visions of 'nation-statehood' – including in the Arctic. It is therefore important to recognise that the ways in which identities become spatialised are neither natural nor unproblematic (Dijink, 2002). And further, claims of 'the national soil' may not only be fertile ground for conflict in itself but may also serve as a foundation for the upholding of asymmetric power relations and hegemonic views of the world. If spatially defined, identity discourses can become bounded and regulated alongside physical boundaries, where rights to belong – inclusion and exclusion – are determined too. In short, what can be meaningfully said, thought, and done is all contingent on locational and relational positioning.

What should be clear by now is that discourses of state identities matter – and that one of the key pillars of them is geography (the other pillar being time, the topic of the next chapter). And equally, it should be clear that geography and geographical imaginaries matter too. When this is articulated by representatives of the state, they potentially take on added significance in and through political practice that may follow. In the remainder of the chapter, these geographies are explored further, in particular through the descriptions and explanations by state personnel from the three Arctic states that this book takes as its cases. The chapter starts by discussing the more traditional concepts of borders and sovereign territories, but goes on to include also environmental characteristics and elements, experiences of nature, and shows that even the naming of space matters for understandings of state identities.

Lines on maps

As the previous chapter explained, a formal title of Arctic statehood tends to be understood as geographically based: latitudinally defined territories from which political claims can be legitimately made. Perhaps unsurprisingly then, the first thing that tends to come up in discussions of Arctic statehood is the Arctic Circle – or, in the case of Canada, often 'North of 60th [parallel]'. On several occasions, the question of what it means to 'be' an Arctic state has been answered with reference to a map and Euclidian lines. This has recently been underscored by the rhetorical moves also of non-Arctic state representatives who attempt to align and affiliate their countries with the region depending on relative distance and proximity. Examples include *Scotland's Arctic Policy* introducing the country as 'among the Arctic region's closest neighbours' (Hyslop, in Scottish Government, 2019: 3) and China's Arctic White Paper's use of the term 'Near-Arctic State' (PRC, 2018). Such examples speak volumes of the geographical basis of Arctic identities, which also state personnel reflected on when asked about their own understanding of the notion. As an illustrative example, a Norwegian official with links to the Ministry of Foreign Affairs explained the meaning of Arctic statehood in the following way:

> The formal, geographical link is that we are one of, first and foremost, one of five coastal states around the Arctic Ocean; we border what we have delimited as the Arctic Ocean. And we have territories in – exactly where the Arctic border runs, that can be discussed, but there is no doubt that Norway, with both North Norway and not least Svalbard,[1] has areas that are part of the Arctic. (N.i)

From this geographical point they went on to explain Arctic identity:

> It defines us in terms of foreign policy, security policy, and implicitly also defence policy, that we – our geography – it is our identity. That is, we are a country far, far north with large ocean areas; limited land area, but still. In an Arctic context, that defines our cooperation patterns, how we act, and more. (N.i)

In other words, not just formal Arctic statehood but also Arctic state identity flow from geography. Latitudes, territories, and ocean spaces all come together to form the idea of the Arctic and identity.

While the kinds of 'homelands' you might first imagine when thinking about national identity tend to be just that, land, the Arctic region is of course largely made up of ocean space. It is therefore interesting to consider how these formally defined Arctic geographies come to re-narrate and re-imagine oceanic spaces in terms of identity. In the case of Norway, recent years have seen a gradual shift in rhetoric to frame Arctic issues increasingly as ocean issues, in turn shifting also identity narratives to the sea. Not least, this ties into continental shelf claims under UNCLOS, whereby the seabed

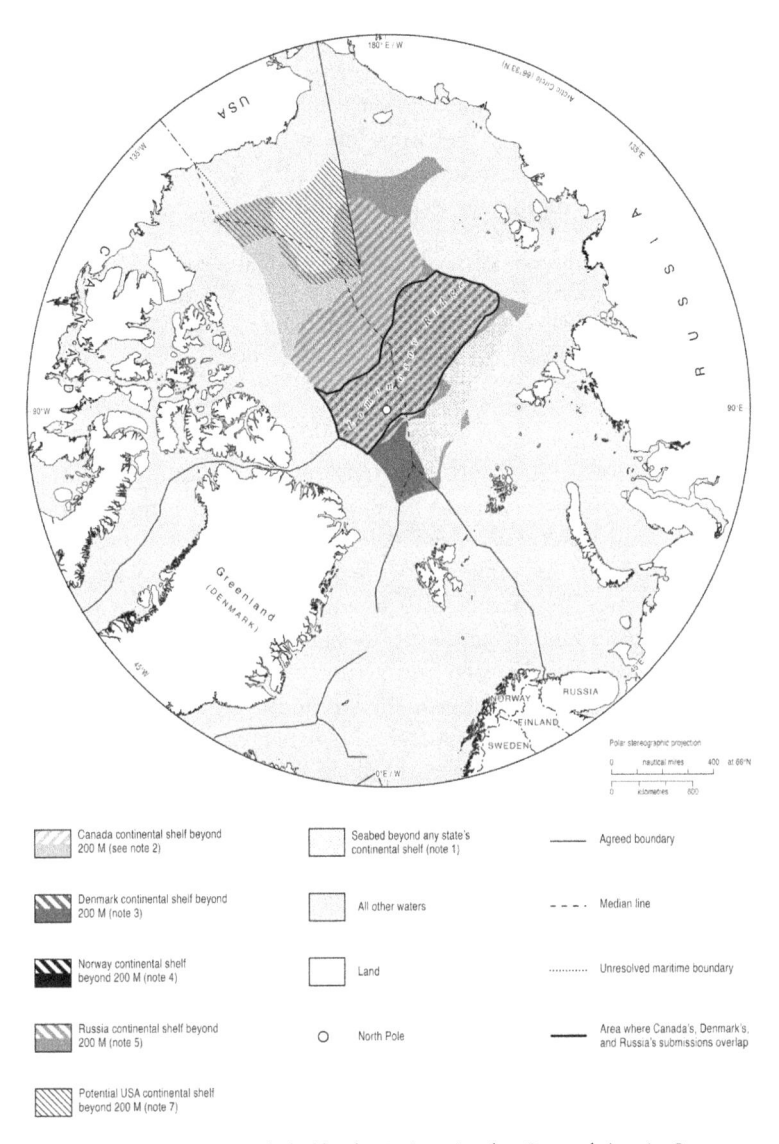

Figure 2.1 Continental shelf submissions in the Central Arctic Ocean (Source: IBRU/Durham University, UK; available at: https://www. durham.ac.uk/research/institutes-and-centres/ibru-borders-research/ mapsandpublications/maps/arctic-maps-series/)

seems to be momentarily imagined as 'land-like' – solid ground extending from the aforementioned 'national soil'. The reasons for such a re-imagination are no doubt in part economic, but with its basis in UNCLOS it also becomes linked to international law and rights (see Figure 2.1). Another interviewed Norwegian official with a background in diplomacy explained this particular dynamic:

> [T]he Law of the Sea is what counts here, and that is based on nation-states [...] And the continental shelf, that is a mountain formation extending from land, outwards; it is continuous – which pertains to the coastal states that manage them. So, Norway as a coastal state has a continental shelf with oceanic areas seven times the size of the land. (N.vi)

The invocation of the subsea extension of the country paints a powerful picture, alluding to an extension also of rights, responsibilities, and potentially even belonging. That is, it hints to an image of what is seemingly solid, *beneath* the depths, where flags may be planted (see Dodds, 2010b) and oil platforms may be built: concrete structures of settlement where Norwegian workers of today may live (see Eriksen and Neumann, 2011). Not only does such a conceptualisation place the Arctic on a globe imagined in neatly divided state-units, whereby borders are as easily drawn on the blue as the green; but it also links the Arctic Ocean to ideas of 'national space', seemingly integral to the very essence of people and their home.

Arctic statehood and membership in the Arctic Council are no doubt matters of geography – yet, with a closer look at the map, it is evident that the Icelandic 'mainland', or main island, lies south of the Arctic Circle (see Figure 0.1). Only a small uninhabited island, Grímsey, provides latitudinally defined Arctic 'soil' on which to base its statehood as such (Harding and Bindloss, 2004: 41). In contrast (and contestation), the official governmental view is, however, that 'Iceland is the only country wholly within the Arctic' (I.MFA, 2009: 7; 2021) – but based on criteria other than cartographic gridlines. And, indeed, this is one way in which the aforementioned contextual and purpose-specific definitions of the region hold political significance too – something which has been a key point of emphasis for Icelandic officials since the state's exclusion from Arctic fishery-related negotiations in 2008 (see Dodds and Ingimundarson, 2012) and the Ilulissat Declaration (2008). Their position on the matter is that the ocean – stretching northwards, and flowing around and enveloping the country – *connects* Iceland to the Arctic Ocean. However, as its continental shelf claims under UNCLOS do not extend as far north as the Arctic Ocean,[2] it is not considered among the five Arctic coastal states – to much political dismay in Iceland. When the Icelandic Parliament, *Alþingi*, in 2011 agreed on a resolution on its Arctic Policy (I.MFA, 2011), a more 'correct' definition was prioritised in several of its 12 principles. For example, the third priority was the following:

> Promoting understanding of the fact that the Arctic region extends both to the North Pole area proper and the part of the North Atlantic Ocean which is closely connected to it. The Arctic should not be limited to a narrow geographical definition but rather be viewed as an extensive area when it comes to ecological, economic, political and security matters. (I.MFA, 2011: 1)

According to the *Alþingi*, it was in other words the Icelandic government's task to promote an understanding of what is here called a fact, and that Iceland therefore belongs. While this is no longer an explicit priority in its 2021 Policy, the opening sentence indeed makes the same point: 'Iceland is the only Arctic State that can be deemed to lie entirely within the Arctic as it is most commonly delimited' (Minister for Foreign Affairs and International Development Cooperation Gudlaugur Thór Thórdarson in I.MFA, 2021: 1). The sense of unfair exclusion from an exclusive group was powerfully described also by several interviewed Icelandic officials, such as in the following quote by an employee in the Ministry of Foreign Affairs:

> I have to insist that when it comes to Iceland's position in the Arctic, then our view is that we are, of course, completely inside the Arctic. We have the [world's] northernmost capital, and [...] we are almost the only country that is entirely within the Arctic. And that means that all the inhabitants in Iceland, in this way, are Arctic inhabitants, so to speak. (I.i)

And indeed as mentioned earlier, according to the *Arctic Human Development Report* (AHDR 2004: 17–18; see also AHDR-II 2015), sometimes considered the 'centrepiece' of Iceland's Arctic Council chairmanship in 2002–4, *all* of Iceland is well within the maps' exclusive coloured lines; lines that are not only drawn according to latitudes, climates, and biomes but also based on broadly inclusive cultural, political, and social criteria, as employed by the Arctic Council's variously focused Working Groups. Across Working Groups and disciplines, competing 'cartopolitics' – that is, cartographic practices that *produce* a spatial reality to which political practice can be applied (Strandsbjerg, 2012) – are here bundled together in an 'overarching', inclusive definition of the region. For Iceland, *full* inclusion (and thus, *full* recognition of its Arctic statehood – also as coastal) is therefore contingent on specific Arctic spatialities. The promotion of these takes place both to domestic and international audiences, and, in the process, re-scripts both the region and the nation-state (Dodds and Ingimundarson, 2012: 27; see also Offerdal, 2014). In this way, it is possible to think of Arctic spatiality as an active *process*: 'becoming' Arctic through the ongoing recognition by others, as well as by fellow nationals and state practitioners. In other words, 'becoming' Arctic is not just as an outcome of an existing spatiality but through a process of spatial*ising* anew both the region and the state.

In contrast to Icelanders' view of themselves as 'wholly within the Arctic', most Canadians have not visited the North themselves. Yet it is a space that features prominently in national conceptualisations of Canada and Canadian identity, as we will see also in chapters to come. Colourful lines on maps, in classrooms as well as in governmental offices, have tended to show Canadian territory shaped as a wedge, most of which lies north, pointedly peaking at the pole. Although this depiction is not uncontested – Canada's UNCLOS submissions are still not determined (Quinn, 2022) – it is a powerful image of Canada's vast geography,[3] showing just how significant a part of it lies north of the Arctic Circle. It will come as no surprise then, that on the question of the meaning of Arctic statehood and identity, many Canadian officials responded along the lines of: 'it's geographical, obviously. I think there is a shared sense of ownership of the North' (C.i). However, as is evident also in Norway and Iceland, what and when space becomes Arctic space is defined not only by the topic at hand but also by interest, positionality, and context. An interviewed Canadian official working on environmental policies explained this difficulty of definitions:

> [W]e still have to define what we mean when we talk about the North and the Arctic every time we go in front of a new audience, or even just – the topic might change. [...] It means different things to different people. There's nothing homogenous about the North or the Arctic. (C.ii)

What or *where* is 'Arctic' is therefore, on the one hand, defined by issue topic; but on the other, the deployment of the term may itself define the topic and what is deemed relevant for discussion. As many Norwegian and Icelandic officials explained, using '*nordområdene*' or '*norðurslóðir*' [both, literally, 'northern areas'] respectively serves as a way in which to circumvent connotations of, *inter alia*, spatial distance and difference; in Canada, a similar terminological selectivity is even more apparent. There, 'the North' is the favoured term to broaden discussions, extending it southwards and making it more relational, while simultaneously narrowing it to a strictly domestic Canadian focus. That is, separate from foreign policy agendas, and disassociated with the Arctic Circle delimitation, 'the North' is generally agreed upon among officials as comprised of the three northernmost territories (as opposed to the ten provinces) – Yukon, Northwest Territories, and Nunavut – or roughly 'north of 60th [degree]'. The Canadian Government's 2019 Arctic Policy applied the following definitional distinction: '"Arctic" is used in the international context, when referring to the circumpolar Arctic (e.g. Arctic states), while "Arctic and North" is used in all domestic contexts' (C.CIRNAC, 2019). As such, state personnel are aware of the overlapping (but not identical) geographies of the North and the Arctic, but the use of either may largely guide what kind of politics is enabled or disabled. Articulating an Arctic state identity – or conversely, a Northern state identity – is clearly a citation of a spatially bounded discourse, but *how* said space is articulated, in which terms, potentially reconfigures the production of new statements and practices, of alternative ways of performing the state.

However, an Indigenous official from 'the North' expressed discontent with the term: 'I don't think it's a proper way of describing it, I think it would be better to describe it as "Arctic". At least the people will understand more, you know, what you're talking about' (C.iii). In their view, it was too vague and they added: 'There was another term, one that comes down to jurisdiction that they use – it's certainly negatively affected us a number of times. It's called "north of 60th"' (C.iii). During the interview, the official pointed and referred to a circumpolar map laid out in front of us, and traced northern latitudes to the Norwegian Arctic. In this case, spatial identity and belonging were articulated along east–west connections rather than north–south. And, as the interview continued, 'they' (the *others*) referred to the Canadian Government and officials who supposedly belonged to another space, Ottawa and the south. Nevertheless, although drawing the line at the 60th, instead of the 66th, northern latitudinal line may seem more inclusive, it does, after all, *draw a line*. Cartographic practice (here, connected to jurisdiction) – the knowledges that go into the act of drawing said line – is thereby complicit in producing a *border-able* and distinguishable 'North' as a 'spatial reality' to which policy may be applied (see Strandsbjerg, 2012). And, moreover, the numerous administrative and practical implications of this line are what in turn produce territory, *produce* a Canadian 'North' (see Painter, 2010). The provinces' northern parts – what some refer to as the 'forgotten north' (Coates and Morrison, 1992) – are thereby omitted from critical discussions, despite potentially sharing similar cultures, livelihoods, challenges, and/or biomes (also Bennett et al., 2016). Another Canadian official explained this particular problem of defining and drawing boundaries:

> [E]ven Canada's provinces which are south of 60th, there are very northern parts of those provinces that have conditions that are Arctic-ish [...] So it's a bit confusing, it's hard to [define the North/ Arctic]. It's remoteness, yeah, and harsh climate. And, sort of, northern Quebec, northern Manitoba – you know, there's polar bears in northern Manitoba, but they're not considered Arctic! (C.iv)

Clearly, neither the Arctic, with its numerous contextual definitions, nor the North, a term that remains relational to a south, are fixed, universally agreed-upon spaces. In the words of the former Canadian Prime Minister Stephen Harper:[4] 'the land of the North is endless and so are the possibilities. Our biggest dreams are at our highest latitudes' (2014a). And, indeed, perhaps what may be considered northern (if not capitalised) really *is* endless, with definitions that shift and change as dreams do. Articulations of Arctic state identities among personnel were unwaveringly geographically based, initially seemingly obviously defined by lines and border. And yet, it was soon evident that the geographical base itself is anything but stable. Nevertheless, though their specificities are contextually contingent, the articulations of a geographically based state identity clearly serve to demarcate topic of discussion, line of action, and production of statement. *Where* we speak of, dream of, and *where* we draw that line inevitably condition the political practices pursued and performed by those 'within' the state; the line may circumscribe geopolitical possibilities.

Filling in the lines

While lines on maps, borders, and definitions – however contestable – are clearly important to how Arctic state identities are articulated, this is not all that is meant by 'Arctic geographies'. Indeed, linking Arctic spaces, the ocean, and subsea continental shelves to ideas of home does not just potentially increase public support for politics but also conceptually transforms a seemingly distant space to a place with meaning for state practitioners too (see Knecht and Keil, 2013). That is, in addition to seeing the Arctic as lines on a map as above, it is also 'filled in' with characteristics, and an environment that is imagined as not just shaped by a nation's resource harvest and usage, but also itself *shaping* the nation (see Dijink, 2002). Imaginations of an Arctic environment may include climates, landscapes, topographies, temperatures, livelihoods provided thereby, and so on. This was how an interviewed Norwegian parliamentarian explained these particular spatial dynamics as influential also in politics:

> I have often participated in international meetings with European top politicians, where you sort of use Norway's Arcticness, with sparse habitation and high mountains and deep fjords and snow and headwind and steep hills and all of that [...] Those kinds of things are raised in these kinds of meetings to create legitimacy and understanding, but also to brag of Norway by emphasising this, because in certain areas we are at the front. (N.ii)

In this manner, firstly to an external audience, 'Arcticness' becomes synonymous with environmental characteristics with which the entire nation may identify; boundaries between periphery and core are blurred. Just as ideas of 'homeland' are extended northwards into the sea, Arctic space is extended southwards, as its characteristics stretch across invisible lines of latitude, rendering it malleable and always relative. Battling wind and weather, coldness and harshness, is something with which ostensibly all citizens may identify (see Bhabha, 1994: 243). This imagery may also serve to provide meaning to state personnel, rendering the Arctic familiar, known, drawn closer through the senses. Described by another Norwegian state interviewee, closeness to nature not only reminds Norwegians of being Arctic – it shapes them as such:

> [In Norway] You live, sort of, closer to nature somehow, to the natural forces; that is part of giving you heightened awareness. That is, when you live in a place [...] where you feel the Arctic weather conditions, you are constantly reminded of it. Sort of like I feel myself [in southern Norway] that the climate is absolutely part of shaping a person and identity, I think, to a very high degree. (N.iii)

They further elaborated on how this might potentially influence political practice as well as general behaviours: '[W]hen you meet others, from other countries, who do not have that, sort of, hard nature, right; then you notice that it affects our character, yes, our identity, how we look at things. And I think this closeness to nature means that we have more respect for nature' (N.iii). In a similarly environmentally 'influenced' manner (Livingstone, 1992), another explained that the political focus on sustainability and environmental protection may likely be traced back to an identity as 'a "fishing-and-hunting people", and in a way, an acknowledgement that you have to take care of both nature and resources' (N.iv).

In this manner, the spatialities of identity discourses, the seeming 'rootedness' in nature and environment, provide state personnel with a framework of political practice and behaviour: a seemingly 'undisputable' explanation for why Norwegians are as they are and act as they do – and perhaps why they themselves perform politics the way they do.

One of the non-latitudinal criteria that is sometimes used for drawing Arctic boundaries is that of temperature, namely the aforementioned ten-degree July isotherm. And indeed, for many state personnel, it is not just latitudes that confer an identity tied to the Arctic but also nature, environment, weather, and climates. In a no less environmentally influenced way than that of Norwegian identity discourses, the Icelandic character is said to be shaped by the hardship of survival in an inhospitable climate (Vasey, 1996: 149). Even the landscape's 'rhythms and clangs' are said to influence the people (Hastrup, 2010: 197). For one Icelandic parliamentarian, nature connects Icelanders not only to their inherent 'Arcticness' but also to the other Arctic states:

> I feel very strongly how my nature, somehow – my inner energy, my nature – is very strongly connected and bound to this country [...] it's just *different energy*. I don't know how to ... I'm not sure if it's the weather or the nature, or ... But the Nordic, the Arctic countries they have all different landscapes [...] but still, it's just the atmosphere, the people, the mentality. Cool on the inside and very wild on the inside sometimes! (I.ii; followed by laughter)

Noted by several of the interviewed state personnel, perhaps particularly in Norway and Iceland, nature is what unites the group of eight despite their differences: 'When you have a common – even if it's only a common physical feature like the aurora borealis and the long dark winters and these glaciers and snow – then that of course helps to have this circumpolar identity' (I.iii). Arctic statehood is here understood as *more* than latitudinal. It is *natural* and environmental – spatialities that in turn unite and *define* people. Representing the state is therefore about *more* than pragmatic border-drawing: it is about the space within these borders from which a community seemingly gain their essence, character, and 'self'.

Imagined as that which has made Icelanders 'who they are', closeness to nature is also the channel through which an Arctic identity is often explained as emerging. For one Icelandic parliamentarian, their sense of Arctic identity was mediated through familiar environments: '*ice*, you know, the glaciers; it's also a part of us. Arctic, glaciers, it's somehow the same. You *connect* with it somehow' (I.ii). This 'connectedness' is one of supposed attunement, making Icelanders 'receptive' to their environments: 'The nature is very much a big part of all of us in Iceland, I would say. So we are very *aware*' (I.ii). This, in turn, serves as an argument for authority in the Arctic, as well as for environmental authority against 'distant', (fishery) quota-setting Eurocrats (Einarsson, 1996a), and today even more distant 'others' in the Arctic (see Medby, 2018). Political emphasis on environmental protection is, indeed, often linked to imaginaries of unique Icelandic nature that has shaped a unique Icelandic people (Dibben, 2009: 143; see also Waage and Benediktsson, 2010). And as will be clear also in later chapters, an identity of environmentalism, sustainability, and 'being green' is a source of national pride and a guideline for political practice too.

Perhaps in Iceland more so than in any other Arctic state do natural *forces* play a crucial role in the conceptualisation of place, landscape, and homeland. The geographer Doreen Massey's (2005) writings about 'migrant rocks' exemplify how space is always dynamic, which in Iceland is epitomised as the ever moving tectonic plates upon which the island state travels.[5] In contrast to a crack that pulls *apart*, Icelanders' particular geographical position is articulated as one of *connection*: 'The position of Iceland is in-between the West and East. And actually, the crack, it goes through Iceland, so we are completely, you know, *both sides*' (I.ii). Or, as another Icelandic interviewee explained it, Iceland has a paradoxical position of dual marginality that becomes centrality: 'We are on the outskirts of Europe; we are also on the outskirts of the US. So, we're in a quite interesting place geographically' (I.vi).

Iceland's particular mid-Atlantic placement has now, in the aforementioned 'age of the Arctic' (Osherenko and Young, 2005), grown a third branch, extending not just east and west but *north* – across the Pole to Asia. Notwithstanding sober assessments of the actual potentials of transpolar shipping (e.g. Humpert, 2013), many evidently see Iceland's geographical position as one of great promise: 'If you take a longer-term perspective, I think we are looking towards seeing a new kind of Mediterranean Sea: a sea that will be open for shipping, for transport, for resource exploration' (I.vii). A sea of *connection* rather than separation is a polar imaginary with a long history – one promoted not least by the Icelandic-Canadian Vilhjálmur Stefánsson (further elaborated later; see Dodds, 2010a; Steinberg, 2016). And while the Mediterranean analogy may, in the wake of the 'European migrant crisis', come with its own problematic imaginary, the role sketched out for Iceland is one of a shipping hub, a node within a network of economic, cultural, and political flows and connections. In this way, Iceland's 'islandness' is not to be considered as one of separation or isolation, but as ever more connected by the waves along its shores (e.g. Mountz, 2015). These oceanic connections are not merely those of transversal *above* fluid depths but the currents, streams, and mobilities themselves – circulations that matter for shipping but also climates and marine life: 'we have to protect this area [the Arctic] – even though it is not just outside, the closest to the coast – because the Arctic streams are from the North Pole to Iceland' (I.iv). Or, as another state representative succinctly explained Iceland's Arctic identity: 'that's quite clear, the connection, because the ocean's currents go back and forth and we are dependent on that. That's one of the main [reasons] behind the identity of Iceland in the Arctic' (I.viii). In other words, conceptualisations of Iceland's Arctic identity are one of the ever dynamic processes where the human and non-human constitute each other (see Massey, 2006; Squire, 2016), in, of, and by Arctic geographies. Hence, despite its seeming constancy, articulations of state identity are equally about being as *becoming*, an ever-evolving process of claiming and inhabiting space that in turn claims and inhabits images of the country too.

Discontent with the inability of lines on a map to convey any *sense* of a place – what a place is like, feels like, looks like – the Canadian geographer Louis-Edmond Hamelin developed a method of calculating what he called *nordicité,* or 'nordicity' (1978).

In brief, level of nordicity is determined by ten climatic, social, and cultural variables, all assigned numerical values, or 'polar units', which are added together to a score of northernness – the maximum being the North Pole with 1000 polar units (Bone, 2009: 290). According to Hamelin's system, the dividing line between northern and southern Canada lies at 200 polar units, and higher values are further classified into Near, Middle, Far, and Extreme North – all part of his extensive new northern vocabulary and neologisms (some more useful than others) (Chartier, 2007). Some fifty years after Hamelin first developed the concept of nordicity, Canadian state personnel similarly speak of the meaning of 'being' an Arctic state as *more* than a consequence of cartography. There may be incremental 'levels' as you move northwards, but for them too it was through climate – cold, ice, snow – that they connected with their Arctic statehood, despite physical distance from the Arctic Circle:

> I think the identity of Canada as a northern nation – as a very cold, and our winter climate – is a huge, a very, very strong national identity [...] Canadians know winter. And because we have a strong winter here, even in the south, they think of themselves as a northern country. (C.vi)

Many noted that, even though this does not mean Arctic conditions per se, southern winters provide an imaginary bond to more northern spaces. 'I think it might blur; like, "Arctic" might blur into Canadian vastness and wilderness. A lot of Canadians [are] very proud of the wilderness and the uniquely Canadian – the vastness as well' (C.vii).

The romanticism tied to the Arctic – as a pristine, vast wilderness that supposedly epitomises the quintessentially Canadian – thereby blurs into national identity narratives in the south that are equally patriotic as nostalgic of a pre-urban, pre-industrial time:

> [I]t gives me, as a Canadian, a sense that in this country there's a lot of space still; there's a lot of wildness, which I identify with as a Canadian. And that wildness is in the Arctic. Now, if you talk to an Inuk, they would not say that it's wild, 'it's our home; we don't consider it as wilderness; it's our place'. But to me, it's important to know that in the world there's still very wild, unspoilt places. (C.viii)

In other words, not dissimilar to the ways in which Norwegian and Icelandic officials articulate what it means, for them, to 'be' Arctic, those in Canada also explained it as *felt* through corporeal senses; environmental and climatic conditions, winter, and cold that, in turn, seemingly shape a people, and shape identity. Here, it is the iterative encounter not with '*the* other' but with other *space* that produces a collective sensory 'surface' – a national Arctic community that gains its self-consciousness through the seemingly universally experienced cold (see Ahmed, 2004). And yet, for Canadians, the Arctic may primarily be a *symbol* for the national cold; the region itself remains distant and intangible, primarily understood through mental and sensory proxies. For southern, non-Indigenous Canadians, including most Ottawa-based state officials, 'being' Arctic therefore requires translation – one that may be corporeal and climatic more than linguistic. 'This idea about what the Arctic and the Far North is all about is just so – it's kind of the extreme of how we try to identify ourselves' (C.ii). The seemingly foreign 'frontier' of extreme colds, extreme winters, extreme winter dark, and extreme summer light thus becomes just that – extremely Canadian: a distilled essence of who, where, and how the national 'we' came to be.

Arctic oceanscapes: coasts, currents, and materialities

In addition to the noted harsh conditions of northern nature – such as coldness, winter, and an inhospitable climate – 'Arcticness' was often described by state representatives in Norway as coastalness; in Iceland, oceanic currents were conceptualised as connections; and, in Canada, references were made to it as an archipelago of solid space. In all, closeness to nature means closeness to the ocean – and in this way, the Arctic Ocean becomes drawn closer to fluid oceanscapes.

Similar to the imaginary of continental shelves as extensions of a mainland, the emphasis tends to remain on land – including that touching the ocean, the coast, and the resources and conditions for life it brings. On the topic of Norwegian Arctic identity, a parliamentarian offered the following:

The Norwegian identity also includes a winter identity; and the transition between that winter identity and the Arctic is not far. At the same time, the coastal identity that we've had, and have, in Norway through many, many years – with all the trade and livelihoods of the mixed society when we conducted both agriculture and fishery – that is also not very far from, well, the Arctic coastal activity that we have. So, I feel that there are gliding transitions and that they aren't necessarily in opposition to each other. (N.ii)

In other words, the ocean matters for life and livelihoods; as another Norwegian parliamentarian succinctly phrased it: 'the entire High North policy has its source in the usage of the *resources* that lie in the High North. In the sea, that is, with the fish that we have managed for a long time' (N.v). In recent years, the political focus on the ocean can also increasingly be seen in Norwegian governmental publications and speeches; the Arctic focus may be moving offshore, becoming more and more embedded in narratives of 'blue economies' (see Medby, 2019a). In this manner, traditional livelihoods are linked to current resource extraction – including that of potentially controversial petroleum – to what has 'always' been, and what supposedly lies at the heart of national life and livelihood, the 'essence' of identity, intrinsically tied to geography. A geography that is more than 'just' land, it is the geography of national life.

Unlike the emphasis on the shorelines per se, Icelandic articulations of Arctic state identities were often made with reference to oceanic currents, as the earlier cited interviewee hinted at. That is, the oceanic flows and currents that envelop the country, flowing to and from the Arctic Ocean proper on either side, are key to Iceland's 'Arcticness'. With them, these currents bring the above noted harsh weather conditions as well as rich fish stocks upon which Icelandic society historically has been dependent. While the Arctic *label* might be new, an island identity – much like the Norwegian coastalness – is deeply rooted, and it is familiar. The majority of Icelanders' settlement along the coast is one such result of a twentieth-century transition from agriculture (Eggertsson, 1996) to fishery (Brydon, 1996: 38; Hafstein, 2000: 95). Even today, fish and fish products remain important exports for the country (Hermannsson, 2005; Mingels, 2014). For several state officials, it was precisely this intersection of geographical position and subsistence that makes Iceland Arctic:

> Because of where Iceland is situated, in the middle of the North-East Atlantic, and [that] we are living on the ocean, that makes us an Arctic nation, in my mind, first and foremost. And the dependence of the Icelandic economy and the Icelandic society on the fishing and fishing activities is huge [...] Iceland, as such, is part of the Arctic because of this connection to the ocean. (I.viii)

For another Icelandic official, it was this wealth of natural resources that 'creates a character of a nation' (I.vi). The mentioned exclusion from the exclusive group of five Arctic coastal states in 2008 is therefore not just contested for pragmatic concerns but is also connected to a self-perception as inherently connected to the sea. Control of their own fishing zones and quotas has come to symbolise historical struggles for Icelanders' independence and national-ism (Bergmann, 2014); a struggle that even sparked the so-called 'Cod Wars' with Britain in the 1970s (Kristinsson and Nordal, 1996: 104; Pálsson and Helgason, 1996: 63), and more recently straining relations with the EU (Robert, 2014). One Icelandic official working on environmental policy explained the significance in the following evocative terms:

> Even if they were not real wars, they're still conflicts – they're sort of like wars of independence, like grabbing your destiny, achieving independence. So, it's very much at the core of Icelandic foreign policy, identity. And more so than just the economic activity; it's of course an extremely important economic activity, but it's a little bit *more* than that. (I.vii)

In this way, Icelanders' Arctic statehood – including their connec-tion (if not their coast per se) to the Arctic Ocean – thereby takes on added meaning, symbolic of the very 'essence' of the country and its people. In these articulations, the ocean is not an 'empty', unclaim-able space but rather the nation's fields of subsistence. Ensuring their influence in Arctic matters is, in other words, closely linked to patriotism and international status for the island state. It is the active performance of authority in matters of the seas, and, as such, the active performance of what it means to be Icelandic.

While Canadians' imaginations of Arctic space as vast distances and cold environments bear similarities to those of Norwegian and Icelandic officials, their descriptions thereof differed in their emphasis on Arctic land, or land-*like* qualities, as opposed to the other cases' explicit engagement with the Arctic as *ocean* (or, even, seafloor). Canadian officials spoke of UNCLOS and international shipping as well, but the ocean was often scripted as *around*, outside, the state:

> [W]e are a nation that goes from sea to sea, which is part of our country's slogan is 'A Mari usque ad Mare', which is 'from sea to sea'. But we all say now from 'sea to sea to sea', because we recognise the Arctic Ocean as also very, very important as one of Canada's oceans. (C.ix)

The geographical differences between the state and the other two are clearly a factor, as Norwegian and Icelandic everyday lives are marked by coastalness and islandhood respectively. In contrast, the majority of Canadians are landlocked in the south, and the sea marks the edges and finitude of a vast state territory.[6] Thus, UNCLOS and the Arctic oceanscape more generally matter to Canada, but perhaps more in practical than emotional terms.

> [Y]ou know, [continental shelf submissions under] UNCLOS will take decades to resolve, but in a way it doesn't matter, because it doesn't – it's not, you know, what we end up with is going to be very much an Arctic Ocean controlled by the Arctic states with perhaps a small area in the middle that remains High Seas or, you know, ocean areas that would be common heritage. (C.x)

However, there is more to it than differences in geography, not least when considering that Canada actually has the world's longest coastline – a quantitative argument for spending taxpayers' money in the North that serves politicians well: 'With 40 per cent of our landmass in the North, and more than 160,000 kilometres of Arctic coastline, Canada is a Northern country' (Harper, 2014a). In fact, it was not long after Harper entered office as Prime Minister in 2006 that he asserted sovereignty over the Arctic archipelagic waters in the Canadian North, specifically the Northwest Passage (Byers, 2010; Byers and Baker, 2013). In brief, the Canadian government claims this is internal waters based on historical usage (granting

Canada full jurisdiction), while the USA maintains that it is an international strait (leaving it open for international transit) (see e.g. Bartenstein, 2011; Elliot-Meisel, 2009; Griffiths et al., 2011; Pharand, 2007; Steinberg, 2014). For Canada, the Northwest Passage holds particular symbolic significance for national identity and statehood. Not only does the search for this mythicised passage feature prominently in the nation-building narrative of Canada's 'frontiers' and settlement (as will be returned to later), but it has also come to symbolise the aforementioned need for distinctiveness next to the USA. This came to the fore in 1969, when the American *SS Manhattan* transited without formally granted permission, spurring vigorous Canadian debate about sovereignty. This specific example was also brought up by an official as he discussed how identity was 'defined maybe in antagonism against another country' (C.xi):

> Even though the US is our closest ally, it doesn't take long in Canada to stoke, you know, the very feeble fires of nationalism when you talk about the US doing something that might be seen as un-Canadian, for example. And, in the late '60s when the US sent an icebreaker through the Northwest Passage without really asking our permission, then Canadians were like, 'well, this is our Arctic, how dare they do that!' and so on and so forth. And certainly from a political perspective that's also part of the discourse, as I'm sure you've seen – especially with [Harper's] government. (C.xi)

For them, it was this incident that marked the start of Canada's concerted efforts to assert and protect Arctic sovereignty; for others, it was the transpolar Soviet threat during the Cold War. As such, Arctic waters hold an important symbolic significance also for Canada and Canadian statehood writ large, but the way that it is framed in officials' statements is not oceanic but *internal*; or, in other words, it matters as between, connected to, or *like* land (perhaps an archipelago, see Vannini et al., 2009). As in Harper's famous 'use it or lose it' approach, Arctic sovereign statehood means active usage of Arctic space (Lackenbauer, 2011a, 2011b). Spatially conceptualised as territorial terrain, political approaches thereto are demarcated – said use becomes that of 'boots on the *ground*'.

The above 'historical usage' that Canada's claims to full jurisdiction of the Northwest Passage are based on is that of Inuit use of the waters when frozen solid (i.e. 'land-like'), thereby ostensibly justifying Canadian territoriality. Under UNCLOS, governance of sea-ice is ambiguous, covered only by the singular Article 234, leaving it open to interpretation (e.g. Kraska, 2014). For Inuit in Canada, however, rights to ice – or, in climate change debates, 'the right to be cold' (Watt-Cloutier, 2015) – are deeply connected to lives and livelihoods: meanings that are not easily (if at all) translated into formal international law:

> When the Law of the Sea Convention was put together [...], they had no conception at all whatsoever how can you own the water, how can you have the rights to the ice when you cannot live on the ice. But, the fact is we have, we still have a lot of people alive today who were born on the ice, belonging, who belong to this area. (C.iii)

Anthropologists have extensively documented not only Inuit use and travel routes on sea-ice but also the ways in which ice is understood and known (see Krupnik et al., 2010; Aporta et al., 2011; Aporta, 2011). What is clear both in their work and the above citation is that frozen water may be known, inhabited, used; however, in Inuit conceptualisations, it is not simply 'like land' – the ice has its own particular materiality that cannot easily be equated with sheer, UNCLOS-instrumental solidity (see Dodds, 2018). Nevertheless, the simplification, rendering sea-ice seemingly static and territorial, is one way in which non-Inuit, non-Northern state representatives may translate an otherwise, for them, illegible spatiality. The official cited above continued that, even as climate change is changing the physical conditions of the space and ice becomes less reliable, it does not change rights, livelihoods, or attachments:

> You're still using it; even if it was frozen ice and then it's melted, you're still using it. And you're still relying on your economy, because your economy – it moves back and forth on those channels and things in there, nature which happens to be a food source or a clothing source. So, your attachment [is] to the [space] – from the top, down to the bottom of the ocean. (C.iii)

In this way, Inuit spatial identity may very well be tied to 'watery' spaces; the Canadian politicisation and subsequent interpretation of this identity, however, is not theirs. Rather, the point that the Canadian North, including its waters, is and has been inhabited and used ostensibly 'since time immemorial' (C.DIAND, 2009: 9) is one of the Canadian Government's key arguments for sovereignty (Steinberg et al., 2015; for a historical view of 'colonising' ice, see Craciun, 2010) – despite the fact that Inuit imaginations (or experiences) may be wholly different. As the above quote clearly states: Arctic space *moves*. And yet, in most Canadian state articulations of Arctic identity and spatial belonging, it is rendered frozen and static – a space that may be bordered and delimited, as it simultaneously, paradoxically itself delimits how said identity may be performed, practised, and stated into political reality. In other words, the spatial imaginary of Arctic 'ground' may in state officials' conceptualisations be static, moved *across*, and devoid of agency – yet, it is precisely through the discursive attempts of fixing it that Arctic spatiality asserts its agency, guiding and conditioning the actions of those by whom it was articulated as such.

Naming and labelling space

Official geographies and boundaries, as well as environmental characteristics, aside, 'the Arctic' is a term that may still ring of distance to many. Returning to the Norwegian example, the state may well be promoted as Arctic, and discursive linkages forged between oceanic space, nature, home, and the supposed national character; yet there is still something seemingly foreign with this largely externally imposed label. One Norwegian official with extensive Arctic experience reflected on this in relation to identity:

> [M]ost people in Norway, I think the majority, define themselves as a country far north. However, using 'Arctic identity' or that Norway is an 'Arctic state', exactly those words, I am a bit uncertain about. Because, 'Arctic', in itself, is a foreign word in the Norwegian vocabulary, and it is not used so much; but that people have a strong identity of being a coastal state, near the coast, and having a northern identity, of that I am quite certain. (N.vi)

Here, an *Arctic* identity is seen as a new label on what was already there, already part of national identity too. Others also pointed out that relative northernness is likely to determine how strongly the Arctic is seen to relate to people's everyday lives:

> I think it depends, perhaps, on where in Norway you are. [In North Norway] they live in it every day. They have the polar night, and all the things you typically associate with the Arctic. So, for them it's completely normal, I think. I think, perhaps, you think less about it in central eastern Norway and southern parts of the country. But … it depends how you phrase the question, because I think, there is no doubt that we are a coastal state, that we lie far north, and that that comes with very particular challenges. (N.ii)

Again, identifying as Arctic is rooted in geography, but geographical northernness is always relative; it matters more when faced with those who are 'south'. 'We are a sea nation and much of the sea is in the north; but, of course, the Arctic identity is perhaps stronger in the north and along the coast' (N.iv). Here, the cited official's view on identity's contingency on geographical proximity mirrored that found among Norwegian youth in a previous study: namely, that relative northernness (as well as context and social relations) matters greatly to your sense of Arctic identity (Medby, 2014). This is a topic we will return to in Chapter 6, namely relative differences within a state. However, in *outsiders'* eyes, all of Norway might be 'the country that is far north and cold' (N.vii). And as always inherently relational, also Arctic spatiality is defined against an external 'other'; for Norwegian state personnel, this means that it may be an identity that matters more when abroad, faced with colleagues who do not come from Arctic states. Viewed from Brussels, Washington, or London, even Lindesnes – the southern-most tip of the Norwegian mainland – is far north, and *all* are northerners, including bureaucrats who may never have ventured to higher latitudes.

Nevertheless, in addition to longitudes and latitudes, language is significant for how Arctic state identity is situated. As mentioned, 'Arctic'[7] is a foreign term and until recently a name not often used in domestic policies in any of the states. By a foreign denomination, it might not be surprising that the Arctic seems distant – primarily linguistically designated to the field of foreign policy. Although any clear domestic/foreign policy binary may be outdated in today's increasingly interconnected world (for example, where Arctic politics clearly relates to both), Neumann (2001) reminds us that such a distinction still continues to determine conditions for action (see also Agnew, 1994). This binary division, illusory or not, is echoed in both popular and official discussions about the Arctic. A Norwegian interviewee acknowledged that it is 'a question of definition that is politically very important' (N.vi). Likely in an attempt to avoid unfavourable linguistic connotations and associations,[8] Norwegian officials have, in place of 'the Arctic', up until recently tended to favour the term '*nordområdene*': literally, 'the northern areas', but usually translated as 'the High North'.[9] As scholars have pointed out, this term has often been more flexible than the Arctic (Skagestad, 2010; Wærp, 2014; see also Keskitalo, 2004; Medby, 2019a), less clearly demarcated by latitudes, temperatures, or treelines, but rather as a north relative to an undefined south. The 2021 *Arctic Policy* (N.MFA, 2021) described the term 'High North' as originating from policy initiatives and strategies. Approaching a definition, it goes on to clarify the following:

> In geographical terms, the 'High North' refers to the land and sea areas between southern Helgeland in the south to the Greenland Sea in the west and the Pechora Sea (the southeastern corner of the Barents Sea) in the east. This term has mainly been used in a geopolitical context and is closely associated with efforts to safeguard Norwegian interests through various initiatives and cross-border cooperation in the North Calotte region and the Barents region as a whole. (N.MFA, 2021: 7)

As this highlights, the 'High North' serves to emphasise the Norwegian 'part' of the Arctic, including the portion of Nordland County stretching slightly south of the Arctic Circle – and it is explicitly connected to policy and geopolitics. In short, to borrow Sverker Sörlin's words, it is 'political rhetoric designed to make the territories north of Norway's Scandinavian mainland seem just a continuation of home' (Sörlin, 2013: 9). By contrast, employing 'the Arctic' term emphasises the international dimension of political practice in the circumpolar north.

Recently, the Norwegian government increasingly uses 'the Arctic' over 'the High North', likely in order to facilitate their participation among international peers (N.i). Despite this, when interviewees were asked about the terms, their explanations were strikingly inconsistent – demonstrating the terms' ambiguity, and, so, contextual malleability. For one person, 'the Arctic' was 'more tied to such Arctic Council work; institutional' (N.viii), that is foreign policy. For another, the two terms were 'overlapping':

> [B]ecause the High North is primarily in the Arctic; at the same time as the High North stretches, perhaps, a bit further than the Arctic. The Arctic is, really, north of the Arctic Circle, strictly speaking, but that is more of a, perhaps, technical view. A popular view is that it can vary a lot. It can run much further south, in fact, than the Arctic Circle; but others can also think that it runs much further north, actually. So, I think it is overlapping. And ... it depends a lot on where you 'stand' when the question is asked. (N.ii)

Ambiguous at best, the concluding sentence sums up on the (lack of any real) distinction between the two: it depends on who, where, is defining and distinguishing, for what purpose. Arctic statehood (and with it, identity as such) is – like internationally recognised statehood in general – defined by distinction and difference, including something as seemingly 'natural' as spatial position. Also geography and physical location are given *meaning* only within discourse; when state personnel speak of the Arctic, it is already bound by the parameters of all its possible preceding and succeeding pronouncements. Placing the state as 'in', 'of', 'over', and so on positions the state not just on maps but also in relations of political power (e.g. Bondi, 1993: 99). Nominal, relational, and relative terms all conjure certain geographical imaginations, and, consequently, serve to position for political practice both *in* and *as* Arctic.

The present ubiquity of an Arctic 'label' might be of even more recent date in Iceland than in Norway. Not only a formal political title, the name now adorns objects, buildings, and events thanks to a growing tourism industry. That is, whereas the fishing industry has historically been at the core of Icelandic economy and life, Icelandic lives and livelihoods have become connected to nature in yet another way: through the rapidly expanding tourism sector (Kristinsson and Nordal, 1996: 106). As more than a space in which to root the state's identity, 'its landscape is big business, from the geological pyrotechnics of ash-spewing volcanoes to northern lights rippling above glacial wildernesses' (Barraclough, 2012: 79). Many of the interviewed Icelanders were also quick to point out that a formal title of Arctic statehood is also a brand that *sells*:

> If you asked a person, 'Why do you want to visit Iceland?' the answer is nature. So, I think that can easily be related to branding Iceland as an Arctic county, because the Arctic, I would imagine in the minds of people is nature, ice. (I.v)

An opportunity seized by marketing companies, it only takes a stroll down Laugavegur, Reykjavík's main shopping street, to see nature-based activities advertised as 'Arctic' adventures, such as glacier walking, northern light chasing, and midnight sun golfing. While the label is relatively new, one Icelandic politician considered it simply not recognised in those terms earlier:

> something you just have; you don't need to label it. But we have been labelling ourselves, and we have been trying to identify more who we are, through the growth of the tourism. We have, for sure, and been very focused on our strengths and what we can show, what we can do, what we can 'sell', if we can call it that ... So maybe our identity is becoming more focused through tourism. (I.vi)

In this way, the booming tourism industry, the outsider's gaze, might influence the ways the Icelanders view their own landscapes and country too (Sæþórsdóttir et al., 2011). For Icelandic state personnel, their own daily stroll to work might thereby serve as a reminder, however banal and unnoticed (Billig, 1995), of living in, being from, and representing the *Arctic* state of Iceland: an island of connections but separations, of relatedness but uniqueness – land embraced by ocean, and a dynamic space with seeming agency to form its people and guide their practices.

Distant as the Arctic may be both geographically and imaginatively, *all* of the state holds the title of Arctic statehood of course, and *all* of Canada is a northern country in relative terms, as outlined above. As the main point of reference from which to distinguish Canada, and Canadian identity, has shifted from the British empire in the east to the American 'superpower' in the south, a sense of *northern* uniqueness has become more important:

> Canadians, they compare themselves with the United States for better or worse, and the big comparison is south–north. So, we're north of the United States and so we always think of ourselves as northerners. That doesn't necessarily mean the Arctic – I think the Arctic represents what we think of ourselves in terms of being northern, being different, and being, I guess, hardier in terms of putting up with the winters. (C.ii)

The point here that the Arctic 'represents' a more generalised sense of northernness is worth noting, symbolic power that resurfaces in other contexts of the state's identity too. As the Peace Arch near the US–Canada border proclaims, the two states are 'Children of a common mother' and 'Brethren dwelling together in unity'. And so, for the Canadian 'little brother', its proclaimed difference – e.g. as above, 'northern [...] hardier' (C.ii) – has become a 'comforting mythology' (Cohen, 2008).

Identifying as northern – relative and relational – becomes a way in which to approximate the Arctic. Arctic statehood is translated to northern statehood, in turn drawing the distant and separate towards the familiar, folding into a sense of Canadianness:

> And I do think that because it transfers or it connects to the Arctic, that it also makes thinking about what would be more properly an Arctic, or an adjacent to the Arctic, sense of what our cultural and national identity is easier to the people who don't have the experience of what it is like to live up there or to be up to there to identify with it. Because there is kind of transference through that term, north, and a feeling that, you know, because we are north of so many others, we get to participate in feeling 'northerly', even though there are those in Canada who are as far north of here [Ottawa] as we are of Florida! (C.v)

Spatiality is, in other words, also a matter of where you are *not*; and identity a matter of who you are not. Northernness and Arcticness merge, blur, and evolve in the imaginations of those who call it 'theirs' before 'home'. The space and the region come to matter and be felt when faced with others – such as those from further south, and those not members of the region. In this way, everyone within the state boundaries may claim a northern identity, and in turn an Arctic identity, living within the contextually defined conditions and geographies of the state.

State geographies

The state's 'geographies' refer not only to (home)lands in which identity may be rooted, but as far more: space as *place* with heterogeneous connections between the human and non-human, to environments, natural forces, climates, weathers, floras, and faunas. In this manner, discursive boundaries are themselves produced in interaction, and collective identity in the sharing of subjective bodily experiences (or the shared lack thereof, as was often the case among southern Canadian state personnel). And interestingly, as a geographical region that is largely oceanic space, the spatialities of 'being' Arctic are – in spite of largely agreed upon lines and latitudes – expressed differently from person to person, as well as from state to state.

Without reducing individuals' views to the overly generalised, there are notable contrasts between the three states in this regard. Again, in brief, Arctic statehood is in Norway often linked to oceanic and sub-oceanic resources; in Iceland as oceanic currents, flows, and connections between the island state and the world; and in Canada as a solid and frozen frontier, land-*like* if not land, and often mythical, fragile, intangible as seen from a disconnected south. These imaginaries clearly suggest widely different political approaches – and yet, in all three they guide the conduct of Arctic statehood in one direction or another.

As is clear, however, geography is not all there is to identity, Arctic or not. Already, in the conceptualisations offered so far, there are references and hints to state histories, futures, and the many contextual relations through which identity is felt. In the next chapter, the second pillar of state identity is explored further, namely ideas of time.

Notes

1 As established in the 1920 Svalbard Treaty, Norway holds sovereignty over the Svalbard archipelago, subject to certain stipulations. For example, all signatories of the Treaty (currently 46 states) have equal rights to engage in commercial activities there (e.g., mining). There are also limitations pertaining to taxation, law, pollution, and military use. A recent controversy has related to whether Norway may claim the 200 nautical-mile Exclusive Economic Zone under UNCLOS in the sea around Svalbard (e.g., for fishery rights), as the Treaty was worded prior to the creation of UNCLOS. The town of Ny-Ålesund is generally considered the world's northernmost permanent civilian settlement. There are at present approximately 2,900 inhabitants on the archipelago, most of whom live in the largest town, Longyearbyen. A high number of different nationalities are represented thanks to the Treaty rights and a highly international researcher community (see e.g. Statistics Norway, 2023; Bykova, 2023).

2 Notwithstanding the ambiguity of determining where one ocean ends and another starts.

3 Canada has the second largest territory in the world, exceeded only by Russia, also an Arctic state of course.

4 Stephen Harper (Conservative Party) served as Prime Minister of Canada between 2006 and 2015.

5 Also worth mentioning, volcanic forces as recently as in the 1960s gave birth to new Icelandic territory: the small island Surtsey (Gimlette, 2009). Interestingly, it is named after the Norse fire giant, Surtr, thereby linking the country's most recent development to myths from its distant past (Halink, 2014).

6 However, see Vannini et al. (2009) for an interesting discussion how a Canadian re-conceptualisations, a re-continentalisation, may take place as the Arctic thaws – an example of the co-production of the social and material, a 'process of transformation of Canada into a peninsular body encompassed within a larger archipelagic entity: a place more intimately attuned to its immense (and growing) coastal and insular routes' (Vannini et al., 2009: 121).

7 'Arktis' (n.) / 'arktisk' (adj.).

8 On the topic of such unfortunate associations, one interviewee was concerned that a common misunderstanding about the Arctic was the following: 'Many think that it is dark and cold and boring and... nothing exciting happens. There are polar bears and Eskimos [*sic*] and igloos,

right. But it is so much more than that. It is – I think people sometimes forget about the fish and oil and gas and such; they think more about polar bears. I think so. Ice and polar bears and cold and darkness' (N.ix).

9 Where the original source or interviewee in Norwegian used '*nordom-rådene*', I have followed the government's example and translated it as 'the High North', although the literal translation, 'the northern areas', arguably holds slightly different connotations (which is relevant for how it is received domestically, of course).

3

State temporalities: the past, present, and futures of Arctic state identities

When asked about their identity, many would refer not only to *where* they consider themselves to be from, as in the previous chapter, but also what ties they have to that identity: ties that extend backwards in time and forwards to an imagined future. These temporal ties can be personal – such as family backgrounds, experiences, and aspirations – and they can be articulated through social connections and wider relations. This is no different when it comes to the question of Arctic statehood and identity: It is a matter of time as much as it is of space, about history and geography considered together – this chapter focuses on these temporalities.

As we have already seen, the Arctic 'label' is relatively new to most northern populations and states. However, while this might mean that a history of explicit Arctic identification is fairly short, the identities that it references can be traced back much further. That is certainly what political speakers do when they exclaim in big words what it means to be an Arctic state on conference stages. But more than being merely rhetorical, the temporalities of state identities – their pasts and futures – matter for decisions and actions that are taken in the present. And, moreover, how state personnel conceptualise their own histories and futures matter for the ways that they relate to the previously discussed changing geographies of the north.

For some, identity is that which remains constant – 'identical' – through time. A sense of self and of community can provide a sense of what Giddens (1991: 92) termed 'ontological security': a feeling of trust in the continuity, constancy, and reliability of both own self and 'the surrounding social and material environments of action'. If surrounding environments were partly what the previous chapter discussed, this chapter will look closer at the ideas of continuity and change through time. For both individuals and communities, this can often include a narrative of a shared past, through a present, and a future in a seemingly linear progression. In the case of Arctic states, then, this would imply that the Arctic state and peoples have supposedly *always* been such, regardless of the noted novelty of brands and titles. What comes to be remembered, as well as what comes to be forgotten, is a matter of geopolitical consequences. The telling of stories and histories may serve to 'materialise' and perform identity discourses into the recognisable shapes of events and monuments – which, in turn, may reify nation, state, and relations of power; or in contrast, they may challenge these.

While the geopolitical significance of historical narratives – national and otherwise – has attracted scholarly attention in geography and beyond, less attention has until recently been devoted to ideas of futures. However, what is clear in the Arctic context is that the (re-)narration of the past as a *polar* past – for example highlighting expeditions, discoveries, and achievements – is often secondary to a focus on Arctic futures: that is, futures based on anticipation, hopes, and fears of what is yet to come. The future – through practices of preparation, pre-emption, and anticipation – therefore materialises in the here-and-now. As such, the future is a product of (and in) the present – not in a predetermined sense, but in that it only ever *exists* in the now, is performed into being today. It is in this manner that 'being' Arctic – and discourses of Arctic state identities – are always an enactment within not just geographical but also temporal boundaries: of histories and futures that intersect in the present, where the Arctic state comes into being.

In this chapter, notions of Arctic state identities are traced from imagined polar pasts, to histories of lives and traditions. The chapter then turns to how Arctic identity narratives often draw on (hi)stories of exploration and heroism, things which are a recurring theme throughout much Arctic discussion and geopolitics. Further, it is clear that present politics is often shaped by future anticipation, and so finally the chapter closes with the forward-oriented and anticipatory nature of state identities.

National pasts as polar pasts

As noted, the label might be new, but the identities described under the 'Arctic' heading often refer to older stories of 'who we are' – not least when it comes to nations. And as states tend to get their legitimacy through reference to the so-called nation, i.e. the hyphenated 'nation-state', it should come as no surprise that Arctic states draw on ideas of Arctic nations too – including national identities. Consequently, Arctic state personnel also link their state's 'Arcticness' to national identity narratives, rearticulating familiar stories for a telling in the present. Although there is never any single national identity, it is worth considering how state personnel interpret what they think of as 'typically' Norwegian, Icelandic, or Canadian in the Arctic context: in other words, how national pasts are reinterpreted as *polar* pasts.

To take one example, the authors of the *Norwegian Polar History* [*Norsk Polarhistorie*] note, in spite of Norway becoming an active 'polar nation' in the late 1800s, a common conception 'of an unbroken Norwegian Polar tradition dating back to the Viking era – at least' (Drivenes and Jølle, 2004: 9). And similarly, state personnel explained ideas of Arctic statehood as simply a re-labelling of something that was *already* there, for example existing identities of being a coastal, environmentalist, seafaring, northern, and/or wintery country – narratives that resonate also with those of their Icelandic and Canadian colleagues. In this way, Arctic statehood does not become a matter of construction or '(Arctic) nation-building', but simply a new word for what is already familiar – thereby placing the Arctic narrative within a broader and longer national history. And those existing narratives of the Viking era, seafaring, and coastal identities, for example, take on new meaning in a new context, while implicitly also bringing with them associated taken-for-granted truths. As such, an Arctic state identity does not immediately open up for reconceptualising who and what is included, but is understood in similar frameworks as those already in place. This is a point we will see again in later chapters too, namely the reframing of the familiar and re-imagining of the state's character.

In addition to a history of seafaring and exploration, for example, being an Arctic state often means a historical position of peripherality. Perhaps with the notable exceptions of Russia and the US, all Arctic states are so-called small to middle powers. This is something the next chapter also returns to in the context of the international state system. However, in the context of history and polar pasts here, it is also significant to note that a sense of global marginality, and even inferiority, likely impacts an Arctic sense of self too. Norway was under Danish or Swedish rule for centuries, until 1814 and 1905 respectively, and was until the mid-twentieth century not only small but also a poor country. The situation today, following the discovery of oil and gas resources (and subsequent wealth accumulation), may look very different, but an identity of marginality in some respects arguably persists – as the above narratives, being on the periphery of Europe may be translated to northernness, and now in turn to Arcticness. The aforementioned symbol of a fisherman becomes recast as harvesting new oceanic resources, and that of the Viking as exploring new seas. Again, the domestication of an Arctic identity means that it becomes an extension of the familiar: 'I think most people think, whether it is the Arctic or the common western coast or southern coast, it is *Norway*' (N.ix). And in this manner, also, political action in the Arctic also comes to be understood as simply an extension, a seemingly inevitable trajectory from past to present:

> Of course, the Norwegian agenda – with responsible exploitation of resources, to summarise – is very much rooted in Norway, or the Norwegian, as a hunting and fishing nation, explorer nation; and there has always been a connection between Norway as a polar nation, a research nation, that wanted to exploit resources. They have historically also gone hand in hand. (N.x)

However new or controversial political practices of today may be, through the lens of a polar past the present too comes to seem familiar and even uncontroversial.

Although an Arctic state identity is not the 'label' that is always at the forefront of people's minds, nor is it always the most relevant among many facets of an identity, that does not make it seem any less constant. As one Norwegian official in the Ministry of Foreign

Affairs explained on a particularly hot summer's day in Oslo, pouring yet another glass of sparkling water:

> [Being an Arctic state] does not define everything the Norwegian state does, [but] it is a permanent condition that we cannot change by government or [political] direction. It is, kind of, we are there and it is who we are. We are an Arctic nation. That everyone in Norway feels that every day – at least on a day like this! – that I do not think, but that is how it is. (N.i)

Note in particular that they describe it as 'permanent', unchangeable, and one might presume unquestionable. A very similar sentiment was expressed by an Icelandic interviewee:

> If you look at us just as a country, being an Arctic country – I don't think that we have, maybe, that we are very aware of, every day, in our daily lives, that we are an Arctic nation. We just are and always have been. So, we don't think so much about it. (I.vi)

As the Icelandic, Norwegian, or Canadian and the Arctic were here woven together in a re-narrated understanding of identity, Arctic statehood becomes part of national statehood more broadly – it is 'domesticated' and normalised. And with that, a geopolitical approach to the region in the present will also seemingly follow those long lines of the past.

National independence is for Iceland even more recent than for Norway – as recent as 1944 and from then Nazi-occupied Denmark (Bergmann, 2014; Karlsson, 2000). Perhaps not surprisingly, for historians 'in Iceland and many other peripheral societies of the colonial order, the primary scholarly task was not so much to understand others but to be understood *by* them' (Pálsson and Durrenberger, 1992: 313). Despite the recency of independence, Iceland proudly claims the world's first proto-democratic parliamentary assembly (Government of Iceland, 2014), dating back to the end of the tenth-century settlement period (Byock, 2002: 3). This does not necessarily equate with statehood (Karlsson, 1994: 180) or nationhood per se, though (Hastrup, 1984: 240). There may not be any scholarly consensus on when indeed the 'nation' – a self-conscious and defined community – emerged, nor is there arguably in most states. In Icelandic history, however, the issue is further complicated by language: There is only one word, *þjóð*, denoting both 'people' and 'nation', potentially leading historians to premature assumptions of the emergence of the latter (Karlsson, 1994). As others have pointed out, following settlement Iceland's inhabitants retained close cultural and political ties with the main source country, Norway (Hastrup, 1984; Karlsson, 1994). It was not until the fourteenth century that sovereignty over the Icelandic dependency was transferred to Denmark (alongside the Greenlandic and Faroese) as a result of the Dano-Norwegian unification at the time (Halink, 2014). Some authors have retrospectively claimed that the Icelandic nation was merely 'fast asleep' during the colonial time (Karlsson, 2003). However, this might be a somewhat anachronistic attribution. As in much of Europe, the nationalist movements in both Iceland and Norway really emerged only in the eighteenth century, thereby politicising cultural difference for the purpose of sovereign statehood (see Hálfdanarson, 2000: 12). It is this difference and independence, however recently articulated, that have come to characterise Icelandic relations in the Arctic. A history narrated as a long struggle for freedom has been transferred also to the Arctic context: regardless of the Arctic label being novel here as elsewhere, the ways in which state personnel understand Icelandic Arctic state identity are as one defined by its past as much as its future.

As is clear from the above, the retelling of an identity as *Arctic* means emphasising certain aspects, qualities, or here historical events: existing histories seen in a new light. This is of course not unique to the Arctic context, as history is always read and understood from a particular present. Public memory, and indeed identity, are actively (if not necessarily deliberately) shaped and nurtured through repeated ceremonies, events, and commemorations. Construction of heritage happens not only through the symbolic but also through affective sensibilities that often have racialised modalities too (Crang and Tolia-Kelly, 2010). During some of this book's fieldwork in Ottawa, there were at least four different venues displaying artefacts from the 'Franklin expedition' – an event and public (hi)story that has taken on added significance in Arctic relations, and which is returned to below. What is important here, however, is that museums and the education of history function as part of this retelling of a national past to shape a national present and future. Many thinkers have pointed to the role of education in constructing a sense of a shared national past (e.g. Anderson, 1983; Hobsbawm and Ranger, 1983), and Edward Said (2000: 176) has referred to the study of history not as neutral facts but 'a nationalist effort' in order to 'construct a desirable loyalty'. Whether or not there is any deliberate construction at play, it is clear that also those who eventually grow up to become state personnel read and learn these stories of Canadian northernness. In the words of one interviewee:

> Our history books, and particularly the history that I grew up being taught, focuses a lot on the importance of the North, and why people from Europe came to Canada in the first place: Looking for a Northwest Passage, looking for resources that tended to be in the North of the country. So, I think kids in Canada grow up with a lot of stories about the North. I think a lot … not quite romantic notions about the North, but certainly a fictional sense of how important the North is to Canada; maybe fictional is the wrong word – it's more a narrative sense, maybe would be a better word for it. (C.v)

Unlike Norway and Iceland, each province and territory in Canada has a fairly high degree of independence in developing school curricula, but shared across all is their important role in the formation of identity. This continues into adulthood, as experts are often seen to have a duty to inform and educate the population. In this manner, political decision-makers and state personnel *may* of course, as some suspect, deliberately try to promote certain identities and perspectives through education, but they may also see it as their professional duty to provide education to the population. A Canadian senator explained how state spending in the North was justified to the public through 'a big effort to *educate* the Canadians as to the value […] it's kind of like the "last frontier", and let's do it right' (C.ix, emphasis added). They continued that this generally successful 'effort' was also taking place through schooling:

> And, I know, school textbooks aren't being rewritten every day, because they're now going online a lot of them; but there are more and more resources online, and we have resources for telling the story of the North and the story of Indigenous Canadians that we never had before. And so, it's going to be part of our education. Some school boards and some education departments are more proactive

than others, but it's not going away: We have the North and it's going to be part of Canada, I hope, forever. (C.ix)

Education generates awareness – and potentially even attachment – to the Arctic from a young age, not only in Canada but likely across the Arctic states. Children who read about proud polar pasts may themselves grow up to become state personnel, showing how state identity has roots also in childhood and pedagogy. Stories and histories may be read in classrooms where maps and flags adorn the walls, where history lessons follow language and maths, and where the Arctic becomes both spectacular and everyday at once.

Heroes and explorers

Among the more spectacular, and frequently celebrated, aspects of Arctic histories are the many heroic tales of explorers and adventurers. In Norway, these past are not only Arctic but Antarctic too, where the polar past is re-interpreted and perhaps reframed for the present context. Although these stories were not exactly forgotten, they have taken on new meaning and importance now, in the so-called 'age of the Arctic'. Explorers such as Roald Amundsen (1872–1928) and Fridtjof Nansen (1861–1930) have regained their status as 'national heroes' (N.iv). One Norwegian official thought that the interest was 'alive again today, with the immense focus [in Norwegian society] on winter sports, expeditions, celebrating that which ties us to the polar region' (N.vi). By no coincidence, the height of Norwegian polar exploration coincided with the mentioned nationalist movement for independence in the late nineteenth and early twentieth centuries, and these two 'heroes' both played vocal parts in the articulation of what Norway should be. 'When we became an independent nation, it was achievements in [the Arctic] that, sort of, created a national consciousness and pride in being able to do something unique on our own' (N.vii). And even in their time, history – particularly a romanticised pre-Danish Viking era – was important for the understanding of both Norwegian nationhood and polar tradition. The Norwegian polar historians Drivenes and Jølle rhetorically ask:

> May it be connected to the fact that the conducts of Nansen and
> Amundsen were written into the great story of Norway, where an
> urge for travel and adventure – the eternal unrest in the blood for
> unknown land and unknown ocean – was often traced back to Leiv
> Eriksson[1] and explorers of his calibre in a distant past? (Drivenes and
> Jølle, 2004: 9 author's translation)

Fridtjof Nansen was particularly active politically, promoting independent statehood for Norway, and his writings – among them
diaries from his expeditions – were important for the growing
sense of national identity. At the time, he was a celebrity adven-
turer, intellectual, and scientist, and his choice to use skis to cross
Greenland was deeply ideological, supposedly exemplifying the
typical 'Norwegian' (Wærp, 2010). Also today it is a common
saying, repeated also by at least one of the interviewed officials, that
Norwegians are 'born with skis on our feet' (N.vii). In Nansen's own
writings about his later expedition to the North Pole, he claimed
that, much like 'our ancestors, the old Vikings', Norwegians are
'characterised by both "love of adventure" and need to discover'
(Nansen, 1897: 3–4; cited in Eglinger, 2010: 11). The Arctic
thereby came to be seen not as exceptional but rather as a space
where the truly Norwegian character could unfold (Drivenes and
Jølle, 2006) – something which resonates also with current Arctic
political speeches, where notions of national characteristics are
applied further to political practices in the polar region.

The idea of and pride in these 'pioneers', who contributed to an
independent state that could stand on its own metaphorical feet (or
skis), echo through today's Arctic relations too:

> [I]t generates pride that we have had big names who also 'break
> through the sound-barrier' internationally; who have been part of
> putting regions of the world on the map, and who have been part of
> taking the lead when it comes to gathering knowledge and exploring
> those areas that, for many, until not very long ago were unknown
> and difficult to understand the scope and details of … So, in that
> way, I think that the polar history, those people's relations, has con-
> tributed very positively to our nation's identity construction. (N.ii)

And as celebrities and groundbreaking discoverers, the active
commemoration of the explorers further amplifies a quest for status

and recognition, including internationally as we will see in the next chapter:

> Because of those – that is, Nansen and Amundsen – we have felt like a 'great power' when it comes to those types of things. I think that probably matters a lot for how we think about the High North; not least, it has contributed to a Norwegian self-esteem that is a bit bigger than it has reason to be! (N.xi; followed by laughter)

The role of 'pioneer' allows histories of Vikings, polar explorers, and indeed innovative petroleum entrepreneurs – or conversely, environmental forerunners – all to contribute to what an Arctic state identity might mean. In any case, the status that Amundsen and Nansen both sought for their country continues through new modes today, where Arctic statehood also means leadership.

Unlike many of the Arctic states, Iceland does not have a long history of polar exploration. Rather than looking north to the frozen seas, Icelandic identity was more often articulated with a view to the east and west: 'The identity has been much more [...] as a hub in the middle of the Atlantic. Northwards we have not had any polar explorers [...], so our thoughts have not been so very strong towards – northwards' (I.x). And indeed looking to the west, two Icelandic émigrés to Canada and later US gave birth to William Stephenson (1879–1962); he would later readopt his parents' identity and took the name Vilhjálmur Stefánsson, before exploring parts of the Canadian Arctic (Pálsson, 2000, 2004). While his own links to Iceland are disputable, he gained fame as the 'Blond Eskimo', and his name has later returned to Iceland through, for example, the Stefansson Arctic Institute in Akureyri's research cluster. In other words, he may be the closest Iceland comes to a polar explorer of its own, as explained by an interviewed parliamentarian (I.iv). However, another seafaring 'explorer' who is more uncontroversially Icelandic was Leifur Eiríksson / Leif Ericsson (c. 970 – c. 1020) (see Figure 3.1) – although, as above, the Norwegians may also refer to him as part of their Viking past too. Although he is not thought to have gone as far north as the Arctic per se, he is thought to have reached today's Newfoundland (I.iv).[2] Although neither Vilhjálmur nor Leifur quite provides Icelanders with an iconic national Arctic 'hero', the ways that their names

Figure 3.1 The Leif Ericsson Memorial (1929–32) in front of Hallgrímskirkja (church) in Reykjavík, a gift from the USA made by the sculptor Alexander Stirling Calder (Source: Rob Oo, CC BY 2.0)

are invoked today arguably highlight a shift of focus towards the Arctic. And with this shift of focus, Iceland too finds its place in the long pasts of the north.

Following mentions of the multiple museum exhibitions, one story of exploration that cannot go unmentioned when considering Arctic state identities is that frequently told and retold of Sir John Franklin's tragic expedition to what we today know as the Canadian North. After their display throughout the Canadian capital at the time of interviews, artefacts from the relatively recently discovered ships have travelled around the world. And the story and recent mystery came up again and again in interviews with Canadian state personnel. In very brief, the expedition led by Sir John Franklin (1786–1847) set off from the United Kingdom in 1845 in two ships, the HMS *Terror* and the HMS *Erebus*, in search of the Northwest Passage. The ships and their crews both disappeared, and remained an intriguing mystery, human tragedy, and the objective of numerous search expeditions in the years that followed – leading also, conveniently, to the charting and study of the region. As one interviewee put it, 'in searching for them they mapped the Arctic channels and the sea-routes through the Arctic' (C.ix). But more than an unanswered question of lost lives, the story of the ships has also entered popular culture, and has remained the subject of many books, films, songs, art, and more (see Figure 3.2) – and has become perhaps the most famous Arctic expedition (Francis, 1997). And as will be returned to, the search for the ships was a key objective for former PM Stephen Harper, forming a much-publicised component of his interest and subsequent engagement in the North. More than a century after their disappearance, the HMS *Erebus* was found in 2014 and the HMS *Terror* in 2016. However, as museum exhibitions and reports present it, the mystery of their fate persists – scientifically, as well as culturally (see Medby and Dittmer, 2021) – as does the significance of it for Canada's Arctic history.

Interestingly, the framing of the so-called Franklin expedition has shifted according to other Canadian relations. Sir John Franklin was himself of course British, and as such the story did not enter Canadian national discourse until the twentieth century – and then, initially, as representing a proud British heritage. As one interviewee rightly pointed out, Franklin 'wasn't Canadian, he was British. The Canadian stamp on the Arctic didn't happen

Figure 3.2 Two polar bears despoiling the remains of a shipwreck in a desolate Arctic setting. Reproduction of an oil painting by E.H. Landseer. (Source: Wellcome Collection).

until the 1950s' (C.viii). This shifted once again in the 1970s, as Canada increasingly asserted an independent identity as distinct from the former empire, and the story of Franklin was retold as one of arrogant and foolish Euro-centrism (Cavell, 2007). And, as noted, the story has once more shifted in recent years to tie in with Canada's assertion of Arctic statehood and sovereignty. When the first ship was finally located, it provided the Canadian government with an opportunity to further promote Canada's Arctic state identity:

> [T]here's been a narrative woven around that story that's given a sense of identity; all Canadians can associate with the Franklin expedition. Because we've been looking for it for a 150 years or something, right! So we finally found it, and the PM says 'we found the Franklin ship'; 'we' being the government of Canada, not the people of Canada. Or, like, 'me, I found it'. (C.viii)

Whether or not *all* Canadians really do associate with it is of course debatable – as many Indigenous people in particular have pointed out, and which is arguably reflected in the 2019 Policy Framework where there is no reference to it. However, at the time, PM Harper did not hesitate to underline the political significance in his statement to the press: 'Franklin's ships are an important part of Canadian history given that his expeditions, which took place nearly 200 years ago, laid the foundations of Canada's Arctic sovereignty' (Harper, 2014b). The fact that there was no 'Canada' as such at the time seemed to matter little in these celebratory statements. So too did the important contributions by Inuit (and their long discounted knowledge on the topic), unfortunately (Craciun, 2012). But whether or not people agreed with these statements at the time, they did bring the ships and stories into public consciousness, and with that also Canada's Arctic statehood and identity.

While the Conservative Canadian government at the time certainly promoted the search and eventual discoveries as emblematic of Canada's position in the North, the retelling of histories also opens up for discussion. Among the uncomfortable, but arguably much overdue, questions raised were high expenditures, private companies' involvement, governmental engagement with media, and eventually, perhaps most importantly, why Inuit had not been heard on this much sooner:

> [A] lot of our history has to do with this, well I guess, colonising or frontier-mentality of people going North and wanting to conquer it, or just like, braving elements to make it part of Canada. There's – the flipside is that it conflicts with a lot of our aboriginal history; because obviously aboriginal people have lived there a long time. So there is conflicting storylines there, but most Canadians relate more to the European history than the aboriginal history side of things. (C.ii)

As in earlier examples too, remembering and commemorating certain events means forgetting others – including those of Indigenous peoples or so-called heroes' less palatable sides. This retelling and reframing was what one referred to as 'an active cultivation of Arctic identity in Canada' (C.vi). It might even obscure lack of real action on societal issues in the North (C.xii), or, as another described it, be an attempt 'to try to stay away of the question of people occupying the territory. So, [Harper is] trying to prove that somebody was up there before. But before Franklin disappeared, the Inuit was already up there' (C.iii). This was perhaps a fact less convenient for the government, but noted by several interviewees, such as the following:

> [I]n reality, for Northern residents, it didn't resonate in any way as something important. Because, for Inuit – and it's totally understand-able, they've been there for so much longer – so like, 'yeah, whatever, you came when? [...]'. That's just a show of ... I don't know, trying to rewrite history; it's an exercise of rhetoric, and not something that concretely means something. (C.xii)

It did, however, mean something for many in the south – voters and state personnel alike. And for a Canadian politician or civil servant who has perhaps never travelled to the North, it may form part of an Arctic imaginary which in turn has practical political outcomes. Invoking so-called 'shared' stories of an ostensibly 'shared' past in the North again justifies political practice as a natural continuation of politics otherwise:

> [G]iven that the [Canadian] national identity includes the Arctic it empowers and enables our political leaders to be very confident if not

> aggressive in claiming its role and influence as an Arctic state [...]. It gives, again, our state – the federal government – the authority, if you will, the democratic authority to claim a place. Because all of Canada sees itself as an Arctic nation. (C.xiii)

And while the above-quoted interviewee may well be wrong in their claim that *all* of Canada would identify as Arctic, what matters is that they believe so as they go about their daily task of representing the nation, making decisions, and planning for the future. Telling and retelling stories of the past to fit the present is a matter not only of deliberate construction but also of making sense of own role, identity, and job – one that is to represent a people with both a shared past and a shared future.

Future anticipations: Hopes and concerns

All of the above (hi)stories are clearly told in and from the present, framed in current contexts, and understood through today's lenses. However, this chapter is titled not 'Arctic histories' but 'temporalities' for the reason that the narration and role of *time* in Arctic geopolitics is as much if not more about anticipated futures. For example, the previously mentioned polar 'pioneers' come to symbolise future leadership too, the countries are positioned for what is yet to come, and even the search for lost ships has an added motivation of finding future resources.

Much as the Norwegian explorer Fridtjof Nansen envisioned the Arctic as a space where the identity of a future independent Norway could unfold, so too do these visions of what is yet to come shape political practices and ambitions:

> Our entire history and our entire identity rest a bit on – it isn't on surfing tropical waves; it rests, in a way, on accomplishments in the north. That this follows us in our way to handle the policy area, that I definitely believe, without being very aware of how. But that it somehow affects us, that I do believe; I think it affects us mainly positively. (N.vii)

And as the Norwegian government's 2006 *High North Strategy* was later summarised:

The Government's ambition is for Norway to be a *leader* in the field of knowledge in and about the High North [...]; for Norway to be at the *top* of the league in key areas of economic activity and the *best* steward of the environment and natural resources in the north. (N.MFA, 2011: 25 emphases added)

Leadership and stewardship are both topics that will come up across contexts and state identity relations, also important for international and national self-perceptions. However, important here is the active articulation of a desired future, which in turn is part of its political materialisation. That is, words and narratives are not inconsequential, but lead to action (Steinveg and Medby, 2023). Published in 2015 and focused on Norway's northernmost counties, the report *Future North* opens its final chapter with the following words by Kriss Rokkan Iversen:

In the beginning the ice created the land. And so the north-facing tapestry of our age extends into the future, just as white and open. Where new weft threads will be woven in. Where patterns in new colour combinations will take shape. Where the future in the north will appear. Woven by the people who call the north country our home – now and in 2050. (N.MTIF, 2015: 148)

The report does not aim to predict but to forecast a range of potentialities. And it concludes, '[a]ll the methods used to look into the future show that there is considerable potential for increased value creation in Northern Norway, but also that such growth will not happen by itself' (N.MTIF, 2015: 153). In other words, the call is for action and investment, the making of an Arctic future. In this manner, the so-called north-facing tapestry is being actively woven in the politics of the present.

Anticipation for the future characterises not just Norway's geopolitical engagement – and identity narratives – in the Arctic, but is likely the case for all eight Arctic states (Dodds, 2013a; Ferdoush and Väätänen, 2022). And perhaps this is a defining feature of statecraft more generally: looking to, preparing for, and planning the future whenever decisions are made today. In the Arctic context this kind of political forecasting is directly connected to scientific planning – Arctic geopolitics is always, inevitably also about climate change. And more than simply a pragmatic means for mitigation or adaptation, science in the Arctic is also of political importance due to the legitimacy and status it may give. So-called science diplomacy, for example, refers to how scientific endeavours, data, and collaborations form an intrinsic part to states' diplomatic efforts. For non-Arctic states wishing an observer seat at the Arctic Council, demonstrating their scientific commitments and contributions is absolutely crucial (see Steinberg et al., 2014).

For the Arctic states themselves, it has therefore become important not just to take part in science but also to show leadership. Clearly, this links back to the noted idea of being 'pioneers' above, and will be a thread running through later chapters too. Geopolitics, economics, and strategy are closely interlinked, as one explained it: 'you still see these connections: connections between Norway's research agenda; what we are interested in economically and strategically. There isn't only altruism in the Norwegian research agenda' (N.x). And, leaving no room for doubt, the Ministry of Foreign Affairs too wrote that, 'Norway will be a leader in knowledge about the north, for the north and in the north' (N.MFA, 2014a: 26). Strategic science is neither new nor unique to the Arctic region of course, however it may be playing out there more obviously than elsewhere. And, often, this science was 'contingent, in its formative phases around the mid-twentieth century, on state concerns about sovereignty, natural resources and national security' (Doel et al., 2014: 79). Scientific knowledge was, in some respects, a secondary gain – as was seen clearly in the searches for Sir John Franklin's expeditions. Having the most advanced technology and equipment are also markers of political status and power. And this means that state identities that are built around these narratives of scientific leadership also necessitate action and investment – for example, guiding research priorities and funding. Being an Arctic state thereby comes with 'a responsibility both to research, gain more knowledge, and work actively on behalf of ourselves and also the great global society' (N.ii).

While anticipatory geopolitics may characterise all Arctic states' articulations of identity, it is perhaps most obvious in Iceland's case. As noted above, there is less of a polar past of exploration and no Indigenous population there, and so positioning themselves as explicitly Arctic is an act in the present for the future. When entering a coalition government back in 2013, the chairmen of the Progress Party and Independence Party, Gunnlaugsson and Benediktson respectively, stated that:

> The government will direct efforts toward making Iceland a leading force in the Arctic [...]. Preparations will begin to take advantage of opportunities created by the opening of Arctic sea routes and emphasis placed on having projects related to this located in Iceland. (Government of Iceland, 2013)

In the years that have followed, such active preparations, as well as positioning, have indeed taken place. These include strengthening ties with China, which is a state that has expressed its interest in polar shipping. When the Chinese icebreaker *Xue Long* [Snow Dragon] became the first to cross the Arctic Ocean from China in 2013, Iceland was its destination. And that same year, Iceland became the first country to sign a free-trade agreement with China – also no doubt in anticipation of what is yet to come. According to Iceland's former Minister of Foreign Affairs, Gunnar Bragi Sveinsson, it may strengthen the state's position as an Arctic shipping hub (Valdimarsson, 2013). And, more than just a matter of geography and history, this relationship to 'others' is significant for Iceland's Arctic state identity (Sumarliðason, 2021). In other words and as is the focus of the next chapter, an Arctic state identity is about international positioning for the future:

> After the Cold War ended, our position was maybe not as clear [as previously]; and our part in the world, you could say in the 'world vehicle', was not as clear. But it's growing again, in a new way, as a part of the Arctic. And that's a good thing for us. We are getting new positive focus, and that's a good thing. (I.vi)

And, as another Icelandic parliamentarian put it, what was key was to 'just, you know, to be part of it, *the making of the future of the Arctic*' (I.ii, emphasis added). In other words, an Arctic state identity necessitates political action, and not just the anticipation but also the 'making' of the future.

The political actions of today are, as above, articulated as a key priority for the state, yet many also recognise the longer timescale to this than what might matter to voters. Future opportunities might not be of the most immediate concern to the average citizen. As one parliamentarian saw it, the Arctic focus 'needs to be explained, because it is not on the short-term list' (I.iv). And a state employee working on environmental issues noted:

> I suppose maybe the Arctic will become more important for Iceland in the future, and the public will become more aware of it; that it's something that is important for us. But on the other hand, [...], we're having so many problems here in Iceland; or at least people are more concerned with the internal problems and the economic situation than they maybe are about the Arctic itself. (I.xii)

In this manner, an Arctic state identity is clearly about the future but explicitly for the state, more so than the nation. It is a priority and key issue for practitioners of statecraft, but potentially less so for citizens and inhabitants – at least those living south of the Arctic Circle themselves. That may be changing, however, as economic prosperity allows people to look further ahead. An Icelandic parliamentarian reflected on how recent positive developments now allowed 'more topics than just one in our political debate [...]. I could easily see that our Arctic role becomes more something that the public would be aware of and would be voting [...] along those lines' (I.ix). For another politician, lack of clarity was an issue for the general public:

> I think that there is a lot of interest, but also a lot of uncertainties. When you talk about the opportunities that the Arctic is creating, what are you talking about? For some, it's only a new way of reaching China [...]. For others, the cooperation itself is an opportunity [...]. So, I'm not sure we are agreeing when we talk about opportunities in the Arctic, that we are focused on the same things. (I.vi)

In any case, state personnel have a duty to look ahead and prepare for possible geopolitical futures. And so, Arctic statehood is *already* important, *already* part of an identity: 'attention to the Arctic and the economic interests are not very close to us now, but of course *we* [state personnel] have to look to the farther future' (I.iv); and the Arctic 'will only develop in the direction of being a bigger and bigger topic' (I.v). And with that, an Arctic state identity may not always be the same as a national one, but, for those performing the state on a daily basis, the future is already present.

While state and national identities may not always be the same, there are of course many overlaps – not least as state personnel too tend to see themselves as part of the nation. In addition, statecraft is about representing a people and their interest, and so Arctic state identities and their sense of futures are always linked to those of the country's inhabitants. As will be discussed at more length in later chapters, the Indigenous populations play a particular role in the Arctic – and so do they for understandings of pasts and futures. While Iceland is an exception, both Norway and Canada devote special attention to Indigenous peoples in their Arctic policies, strategies, and statements. In the latter's case, the previously discussed Conservative government of PM Stephen Harper had its explicit focus on the future, for example presenting the Arctic engagement as 'a legacy we will leave for generations of Canadians to come' (Baird, 2013). However, the Liberal government of PM Justin Trudeau has presented a policy framework that includes Indigenous peoples to a greater extent. And not only does the framework start by acknowledging the need to right past wrongs, but the longer section on 'Our Future' also opens with discussion of peoples. It promises that '[t]he clear and ambitious goals and objectives of this framework point the way to a vibrant, sustainable and prosperous future' (C.CIRNAC, 2019). For Harper, the North represented 'our destiny' and claimed that '[t]o not embrace its promise now at the dawn of its ascendancy would be to turn our backs on what it is to be Canadian' (cited in C.FATDC, 2010: 26). The newer framework is deliberately and self-consciously different from these former grandiose statements of Canada's Arctic identity, yet is just as future-oriented – if, arguably, towards a different and more inclusive future. As such, Arctic state identities are not singular, but always articulated in specific contexts and specific presents – and with that, their futures too remain plural.

State identities through time, with time

State identities are about not just geography and space, as in the previous chapter, but also about history and time. And state identities' temporalities extend from the past to the present and into the future. Many would in fact say that much of Arctic statecraft and geopolitics today is anticipatory, planning and preparing for a future yet to come. This future may be one of challenges, opportunities, or a bit of both. In any case, the ways in which state personnel articulate their state's identities in the north include both looking back – to polar explorers, seafarers, and Indigenous histories too – and looking forward to what might be on the horizon. Depending on past narratives and established practices, Arctic state presents and futures may also follow the same tracks. That is not inevitable, however, as discourses and narratives can always be told anew, in a new light, or from a new perspective. If national histories can be re-narrated towards a polar past, so can they be retold otherwise – as examples above have also shown. The past is never uncontested, and the future is never predetermined.

As this chapter has shown, focusing on the views of state personnel, the pasts, presents, and futures of statehood are as varied as the people articulating them. Understandings and feelings of a state identity will inevitably vary across contexts, situations, and circumstance – and this is a strength, not a weakness. Identities are perceived through space as well as time, and always in relation to others. Having explored various aspects of Arctic temporalities in this chapter, the next section of the book turns to the relationality of identities: how we see ourselves and our states always depends on an 'other'.

Notes

1 Note the use of specifically Leiv / Leif Ericsson as a national symbol. As the offspring of a Viking émigré from what is today Norway, and travelling onwards to Greenland and Newfoundland himself, he most likely never set foot in Norway; and so, importantly, he is also considered Iceland's most important national hero, there spelled as Leifur Eiríksson.
2 See note 1.

Part II

State relations

4

An Arctic state among states: positions and positionings in an international region

While the previous part of the book has presented a 'spatio-temporal' frame for state identities, in this and the next chapters we will turn to the relations through which state identities come about. While space and time may provide something like a scaffolding of identity discourses (the 'where' and 'when'), state relations refer to a sense of identity vis-à-vis a contextual 'other' (the 'who' and 'whom'). The following four chapters on state relations are structured according to what we might think of as political 'scales' that range from the level of the state to its constitutive populations. For instance, how may a state identity look different for an Icelandic state employee speaking at the Arctic Council than when speaking to local voters, to colleagues in a ministry, or even to a spouse after the end of the working day? In structuring these chapters according to scales I do not, however, intend to suggest any hierarchy between them, any directional transference from one to another, or 'high/low' politics. Rather, political scales serve as a pragmatically useful (if imperfect) structure, which resonates with how many people imagine geopolitics.

In this first of the four relational chapters, the focus is therefore on the 'international scale' – or how the Arctic region and concepts of statehood and identity fit into a wider global system. For Arctic states, their title as such holds different meanings depending on context, but for all it is one of geopolitical importance. It is about international position and status, and it is about active position*ing* and status-seeking. Arctic statehood is also state*craft*, and state identities are about not just 'being' but also 'doing'.

Any identity is arguably relationally understood and articulated depending on who you are defining yourself against, an 'other'. Just as the Arctic is not simply about where it is but also about where it is *not* – boundaries that also exclude – identity is always about difference. As the well-known theorist of national identity Benedict Anderson (1983: 7) explains, 'even the largest of them [nations] encompassing perhaps a billion living human beings, has finite, if elastic boundaries, beyond which lie other nations. No nation imagines itself coterminous with mankind.' And likewise no region would be such without other regions beyond its boundaries, and no Arctic state would be so without non-Arctic states. Just as there is no self without the other, there is no north without the south. In some ways, the Arctic can therefore be considered exclusive, as membership that comes with certain privileges, as well as certain responsibilities. Both the previously discussed geographies and environments, and histories and imagined futures feature in these relational positions vis-à-vis non-Arctic others.

Additionally, the Arctic is itself an international region, a circumpolar north of intergovernmental discussion in the Arctic Council, where state representatives meet other states' representatives. An Arctic state identity is therefore articulated in relation not only to the non-Arctic but also to other Arctic states. For example, a Norwegian sense of Arctic leadership may be about Norway's role in relation to China or the UK, but it may also be that in relation to its Arctic neighbours Sweden, Finland, or Russia – and, in either case, different aspects will be highlighted as more or less important. What this brief example shows, and as will be elaborated in this chapter, is also that Arctic state relations always change and will continue to do so no doubt also after this book's publication – yet the outlines of different state roles are discernible. Colonial histories are one factor, another is more recent geopolitical tensions and even war: state identities are never fixed.

This chapter starts by outlining state identities as status and privilege – Arctic state identities as exclusive in relation to the non-Arctic. It returns to ideas of leadership and the 'pioneers' as mentioned, and the responsibilities states are considered to have. The topic of status comes up again in discussion of relatively small- to middle-power statehood, where an Arctic state title can be seen as a particular asset. The chapter then turns to relations within the circumpolar region itself, where membership becomes a defining feature – as well as to ways in which each state is distinguished from others.

Polar privilege and leadership

Considering the title of Arctic statehood, the international meaning might for many be what first comes to mind. As noted, it is an international, multi-state region in which each of the eight Arctic states holds a particular role. And, given the previously discussed non-Arctic (Greek) origins of the regional name, it is perhaps no surprise that, when asked about 'the Arctic', specifically, international relations may be what first comes to mind. As a circumpolar region, its governance regime rests on the two pillars of the Arctic Council and UNCLOS that were introduced in Chapter 1 – and so, unsurprisingly, membership in the former and adherence to and promotion of the latter are key characteristics of Arctic statehood too. This, in turn, means that state identities are also often tied to notions of both privilege and of international cooperation and law. Participation in Arctic fora and political engagement under that banner likewise are ways in which the Arctic state is performed – the state becomes so only through political practices (Abrams, 1988).

For Arctic states and their representatives, and particularly for the three states this book focuses on, the Arctic provides an important avenue for international political engagement. This remains the case even if the engagement has changed following Russia's full-scale invasion of Ukraine in 2022, pausing some of this now long-running work. In one interview, a high-ranking Norwegian official explained that participation in the Arctic Council presented a co-operative image of the country, useful for when they were confronted with questions of why Norway has not joined the EU: that Norway also knows how to 'play ball', and that its Arctic role therefore 'is an important asset' (N.xii). A Norwegian parliamentarian explained how Norway's Arctic statehood allows the small state a larger role internationally:

I would say [being an Arctic state] affects us because I think all nations, all people, want to be a bit bigger and a bit more significant than you often realistically are. And Norway, as a tiny country – at least in terms of inhabitants – that we are here an actor in the 'great game', with everyone from the US to Russia, China; yes, I think that can make you 'inflate' a bit too. (N.xiv)

In addition to participating in meetings, contributing to scientific reports, and investing in the region are other ways that the state gains legitimacy as an international player – and even as a leader, or, as we saw with reference to historical explorers in the previous chapter, a 'pioneer':

We have a very large Arctic territory, and Norway is a country that uses – compared to how big we are, at least in population numbers and such – a lot of resources on Arctic collaboration [...] Well, per capita there is no one that uses as much resources and money as Norway does. And that gives us influence, right [...] But it also gives us some, kind of, annoyance from the other countries that we take too much ownership, too much of this cooperation, and it becomes too Norwegian. (N.x)

This perspective suggests that other states may find Norway *too* active in Arctic geopolitics, yet interestingly state personnel from other states also see *their* state as a leader in the region. Relations between Arctic states are returned to later in this chapter, but in relation to those external to the region itself there is no doubt that this 'influence' matters. And given the exclusivity of Arctic membership – only eight states can claim that title – it can be a useful asset in wider international relations. An official from the Norwegian Ministry of Foreign Affairs explained that the government 'highly deliberately' uses that, continuing 'we are not the largest nation in the Arctic, but at least we are a *leading* nation in the Arctic' (N.i).

For the three relatively small states we are focusing on here, such a title as Arctic can therefore be considered useful, even valuable, with the increased interest and opportunities that come with that. Not unlike the Norwegians 'playing ball', an Icelandic parliamentarian described that, in the view of non-Arctic states 'it makes us a better-looking dance partner' and gives the country 'a ticket' to be used in diplomacy (I.ix). And more than simply a useful means for a small state to be heard internationally, the title gives an elevated role. As such, being 'in the club' is always about who is not, the 'others'. Again echoing the sentiments of their Norwegian colleagues, another Icelandic parliamentarian explained that 'the Arctic states, they will lead in the Arctic. They will have the rights in the Arctic, and they will set the rules. So other countries, they will not be *leading*, but they will of course *play with*' (I.ii). In other words, in the Arctic region it is the others who may need a so-called ticket, while the eight Arctic states are those determining the rule of the game, or the steps of the geopolitical 'dance':

> Because this is a huge area – it's very remote, sparsely populated, dark hours during half of the year, things like that – you need all kinds of support to do whatever you want to do. So, a close cooperation – be it [with] China, be it India, be it Singapore, the EU, whatever – you should encourage a cooperation about special things like that in there, but I would not like to see those as full-fledged members of the Arctic Council. I think that would be, quite simply, a step towards destroying what the Arctic Council is. (I.viii)

While full membership for non-Arctic states has never been a serious topic of discussion, the above points to an often-expressed view that current Council observers should know their place. If an Arctic position is one of privilege, that of non-Arctic states is firmly one of observation, potentially contributing but not leading.

Playing 'ball', a 'ticket', or in a Canadian official's words, Arctic statehood 'definitely is a card that comes into play in terms of inter-national negotiators or diplomatic policies' (C.ii). While Canada is significantly larger than the other two states, it is often con-sidered a middle power internationally, so many perspectives on the significance of the title are certainly shared. Several Canadian state personnel described Arctic statehood as something that could be used for leverage, saying that it makes Canada 'someone you have to invite at the table. And the Arctic Council as well is an important forum where we have visibility' (C.xii) (see Figure 4.1). Not only is this international status of relevance in diplomatic negotiations with other states, but in terms of Arctic identity it may also register at home: 'While [...] Canada has always had a strong sort of Northern and Arctic identity, I would have to say though

Figure 4.1 Arctic Council ministerial meeting in 2015 in Iqaluit, Canada, where Leona Aglukkaq (Canada) was Chair, with Ministers of Foreign Affairs and Indigenous organisations' leaders sitting around the table (Source: US State Department/Public Domain)

that we are going through a significant pivot point, where we are recognising that the entire world now is very interested in the Arctic as well' (C.xvi). In other words, the international interest may *generate* a stronger sense of an Arctic identity – and not just among state personnel, but also potentially the wider nation. However, the very assertive expression of Canada's Arctic state identity, in particular during the Conservative government of 2006–15, could also harm the country's image – for example, seeming at odds with an existing identity as a 'bridge-building' middle power:

> And we're hearing it; I've heard it myself in different multilateral international meetings: [...] 'what's happening in Canada? You guys used to be this, that, and the other thing, and that's not happening anymore, and now you're doing this, and we don't understand. And we're concerned.' [...] At the officials' level, people are starting to hear the concern of other state officials around some of the policy directions or some of the politics that are having a bit of an impact, a negative impact, or – not a positive impact. (C.xiv)

Whether perceived as positive or negative, the above clearly demonstrates that the articulation of a state identity is simultaneously a product of international and domestic processes. It may be a privileged position to be among the Arctic states, yet it is a title and an identity that require continual performance as such.

Regional responsibilities

The political practices and performances expected of an Arctic state involve not only the above rights and privileges but also responsibilities. In the view of a Norwegian official, this was only rightly so: 'multilateral cooperation in the High North is highly necessary, but it will still be the states that *are* Arctic states that have the greatest interests in these areas, and that *should* have the greatest interests in these areas' (N.xiii). They continued that, in their view, non-Arctic states tend to have 'purely economic interests', and so it is up to the Arctic states to include issues relating to 'minorities, the climate, pollution, etc. – that [which] we have traditionally seen as important'. And while 'open dialogue' is to be welcomed, decision-making should be left to the Arctic eight (N.i). As such, an Arctic state identity does not only enable but in fact *require* certain political practices to follow. The privilege that was discussed above is therefore also a matter of responsibilities.

While the view that international interest in the region is welcome, and for the Arctic states often gives them an advantage, this does not mean that their hospitality as Arctic 'hosts' is unconditional. In the words of an Icelandic parliamentarian: 'Of course it's an opportunity, but it must be based on our premises [...]. They [non-Arctic states] are *guests* in Iceland. And, as they are guests in Iceland they must comply with Icelandic legislation. Without any exemptions' (I.v). And non-Arctic states and actors, 'guests', have to comply not only with national legislations and decisions but also more broadly with regional norms and expectations. The contributions they not only can but *should* make, for example as observers in the Arctic Council, include scientific research and investments. Demonstrating a commitment to the region's prosperity, adherence to UNCLOS, and respect for Indigenous and local peoples are among the explicit requirements of an observer seat at the Arctic Council. In other words, the Arctic states have written the rules of engagement in the region, ensuring fair conduct and standards – and in the process reiterating their own status too.

With these responsibilities that Arctic states ostensibly have, there is an implicit political hierarchy of voice and legitimacy – and perhaps an implicit sense of superiority that is part of Arctic state identities. This view seems to be shared across the Arctic states. A Canadian state employee explained their position in line with traditional images of an international system of states:

> [T]his is a part of the world like any other part of the world occupied by states. So I think their role in the Arctic is welcome; they can certainly play a role in doing what, you know, what states do internationally, or what companies do internationally, or what people do, but recognising that this is an area managed by, in particular, the five coastal states that occupy the area. (C.xv)

Limiting non-Arctic states roles may therefore be useful, in some people's views: 'I don't know what role they can play, because they don't have direct interest in the Arctic, other than the resources that come out of it, or the transportation that it offers, or tourism potential' (C.viii). In other words, those not 'belonging' to the region are framed as not just geographically but potentially also *morally* disconnected, prone to pursuits of self-interest.

The above perception of other, non-Arctic states' behaviours in the north, in turn, seems to necessitate the noted political practices of protection – or, in Canadian terms, often framed as 'stewardship':

> Where the interest is being expressed by non-Arctic countries, I think we find it's often fairly self-serving. There's an interest in getting at resources that are in the Arctic, and a complete lack of recognition that the climate change problem that is causing the loss of ice and environmental change in the North is being caused by the south. (C.xv)

They continued, explaining the leadership needed from an Arctic state:

> Canada has a very special role to play here: To say that we recognise that we are responsible for this area; we recognise that we have things

to do, but that responsibility – there's only so much a country can do on its own. It has to, in terms of a problem like climate change, it's a worldwide problem; it's not something that one country can address. And everybody has to come together to do something about it. (C.xv)

Another Canadian official explained that non-Arctic others also 'have an interest and, as members of our global community, a degree of right to be engaged in Arctic issues' (C.xiii). Yet, in order to do so they 'need to deeply understand that the North is populated and to respect the interests, rights, of the peoples who already live there. It's not open territory, it's not the Antarctic' (C.xiii). It is hard to disagree with this point, of course, but implicit in the statement is also a sense that Arctic states may have a 'deeper' knowledge or a truer understanding somehow – again, reinforcing the sense of superiority that is so common to identity discourses (Connolly, 1991). The power and agency to act remain the privilege of the Arctic state, and the non-Arctic 'others' need to learn, observe, or follow the rules of the game.

Intra-Arctic, interstate relations

While Arctic states and their identities may at times be defined against those beyond the region, the articulation of each particular state's identity will also be defined against the seven other Arctic states. That is, identities are both about group membership and about perceptions of uniqueness within the group. We have already seen above how Norway, Iceland, and Canada are each presented as leaders in the region, and this is a recurring theme in much of the policies and statements relating to the region. Being one of the Arctic states is described as 'placing us in a position where you are perceived as important, and the decisions we then make in this policy area will also be important for how other countries see us' (N.iii), continuing that 'it is a dimension where Norway can, sort of, assert itself' (N.iii). Adding to the previously mentioned perception that the state is *overly* active in Arctic geopolitics, investing and influencing, it is also one of the five Arctic *coastal* states. This is a somewhat contested title, as Icelanders argue, but nevertheless there has been a distinction between the Arctic eight and the even more exclusive group of Arctic Ocean five:

> There is kind of an 'A' and a 'B' team in the Arctic Council, as there are five states that have borders to the Arctic Ocean, and Norway is one of those [...] So that is, in a way, the 'A team': those who have direct interests and territories in the Arctic Ocean; while the other states – with areas north of the Arctic Circle, but no border to the Ocean – they are kind of part of this game without participating to the same extent. (N.x)

Clearly, an Arctic state identity is here articulated through a pre-existing desire for importance and influence of a small state on the edge of Europe.

Given that the Arctic Council's chairship rotates between the eight states every two years, there is an added temporariness of *actual* leadership of the Council. While neither the Council nor its chair has decision-making powers, the chairing country will decide priorities for its term and usually a number of projects. Canada was the first country to chair the council when founded, in 1996–98, and did so for a second time in 2013–15. Iceland chaired most recently in 2019–21, and this provided a timely opportunity for the state to update its Arctic policy. Among the updates and revisions in the parliamentary resolution on *Iceland's Policy on Matters Concerning the Arctic Region* (I.MFA, 2021) was a strong statement on the importance of the Arctic Council. In fact, the first of 19 'points of emphasis' is '[t]o actively participate in international cooperation on matters concerning the Arctic region, based on the values that have guided Icelandic foreign policy, including peace, democracy, human rights and equality' (I.MFA, 2021: 3). In other words, the state's role in the Arctic is both about international participation as well as its own 'values' within it. Norway took over as chair in 2023, and, while the situation in the Arctic has been significantly impacted by Russia's aggression elsewhere during its own chairmanship 2021–23, the emphasis remains on cooperation in the north. In line with the consensus-based structure of the Council, priorities often follow similar lines – for example focusing on the ocean, climate, sustainable development, and Arctic peoples. But in a time where geopolitical relations elsewhere are difficult, the relatively steady pace and unsurprising interests in the Arctic are arguably to be welcomed – Arctic statehood remains articulated as active membership, even if relations may differ between and with each of the states.

With the emphasis on membership, the expressed dissatisfaction among Icelandic state personnel of their exclusion from the negotiations among the five Arctic coastal states leading to the Ilulissat Declaration (2008) is perhaps less surprising. For them, it was about more than just wanting to have a say on the particular topic: it was also about a deeper sense of exclusion and rightful participation. Being one of the Arctic states 'gives us a role in the society of other countries' (I.vi). Perhaps unsurprisingly then, the Arctic Circle Assembly – an annual event in Reykjavík, bringing together Arctic stakeholders – was launched in 2013 to facilitate further international engagement in the region, as mentioned. Some would suggest it was also a direct response to the exclusion in 2008, a topic that comes up again in Chapter 7, but suffice it to say it has become an important forum in its own right that also positions Iceland as host (Steinveg, 2020a). And, as noted in the previous chapter, the relatively recent independence from Denmark (in 1944) means that Icelandic foreign policy has been marked by a desire to assert itself as an equal actor on the international stage (Hermannsson, 2005). It is also worth noting that, like most Arctic states except Russia, Iceland is an active member of NATO,[1] hosting exercises such 'Northern Viking' and 'Northern Challenge'. Military practice and presence are therefore among the ways in which Arctic statehood is experienced in everyday life in Iceland: 'We have exercises on that yearly – that brings into the minds of people here that we are [...], definitely, on the border of the frozen north and the warmer south' (I.x). And participation in fora such as NATO and the Arctic Council is among the key outcomes of having achieved 'sovereignty as an independent republic' (I.iv) – and, indeed, some Icelanders consider their country among the founding members of these, noting again different meanings of leadership that re-emerge across articulations of state identity.

A sense of leadership among the Arctic states was something that also Canadian state personnel articulated, but again in their specific ways. In contrast to Norway and Iceland as invariably small states, Canada is a country that is often internationally considered a middle power, on the basis of its position between former empires and small states within the UN. The so-called middle-power myth – the construction of an image as such – has been instrumental both for Canadian political relations and for identity (Chapnick, 2000). And this is a role, identity, and arguably a myth that is brought also to Arctic cooperation – for example, a preference for 'soft power', multilateralism, and international-ism in foreign affairs, as well as being a peace-keeping country (Berdahl and Raney, 2010; Munton and Keating, 2001). As such, Canadian self-perception is – not unlike the Norwegian – based on a sense of moral virtue and responsibility. In turn, the identity carries a set of expected actions and behaviours, relevant also for international relations in the Arctic. A frequently noted example is Canada's leadership in the establishment of the Arctic Council with the Ottawa Declaration in 1996 (Keskitalo, 2004) – 'Canada spearheaded the Arctic Council' (C.ii). While the first environ-mental protection collaboration[2] in the Arctic was initiated by the Finns, and it was the Soviet leader Gorbachev in 1987 who famously encouraged further peaceful cooperation in the region, it was the Canadian state at the time that saw establishing the Arctic Council as a particular priority (and opportunity): 'For Canada, a country that was constantly searching for its own identity, the North would have something to give, in fact what was genuinely theirs' (Heikkilä, 2019: 36). The Council is now, as noted, based on unanimity and rotating chairships so not likely to be dominated by any one state, but nevertheless it is an international arena for each to enact its particular state identitiys:

> [T]he Canadian element of the Arctic Council is to get everybody with an interest together, and say 'okay, can we agree on everything that needs to happen?'. And then, based on who's got the resources to make it happen, 'let's figure out how to work together and make it happen'. (C.v)

And so, regardless of changing party politics within the state, there are seemingly more deeply rooted characteristics that define state performances and geopolitical practices.

Small states, Arctic status

The significance of Arctic membership, or even leadership, takes on added meaning for the otherwise small to medium states, who all have an equal vote in the consensus-based Arctic Council – alongside big players such as the US and Russia. Being a small, 'peripheral' state that 'punches above its weight' internationally is a source of some pride for Norwegian state personnel (de Carvalho and Neumann, 2015; Medby, 2015; see also Steinveg, 2024). In their case, the sense of international importance is also expressed through the annual awarding of the Nobel Peace Prize in Oslo, attracting international attention and performing a role of peacebuilder and team-player. The attention surrounding the annual event 'is actively used to present Norway as a good power through various practices and performances' (Johnsen, 2015: 116). Clearly, there are similarities between the Norwegian and Canadian images in this regard. And more than just a deliberate act for international audiences, these are practices that also influence self-perception: '[Identity] is, kind of, about the experience you get from seeing your reflection in others' (N.viii). Global interest in the Arctic may therefore also be generative of further identification and attachment to the region. For state personnel, these understandings of community and self are also likely important, guiding everyday practices and decisions: an existing international role, and national pride, that influence both Arctic and domestic relations.

The arguably idealised image of Norway being a country of peace (and environmental responsibility too) clearly carries to its Arctic geopolitical engagements too. One often highlighted story is the successful maritime delimitation agreement between Norway and Russia in 2010: 'a diplomatic victory for both states, which many states have a lot of respect for' (N.iv). Reflecting on the state's image and identity, others described it as 'mediator and peace nation' (N.iii) and a 'rational and relatively sober actor' (N.xiii). The pride previously expressed in Norway's historically exceptionally peaceful relations with its Russian neighbours, and the 'success-story' of Barents regional cooperation[3] (Medby, 2021), have unsurprisingly been deeply affected by Russia's full-scale invasion of Ukraine in 2022. Norway's relationship with Russia is a defining feature of the former's Arctic engagement. During the Cold War, the Soviet border contributed to Norwegian identity, and to this day is the reason 'that we maintain defence on the level we do' (N.xi). While the 2011 *High North Policy* (N.MFA, 2011) included references to an improved post-Cold War relationship, 'normal, good neighbourly relations', the 2021 *Arctic Policy* (N.MFA, 2021) more cautiously referenced 'some challenging developments' and '[t]he general deterioration in Russia's relationship with Nato and Western countries'. Only the year after its publication, that wording too was rendered an understatement. Needless to say, Arctic co-operation and membership have changed for all states involved, and the future of the international roles of each remain to be seen, but will no doubt continue to be based on the same self-perceptions and imag(inari)es.

What is clear, however, is that the Arctic continues to provide an opportunity and venue to be heard – and to sit around the table and work together with 'great powers' such as the US:

> The Arctic Council, for Iceland, is very, very important – both because it is easier that your voice will be heard, and also easier that you can have an effect on some decisions in the direction that you think is good for your country. So, my personal view is that because of limited manpower in Iceland, regional conventions or agreements are where our voice is best heard, and it is the most fruitful way to bring forward the view of Iceland. (I.viii)

An Icelandic ministerial adviser explained that 'many politicians, they see an increased role for Iceland as being a player in the Arctic field', where 'Iceland is in many ways among equals' (I.xi). And in contrast, not being included or not participating becomes akin to an identity crisis. When the US troops left Iceland in 2006, 'some Icelanders felt that that was somehow a loss of importance, of geopolitical importance. So when you had this increased discussion of the Arctic, that sort of replaced that a little bit' (I.vii). Growing global interest in the Arctic therefore means not only renewed geo-strategic importance for the state (Ingimundarson, 2009), but also a re-affirmation of identity.

It is also through this kind of international cooperation that we have, sort of, developed our identity as an Arctic country. I think it is quite natural, as identity is not always what you decide, but how other people view you and how you view other people. (I.iii)

For state personnel, performing Arctic statehood is therefore always relational – it is about membership and groupness, and about self-perception in the views of another.

Membership and belonging are key across different views on state identities, but, in the Canadian case, Arctic state identities have arguably been more explicitly linked to defence and security also prior to the 2022 war. And, there, the previously mentioned distinction between 'Arctic' and 'Northern' is also political and even practical, where the former relates more specifically to the international region:

We aren't often using the word 'Arctic' unless it's being specifically used to speak around the High Arctic, and certain activities that the federal government is responsible for in the High Arctic – which often kind of overlaps with the international dimension of our Arctic foreign policy and those kinds of things – generally around security, offshore boundary issues, those kinds of things. Otherwise we generally speak of 'the North' from a domestic perspective. (C.xiii)

The explicitly Arctic region fully entered southern Canadian public consciousness only during the Cold War, due to the perceived Soviet threat across the Pole. And it has remained associated with a 'complex interrelationship between: sovereignty, stewardship, and national security' (Grant, 1988: xv). While, at the time, the 'stewardship' often referred to the government's relationship with the Inuit population, the term has now been transferred to the land and geography itself. 'Stewarding' the Arctic is closely linked to ideas of leadership as expressed in Arctic state discourses more generally. Arctic statehood has been summarised succinctly as 'stewardship and sovereignty' (C.xi), and former PM Harper stated that 'This magnificent and unspoiled region is one for which we will demonstrate stewardship on behalf of our country, and indeed, all of humanity' (2008, cited in C.FATDC, 2010: 16). Being an Arctic state therefore necessitates political practices both *with* and *for* fellow states – and indeed, the importance of sovereignty as a defining feature is something that we will return to in the next chapter too.

Considering the relational and social bases of identities – and, as above, the fact that identities are also a reflection of self as seen by others – it is worth noting the influence of Canada's southern neighbour, the US. That is, if Norway's Arctic state identity is in part characterised by its relationship with Russia, and Iceland's with its position between Europe and America, the arguably most influential inter-state relationship for Canada is not the former British empire but rather the USA. A national as well as state identity that is a result of its neighbourhood is a topic that recurs in later chapters too. In the international context, the USA is of course also an Arctic (federal) state because of its state of Alaska, but it is undeniably a proportionately much higher priority for Canada – and more significant for identity. It has been suggested that, during the Conservative government of 2006–15, Canadian Arctic policy actually moved in the direction of a US model – including increased military engagement, reduced taxes, and a rejection of climate change reduction targets (Harrison, 2014). Yet, in more recent years, Canadian foreign policy has moved back towards previous middle and soft power ideas under the Trudeau administration that came into office in 2015. And in the US, Trump's presidential period in 2016–21 widened the gap between the two, only for it to narrow again under Biden's from 2021. Most recently the war in Europe has united all of the Arctic states except Russia, emphasising their shared positions and values in the face of international aggression also beyond the region per se – including the Arctic states Finland and Sweden joining NATO. Nevertheless, distinguishing themselves against both the US and generally other states is a key aspect of state identity, also in the Arctic:

> I think that Canada is being viewed as a more confident nation, and one that maybe is a bit more independent. We'll not just go along with what everyone else wants to do, but we'll assert our own position. (C.xviii)

He continued that 'Canadians often think, because we compare ourselves to the [United] States, they think we're a small country. We're not! We're the eleventh largest economy in the world, so we should act like that' (C.xviii).[4] Assertive and strong, sovereign and free – as well as co-operative and morally just – these are ideas that may characterise Canadian state identity, but are not too dissimilar from other states' too. Yet, few if any would argue that a singular and common Arctic state identity exists (or should exist). What is shared across the states and throughout this chapter, though, is a sense of pride in their own state and their role among other states – as is likely needed for those whose job it is to represent it in the day-to-day.

International state identities

State identities might follow the lines of geography and temporality, but are always also about relations with others. Considering those international relations, this chapter has shown that state identities are intersecting understandings of position in the world, roles and leadership, rights and responsibilities, and about relations with other states within the region too.

Across the three Arctic states considered here is a shared sense that international cooperation and intergovernmental work really matter. As a circumpolar region of multiple states, it is not surprising that the Arctic would require collaboration, but it is clear that for these states' personnel it also provides an arena for deeper-rooted self-perceptions. As members of an exclusive group of eight, the states are here relatively big players – and with equal decision-making rights as otherwise 'great powers'. The Arctic is, in other words, a place where small to medium states can enact a desired role of influence, and it provides a venue to express interests. Further, it provides an opportunity to enact existing identities tied to ideas of peace, moral values, and so on – continuing some of the historical pursuits of polar explorers and their quests for national independence in the north.

Additionally, the exclusive title as Arctic state is one of privilege and rights, setting the rules, as well as one of responsibilities. The latter is articulated variously as stewardship and protection, noting the different characteristics of political practices for and from the region itself compared to those of more southern actors. It is considered an 'asset' or 'ticket' in international affairs, but one that requires continual performance and even protection from threats. And these enactments are never predetermined, but can be understood and performed in a variety of ways – identities are always contested and contestable. State identities are, like other identities, defined against others – be they Arctic or non-Arctic states, neighbours or further afield. And these identities are not just expressed 'over there', or in international fora, but also at home. State identities are undeniably tied to – simultaneously affecting and an effect of – national identities. Continuing the discussion of how states assert themselves as different, the next chapter looks within its borders, to the Arctic at (or as) home.

Notes

1 Iceland is actually the only NATO member without a standing army of its own, but does have a coast guard that performs many similar functions, and a security force. Additionally, defence is a sector in which Iceland and Norway have maintained historically close ties, with the latter contributing to e.g. surveillance.
2 The Arctic Environmental Protection Strategy was proposed in 1989, and adopted in 1991 in Rovaniemi, Finland.
3 The Barents Cooperation is a political initiative for peace-keeping and people-to-people cooperation in the border regions of Norway, Sweden, Finland, and Russia. Launched in 1993, its long-running work has been seriously affected by the war in Ukraine.
4 They linked this to Canadian politics in the Arctic, using the recent cooling of bilateral relations with Russia as an example of how they are capable of asserting themselves.

5

The Arctic state and the nation: narrating identity in and as the north

A state identity is articulated among other states, as state representatives meet their international colleagues – yet is also closely tied to ideas of national identities and feelings of belonging. While it may be analytically correct to separate state from nation, the ideology and illusion of hyphenated nation-states run deep in societal understandings and socio-political orderings (see Antonsich, 2009). In other words, many often assume that a territory and political institution link neatly to a self-defined 'people'. For example, the idea would be that the borders around Norwegian territory corresponds with governing institutions and 'the Norwegians', including Norwegian language, customs, and so on. Given the power of this idea(l), it is impossible to fully grasp a state identity without also looking to the nation and national sense of communal self. As we saw in the previous chapter, this communal sense is often a product of external relations – what distinguishes one country from another – yet it also looks inwards, towards what unites. For state personnel whose job it is to represent this seemingly hyphenated nation-state, ideas of shared identity therefore matter: they may guide political practices and behaviours, and invisibly shape what comes to be seen as 'right'.

How we understand the 'nation' and with it nationalism – the ideology that nation and state should (and can) correspond – is a debated topic among thinkers and theorists. Some have developed typologies of nationalism, chronologies, or even binary distinctions between for example ethnic or civic nationalism (see Hechter, 2000; Özkirimli, 2000). Others again emphasise the important role of factors such as language, religion, values, and so on. More often than not however, many of these aspects will be present all at once, and vary in prominence according to time, place, context, and momentary 'other'. That is, it is, like any identity, always articulated through interactions, again and again, and open to contestation and change. However, it is when any of these factors become politicised and tied to inclusion in the so-called nation (and, of course, exclusion from it) that nationalism takes on a role that can reach deep into people's lives and experiences. In the Arctic as elsewhere, what comes to be defined as 'essentially' so – a 'core' of an Arctic identity – is therefore a question of very real consequence. While this chapter can only outline the expressed views at the state level, it is no doubt a factor in states' geopolitical decision-making – and, again, potentially highly consequential and powerful.

Although a title of Arctic statehood is, as we have seen, relatively recent, often entering public discourse only via the Arctic Council's founding in the mid-1990s, it is already clear that much deeper-rooted and longer-running identities impact the articulation of an Arctic as such, across any country's context. It is this national articulation of 'the Arctic state' that this chapter will explore, first charting its ties to such pre-existing notions of shared self – a topic already touched on in previous chapters too. It then goes deeper into the factors often thought to set a nation apart, its uniqueness in relation to neighbours and others. It then turns to how these factors are neither expressed nor experienced only through spectacular celebrations or 'hot' manifestations, but also the everyday, popular culture, and what Michael Billig (1995) famously refers to as the 'banal'. By this he means the often unnoticed 'flagging' of the nation in seemingly mundane ways: 'The metonymic image of banal nationalism is not a flag which is being consciously waved with fervent passion; it is the flag hanging unnoticed on the public building' (Billig, 1995: 8). How these so-called banal reminders of nationhood, including education, affect also those in power is a topic that has arguably not been given the attention it deserves. In short, the chapter starts exploring how ideas of national 'Arcticness' are experienced and understood by state personnel – also in everyday and even taken-for-granted ways.

National independence and sovereignty

Even if, as noted, Arctic statehood is a relational title – northernness in relation to a south – and a position in an international system, Arctic state identities are articulated differently across each country. No Arctic state identity is singular or the same, nor is it static, but always understood in a relational sense vis-à-vis others. For state personnel this means performing political practices of Arctic statehood in their particular ways, for example a specifically Norwegian, Icelandic, or Canadian approach to Arctic geopolitics. For Norwegian state personnel this means that their Arctic state identities are also anchored in an idea of what Norway is, has been, and should be. For example, the previously discussed historically iconic Norwegian Vikings or traditional fishermen have become metaphorically connected to a wider Arctic coastal identity. As such, histories of Norwegian nationalist struggles for independence in the nineteenth and early twentieth centuries continue to influence, implicitly emphasising difference from the Danish and Swedish (Burgess, 2001; Tønnesson, 2009). Historical imagery and imaginaries of pre-industrial national romanticism and fairy-tales, such as trolls, represented Norway when hosting the Winter Olympics in 1994 and featured in EU-membership debates, for example (Eriksen and Neumann, 2011). Arguably more defining of Norwegian identity today than the nationalist movement and independence, however, was the discovery of 'black gold' – namely oil – in the North Sea in the late 1960s. The oil quickly transformed what had been a rural and poor country into one of the world's wealthiest petroleum producers – what has been described as the 'oil fairy-tale' (Kristoffersen and Young, 2010). Yet, the self-perception of being a country struggling to assert itself and be heard internationally persists, and features in politics also today – and is, in some ways, related to Iceland's continued emphasis on independence and Canada's on sovereignty. Drawing this together with ideas of space and time, as discussed in the previous chapters, state personnel reflected on these interrelated factors too: 'Polar history has been very central to building the Norwegian identity from the seventeenth and eighteenth century, with the focus on skiing, on winter – that which made Norway special in relation to the union with Denmark' (N.vi).[1] While the union of course no longer exists, the 'struggle' is today transferred to being heard internationally – including in the Arctic, where an identity as such is continually performed through political practice.

Recalling the history of the even more recent national independence of Iceland discussed in Chapter 3, this has come to be a key concept for understandings of self there too. And whereas it might be the symbols and imaginaries of the Norwegian nationalist movement that have persisted there, the very *concept* of independence has a prominent role in Icelandic discourse. Across interviews about Arctic identity with Icelandic state personnel, independence was a frequently recurring theme, described as a key characteristic of Icelandic people: 'We're independent, we make our own decisions, and no one will tell us what to do. I think that's sort of like the core of the Icelanders' (I.xii). And not only to its history as a Danish dependency, independence is also linked to Iceland's geography as an island state and an open environment – what could be seen as isolating difference can also be viewed as uniqueness to be proud of.

> Involved in the feeling of wanting to be independent there's also that we are a people who need a lot of freedom. I think that comes from being brought up in an environment where you are totally free […] You have a lot of space; you run; you start by sleeping outside when you are a kid, when you are a few months old. And then, when you start running around, and you have something between your ears to control what you're doing, then you start running around free in the streets and in the nature. And that also makes a country that is brought up like that. (I.vi)

In the above quotation, national 'spatio-temporality' is brought together to explain uniquely Icelandic political practices as a result of identity, also as experienced and enacted in the Arctic.

National identity and what is considered 'typical' can be articulated as similarity, belonging and difference at the same time – and in particular in relation to close neighbours and imperial powers, as in the following Icelandic example:

Our identity as a nation, it is, you know, it is Nordic, but we are different. There is more individualism, and it's regarded as somewhat positive to be able to stand on your own two feet, to not be dependent on others, and to not receive benefits. (I.ix)

In other words, it is possible to see yourself both as different and distinct within the international system and *also* as equal, taking part, and fully included (Adler-Nissen and Gad, 2014). There can, of course, be a tension between internationalism and individualism: 'We're a small nation, but we want to have a big voice internationally. I think that's sort of like how we *want* to be – I'm not so sure if we can' (I.xii; followed by laughter). But these can also co-exist, and the Arctic region arguably provides one avenue for the enactment of both what is typically Icelandic and what is shared in an international region – and to enact a desired role of influence beyond size. It is here, at the confluence of the particular and the universal, where the national community looks inwards and becomes aware of itself as Arctic, that an identity emerges.

Much like the idea of independence has done for Icelanders, that of sovereignty (alongside stewardship) and its protection has defined much of Canada's engagement in the Arctic and beyond, as alluded to in the previous chapter too. While the Canadian anthem suggests it is 'strong and free', the end of formal *legal* dependence on the British Parliament ended only as recently as 1982, and the British monarch remains Head of State. It is therefore, like Norway in 1905 and Iceland in 1944, fairly recently independent, and the search for its own identity is not a closed matter – but in Canada's case more often articulated through the language of sovereignty rather than independence. And while its population is bigger than that of both of the other two states, due to its large geographical size it is in fact very sparsely populated on the whole. It is therefore perhaps not surprising that the three states share a sense of being a small player in a big world, each needing to protect its own (sovereign) spaces. The Arctic then, or 'the Myth of the North' (Grant, 1988), has served as one such way for Canada to distinguish itself from the former British empire – not wholly unlike the explorer Fridtjof Nansen's quest for national identity in the north as a means to distinguish

Norwegians from Danes. Grant (1988: 3) describes this myth as a perception that for the 'adolescent state the key to maturity lay in development of its northern "hinterland"'. In this way, the Arctic offers an opportunity for the state to enact its identity in the face of an imagined and re-imagined threat to sovereignty. And, in turn, the perception justifies spending and activity in the region, and indeed identity:

> [The Conservative party] see security-threat as a way to unite Canadians with a common objective, and the threat of having maybe other countries wanting our territory and the – like, we don't really have enemies [*laughter*] as a country, so to have something to defend, I think, as an ideology is really important in [the Harper] government. (C.xii)

In short, Canadian state personnel share their Norwegian and Icelandic counterparts' sense of Arctic statehood being characterised by membership, intermittent and contextual leadership, and an opportunity to engage internationally; but also they see a need to continually perform their own sovereignty and indeed identity in the Arctic and elsewhere.

Sustainable identities, sustaining the nation

The sense of national exceptionalism or even superiority discussed in the previous chapter – being a 'peace nation' and morally just – is also transferred from one sphere to another. In the Arctic geopolitical context, it includes the notion of environmental responsibility and stewardship, and indeed being ahead of others on this. In Norway, it is a matter of some pride that the now-famous concept of 'sustainable development' [*bærekraftig utvikling*] can be traced back to the UN report *Our Common Future* (UN, 1987) produced under former Norwegian PM Brundtland's leadership. And the previously noted 'closeness to nature', as well as outdoors activities such as skiing, are aspects of Norwegian identity that become enrolled in the project of sustainability and 'sustainable development'. The concept has become so frequently used that it is now verging on cliché both in the Arctic and in wider geopolitical discussions: it is hard to argue with sustainability. It serves as key for political credibility, while keeping the definitions of what is meant by both 'sustainable' and 'development' often vague.

In any case, sustainable development is an idea that simultaneously links to ideas of national identity and guides political practice in the Arctic region. According to one Norwegian interviewee, 'today, the Norwegian identity [is tied to] us being the nation that exploits natural resources but in a sustainable way' (N.x). And it is a theme that runs throughout Norway's Arctic policies too: the *Norwegian Government's Arctic Policy* (N.MFA, 2021) includes mention of sustainable business development, sustainable communities, sustainable use of natural resources, sustainable ocean-based industries, sustainable economic development, sustainable resource management, sustainable production of goods and services, and sustainable job and growth creation – to mention just some examples. It is, of course, no small paradox that a country whose identity centres on ideas of sustainability – such as its own reliance on renewable energy from hydropower – receives most of its export revenues from fossil fuels (see Rimmer, 2016). Yet, even in the face of this paradox, some maintain the image and self-perception with reference to their Russian neighbours, claiming that, unless Norway extracts the hydrocarbons in a 'sustainable' way, Russia would surely do it but with much less concern for the environment. This is what Leif Christian Jensen refers to as 'discourse co-optation', where the environmentalist argument is appropriated *for* Norwegian petroleum extraction (Jensen, 2012). In recent discussions about potentials for controversial deep-sea mineral mining in the Arctic – something which critics caution has not and should not be conducted for environmental concerns – the same argument has been made: 'that the country's track-record when it comes to *responsibly exploiting natural resources*, makes it a good candidate to open the door to this new industry' (Humpert, 2023 emphasis added).

Sustainability is, as we can see, a malleable term that is clearly employed for various, even sometimes contradictory, purposes. And it serves to promote a certain image: 'we are, perhaps, better at managing the areas than for example Russia, etc., I do believe that; and we are also very preoccupied, so to speak, with showing that off (N.11). And through the idea of 'sustainable development', the two often oppositional priorities of environment and economy are wedded together as an opportunity:

> [W]e have had a, sort of, leadership in relation to climate research and in relation to resource exploitation – that is, the new resources, oil and gas, etc. – and we have managed to raise interest for the High North globally, and particularly in Europe, abroad. (N.v)

In other words, the country's particular, 'sustainable' political approach is a source of pride and of identity, and it connects to the aforementioned search for international status. It renders what is otherwise a potentially controversial practice, such as fossil fuel extraction, as 'normal' and even something to celebrate. As such, it demonstrates how identity discourses can frame and guide political practices – but how, exactly, remains open to interpretation and interests.

Notions of sustainability and environmental stewardship may be broadly shared across the Arctic states, but, again, it is important to note that *how* these are understood within and through national identities will differ. Even though Arctic statehood includes circumpolar membership, an identity as such also 'means specificity – you have something special to provide' (I.v). In Iceland, too, ideas of environmentalism are important – there, often linked to the ocean and renewable energy. As we saw in Chapter 2, understandings of the Icelandic nation-state and its relations in the Arctic were often connected to ideas of nature: 'connections' to ice and glaciers, rhythms, and an intrinsic part of the self. And again, these in turn become arguments for authority in the region, based on particular experience, knowledge, and awareness. With nearly all of Iceland's energy coming from renewable sources, such as geothermal and hydropower, pride in being 'green' is widespread in state-level explanations of identity: 'It is of course very important for Iceland to be a clean country – without any smoke, without any nuclear waste, without any other kind of waste. Clean. That is really a huge issue for Iceland' (I.iv). Iceland's particular role in the Arctic was also described by many as guardianship of oceanic environments, protecting it from less environmentally conscious actors. In this manner, a self-perception of being a people of nature was extended to mean a people of *Arctic* nature. As one Icelandic official explained, 'in the Arctic cooperation we bring to that table the same principles as we apply elsewhere. [...] Sustainability is something that goes through everything we preach and all our policies' (I.v). In other words, an Arctic state identity is *part* of what it means to be Icelandic: performing Arctic statehood means performing the Icelandic, deeply rooted in the nature of the nation.

A relationship with nature, the environment, and climate may also be significant across Arctic statehood in general. But what in Norway and Iceland is often discussed in terms of sustainability, sustainable development, and 'being green', in the Canadian context often comes up under the banner of 'stewardship'. And while this matters for Canadian identity writ large, it is particularly so in the Arctic context, where the concept has a long, and problematically colonial, legacy. Tracing its history, Danita Burke (2017: 36) links '[t]he notion that Canada is the steward of the fragile Arctic environment' also to the 1970s Arctic Waters Pollution Prevention Act legislation, arguing that it 'is a part of the fabric of the Canadian narrative about the country's relationship with the Arctic region' (2017: 36). In the North, Canadian identity as 'strong and free' can indeed play out (see Burke, 2018), but it is also a space to be protected from others – and today that often refers to protecting the environment. In 2017, Canada set an international example by agreeing to establish its largest marine protected area (at least at the time of writing) in the North, the Tallurutiup Imanga – Lancaster Sound National Marine Conservation Area (IUCN, 2017). The agreement was signed not only by the Government of Canada (Parks Canada), but also the Nunavut Government, and the Qikiqtani Inuit Association – this, in turn, ended oil and gas exploration, mining etc. in the area, while protecting the rights of Inuit to continue their traditional activities. As such, the decision both protects the environment and gives some power back to Inuit communities – and it is an international demonstration of consciousness and stewardship. However, big headline initiatives, no matter how positive, can often overshadow the more grounded realities of day-to-day life. For example, vital energy use across the Canadian North is still often far more reliant on imported non-renewable fossil fuels than other parts of the country. As such,

Canadian Arctic statehood, and its stewardship, may lead to certain practices, initiatives, and investments – but it does not consistently and equally extend to all aspects of Northern policy.

Uniqueness as usual

Identities are, as we have already seen, a combination of that which is unique or *exceptional*, and indeed something to be proud of, as well as the taken-for-granted and familiar. For Arctic states, this means the coming together of this statehood as status and even superiority among other Arctic and non-Arctic states, and it means that the title is articulated as 'just how it is', precisely non-exceptional and normalised. This latter aspect means that approaches to the Arctic come to be talked about as 'business as usual', as unsurprising, and matter-of-fact – and, in turn, difficult to disagree with.

The environmentally conscious discourses sketched above are seen not as limited to a state's Arctic identity but rather as part of an already existing identity or image that has been extended to this new political context. In Norway this means that the Arctic region is often discussed not as a unique space in need of particular policies but rather as 'just another' part of the country. In other words, questions of perhaps different approaches or sensitivities may seem out of place if the region is an extension of Norwegian practices and policies elsewhere. Norwegian state personnel's views on environmental protection in the Arctic were as varied as their political, partisan, and professional positions – but, notably, extended to their views on protection elsewhere too. Whereas many were proud of Norwegian concerns for nature, one interviewed parliamentarian expressed a more critical view:

> I think the, let's say, 'oddball' Norwegian mind-set – that we are best and we are best at environmental protection, and we are a bit careful – in my head, really, a bit over-preoccupied with it, and a bit too, perhaps, a bit too environmentally conscious [...] I feel that [...] is just continued into the Arctic. (N.ix)

They saw this Norwegian state identity of environmentalism as a hindrance in today's Arctic; in their words, making the state 'almost fanatically preoccupied with those things' (N.ix). Another parliamentarian from the same party shared some of these concerns, suggesting that the best approach would be 'accepting that it will be a while until you get new resources, etc., and therefore Norway should also, of course, make use of the natural resources we have and earn money from them' (N.xiv). However, recognising the symbolism of the debate, they continued:

> Not that I am personally in favour of it, but if there is one nation on this Earth that could, perhaps, have limited oil extraction based on a climate reasoning, so to speak, and had the economy to miss that income etc., then that is Norway, right. And also, to show the importance of taking care of the climate and environment – among others, because of the Arctic. (N.xiv)

Nevertheless, they saw also symbolic power in the opposite, here echoing some of Leif Christian Jensen's points about 'discourse co-optation', further suggesting that

> the extraction we conduct is more secure and safer than in many other countries. But also, not least, this will create more employment and a lot of activity in our High North areas, and that I think is important in order to secure a claim to the areas also in the longer term. (N.xiv)

What is clear in both of these cases is that pre-existing views of Norwegian identity are brought to Arctic politics, re-interpreting the new context in order to fit a familiar frame. As one performance of the state identity is accepted – be it acting as a steward or ('sustainable') extractor – certain political practices follow, while others become ruled out. In both cases, articulating the Arctic through seemingly stable identity discourses, Arctic geopolitics become normalised and 'Norwegianised'. And, moreover, the state official's own subject position remains the same, and if nothing else, their own professional role and identity are 'sustained'.

All Arctic geopolitics is to an extent oriented towards what is yet to come, and as previously discussed this is perhaps most clearly so for the Icelandic state – extending also to its environmental engagement, identity, and sense of how it brings this to the Arctic sphere. Decoupling climate change from opportunities it may generate has been described as 'opportunistic adaptation' in the Norwegian context (Kristoffersen, 2015), and the polar thaw might provide potential advantages for the Icelandic state too. These potential opportunities include increased use of polar shipping routes, new resources, and a new international status – all of which may either reinforce or re-narrate Icelandic identity. One prominent example includes the discussions around hydrocarbon exploration on the Icelandic continental shelf – and this in spite of Iceland's own energy use being largely renewable. Exploration ended as recently as in 2018, when the Norwegian and Chinese companies involved pulled out. Discussing this four years earlier, an Icelandic parliamentarian explained that the main thing was 'to be prepared, and a plan', and 'to be part of it, the making of the future of the Arctic' (I.ii). Even when it comes to possibly controversial resources, 'we have interests, and we don't want to be outside the club' (I.iv). In other words, potential resource extraction is about anticipation for the future as well as international inclusion. However, if oil or gas *had* been found, it might not just have been an opportunity for export revenues, but, on the contrary, its active disavowal could also be an opportunity for international status – a symbolic performance of Icelandic identity (not dissimilar to the Norwegian statement above):

> Our nation is, you know, one of the better-set nations in the world; our living standards are really high. And it would be something that the rest of the world – rest of the universe even – would notice, if we said that 'well, we're not going to pursue our interests when it comes to oil, because it's just environmentally really irresponsible to do it'. So, that would be a role that would matter much. (I.ix)

Again, state identities are malleable and contextual, and never fixed – as is clear from the above examples. What is also clear, however, is that elements of existing identities can serve to guide geopolitical practices in the present and for the future – though never wholly determine them – as identities continually evolve and change.

While uniqueness within an international community of states tends to focus on relations *between* states, also relations within the state's borders can serve to distinguish it from other states. This is also the topic of Chapter 6, but especially in the case of Canada this internal diversity has itself become one of these national identity markers. As a collection of former British and French colonies, and importantly numerous Indigenous nations, Canadian identity tends to be described less in terms of cultural homogeneity than is the case for the other two states. Indeed, some have gone so far as to say that the only thing that truly unites Canadians across their vast territory is their incessant preoccupation with locating an elusive national identity. In the words of Hillmer and Chapnick (2007b: 11), 'Canadian nationalisms remain in the search, seldom the arrival'. Or Manning (2003: xvii) goes as far as to describe Canadian belonging as 'coterminous to homelessness'. In Québec, this strong identity has even led to nationalist aspirations among some, and, in 2006, the Canadian Government formally recognised the Québécois as 'a nation within a united Canada' (Bélanger and Doran, 2013: 163). As such, Canadian identity is numerous – a multinational state – where diversity itself becomes part of a shared perspective on the state. Perhaps for this reason, a shared space offers a unifying feature – a shared state territory for numerous nations. The question of the 'quintessentially Canadian' may therefore be a question not just of 'who' but also of 'where' (Frye, 1971; see also Arnold, 2012).

Cohabitation, the sharing of space, and the aforementioned nature, cold, and winters therefore play an important role in uniting diverse and distant peoples within Canadian borders. In 1936, Canada's longest-serving PM, Mackenzie King, stated that 'while some countries have too much history, we have too much geography' (cited in Barnes, 2007: 161), referring to the country's vast distances and lacking infrastructural connections. And, not unlike in Norway and Iceland, the shared geography has been credited with 'shaping' the peoples' character. Arnold (2010) traces what she calls the 'northmen thesis' back to Canadian nationalism of the late nineteenth century, when the idea was that the climate had brought about a Canadian race[2] that was different from European ancestors and empires:

> As long as the north wind blows, and the snow and the sleet drive over our forests and fields ... we must be a hardy, a healthy, a virtuous, a daring, and ... a dominant race. (cited in Arnold, 2010: 453)

Since the 1970s, discourses of Canadian identity have changed to be one of 'multiculturalism' (as we will return to below). Yet, some argue that ideas of Canada is still deeply racialised: the idea of a 'frontier-land', ready to be conquered by the white man, still has a role in popular imaginations (Baldwin et al., 2012a: 4). And, while ideas of environmental determinism may (hopefully) be a thing of the past, the state's environment does play a part in the sense of a Canadian collective – sharing the experience of cold northernness beyond latitudinal boundaries, in turn serving as a uniting factor:

> I guess it's because we're a northern country and we have rough winters. Canadians always like to see themselves also as hardy and winter-country people. So they do have this psychological connection, whether appropriate or not, it's there: they see themselves, they see Canada as definitely an Arctic nation, beyond the legal fact that we are. (C.x)

Note that the interviewee here refers to 'they' rather than 'we', indicating that they are likely talking about a more generalised Canadian public – while possibly not including themselves. Chapter 7 returns to ideas of personal and professional identities of state personnel, and how this weaves in and out of a wider national collective. However, state personnel also share the embodied experiences of geography, which in Canada was a topic returned to frequently when speaking of Arctic identities. And they may also share experiences beyond the professional, such as hobbies, sports, and seeing this 'vast territory' displayed in classrooms. As such, that which is typically Canadian – 'cold and winter and ice and skating and skiing' (C.viii) – becomes a gradual and unconscious reminder, also for state personnel, of their country and their job as 'Arctic'.

Banal Arcticness and branding

As we now know, the title 'Arctic state' was an outcome of the Ottawa Declaration that in 1996 established the eight member states of the Arctic Council as such. While the term may well have been in usage prior to this, the official recognition of it is notably recent – and so, unsurprisingly, this label from a political document is a new one to many of the people living within these countries. Nevertheless, as we have seen so far, it has quickly become linked to already existing identities, and normalised in this way. And, using Billig's (1995) famous term of 'banal nationalism', we can think of 'banal Arcticness' as the many unnoticed ways in which Arctic statehood is 'flagged' in the everyday.

According to the historian Sverker Sörlin (2013: 9), Norway maintains an 'active polar lore' and 'boasts about its national polar explorers and stresses its polar identity, even in the form of a "banal nationalism" manifest in the daily posting of temperatures for both the South and North Pole in Norway's largest daily, *Aftenposten*'. And not only in the form of weather forecasts, but Arctic headlines in both national and international media remind state personnel and others of the title, and may even influence Norwegian self-perception. While perhaps not immediately geographically close, the Arctic can thereby provide a symbolically shared space, existing with the abstract 'homogenous, empty time' of a national present (Anderson, 1983), and a feeling of connectedness in spite of distance. However, as one Norwegian parliamentarian noted about the lack of specificity of such stories:

> I also think it is very vague [...], and I sort of see 'the Arctic' being spewed out everywhere. And I think [...] that, perhaps, places that are not part of 'the Arctic', there it becomes, maybe, sort of mythical; it is something very exotic, something fun to talk about. (N.ii)

In their view then, being 'Arctic' may hold more meaning outside the borders of these countries themselves, as something 'exotic'. Certainly for the tourism industry, this has been a label that they have seen value in. Another Norwegian official explained that Norwegians are aware of Arctic statehood due to the three interlinked issues of climate change, oil and gas extraction, and spectacular nature: 'ice, walruses, polar bears, and all sorts of things up there that people think are great to see, great to visit' (N.x). Again, this hints at tourism – but also at pride in one's own country. Through such branding, local inhabitants are also reminded of the external view – in turn influencing self-perception. And moreover, for state personnel (and everyone else) who do not work directly with Arctic issues, it nevertheless becomes part of the everyday.

If identities, including a state identity, are in part the relational outcome of realising how you are seen by others, then this kind of branding – including the 'banal' flagging, the prosaic, and the everyday – matters (see e.g. Benwell, 2014; Edensor, 2002; Painter, 2006). Also in Iceland, 'Arctic' is an adjective, adverb, and noun seen attached to products and experiences with increasing frequency. And so, while there is no allegorical Arctic flag hanging unnoticed outside the *Alþingi* (see Billig, 1995), there are plenty of reminders of the state's title and geographical position in the world. Strolling around the city centre of Reykjavík, such posters, signs, and advertisements all contribute as silent reminders of what the former Icelandic President Grímsson has proudly called 'a dynamic Arctic village' (Grímsson, 2014a). Through the active use of an Arctic title, directed perhaps primarily at external audiences, the local inhabitants may also gain a sense of pride in this. And, gradually, what was originally directed at others can later become reproduced to domestic audiences as celebrations of heritage: 'they [Icelanders] need witnesses to confirm their identity' (Einarsson, 1996b: 226) – as arguably most do. One of the interviewed Icelandic parliamentarians reflected on this, stating that 'people become more aware of their heritage than they were otherwise, because it becomes a merchandise to sell to tourists' (I.ix). For some this may become a source of great pride, while for others it can also serve more cynically as the previously mentioned 'Arctic ticket' (I.ix) in diplomacy: 'Clearly there is some attempt here in Iceland to cater to the image, or to a brand or something exotic, and … you see a polar bear outside. We don't have polar bears!' (I.vii) (see Figure 5.1). The same interviewee continued that the popular puffin has become somewhat of a national mascot for the country, yet the actual national bird, the gyrfalcon, was nowhere[3] to be seen, apparently not being 'very exciting or exotic' (I.vii). Similarly, the much publicised Icelandic belief in elves and hidden people, the *húldufolk*, has been described as nostalgia for the 'pure' or 'traditional' Icelandic identity in a modernising world (Hafstein, 2000). However, as the above interviewee remarked drily, 'Icelanders themselves sort of cater to that a little bit: "yeah, we all believe, sixty per cent, eighty per cent, believe in elves". And, basically, it is a lot of nonsense, but maybe harmless' (I.vii). Neither puffins nor hidden people are specifically Arctic of course, but their promotion to non-Icelandic audiences as something 'exotic' is another example

Figure 5.1 A souvenir shop in Akureyri, Iceland, with polar bears and trolls outside (Source: Patrick Nouhailler, CC BY-SA 3.0)

of how a national community is reminded of its own differences through interactions with others – be that tourists, foreign investors, or non-Arctic politicians. At times spectacular – such as during the annual Arctic Circle Assembly in Reykjavík – but more often banal, Iceland's Arctic state identity is in this way 'flagged' to both visitors and locals in the everyday. Although the reception of such symbols will vary (see e.g. Jones and Merriman, 2009), their continual iteration can also lead to seeming insignificance, boring familiarity as that which was 'exotic' becomes folded into daily routines (see e.g. Anderson, 2015). For representatives of an Arctic state as well as for others, the title of Arctic statehood may then become part of daily life, as a background to professional and personal practice.

Continuing on the topic of symbols – both everyday and 'exotic' ones – in the Canadian case, the most obvious example would be the maple leaf, which is both widely recognisable and ubiquitous as symbolic of the nation-state. Linking two symbolic signifiers of Canadian identity, former Conservative PM Harper asserted that 'as Canadians, we see ourselves as a Northern people. The great white North is as much a part of Canada's identity as the red maple leaf' (Harper, 2008). Although there are of course no maple trees growing in the North, the leaf is present across flags, governmental icebreakers, and everyday tuques, reminding Northerners of nation and of state (see Billig, 1995). But it is not just southern leaves that travel North, but also Northern symbols that make their way south: the polar bear being a case in point. As an animal that most Canadians will (fortunately!) never encounter, it is nevertheless one that many may feel somehow connected to – as one Canadian senator reflected:

> Canada has a strong sense of identity with the polar bear. [...] they have this massive stamp where there's this gorgeous polar bear on it ... I think it's a $20 stamp or something like – not a cheap one, I know that. But there are different things that are, you know, things that are North, and Canada – it's just part of our national identity. (C.xvii)

Similarly, another Canadian interviewee explained that 'things like polar bears are on our *toonies* [two-dollar coins] ... It's a big symbol for what Canadians feel like their Canadian identity is' (C.ii). In other words, everyday objects such as stamps and coins serve as often unnoticed reminders of something bigger and something shared – not just as Arctic or Northern but as more generally Canadian. When a state official sticks a stamp to a letter it is not a conscious and deliberate performance of identity, but it is a 'citation' of a discourse (see Butler, 1999), reinforcing and enacting Arctic state identity in the everyday (see also Dumas, 2023; Wood-Donnelly, 2018).

Another notable example of Arctic state identity symbolism was the use of an *inuksuk* to represent Vancouver's hosting the Winter Olympics in 2010. The *inuksuk*[4] (or actually *inunnguaq*) is a humanoid stone figure, traditionally an Inuit 'helper', both spiritual and practical. Rather than representing something 'typically Canadian' however, Indigenous cultural symbols are often presented as a distillation of Canadian difference (Pupchek, 2001); or, as Dumas (2023) describes the use of Inuit imagery on postage stamps in the 1950s, 'banal colonialism'. One interviewee reflected on how the choice of the Olympics logo tied in with identity narratives and idea(l)s: 'We used it as the symbol for something that was very much a national event in one of the least Arctic parts of our country. It was a very telling decision for how we wanted to portray ourselves on the world stage' (C.v). The choice of symbol was at the time controversial, not least as it is associated with one specific Indigenous people – and whose traditional homelands are far from Vancouver – rather than something more widely shared. However, others considered this part of the image's strength, a marker of Canadian diversity. A senator explained that some had initially thought a totem pole would be more representative of the Indigenous peoples in the province:

> But, in the end, the case was made that we want the 2010 Olympics to be all of Canada's Olympics. Yes, it's being held on the West coast, in the coast mountains, but we want it to be part of – to be all of Canada's Olympics. And the committee decided very strongly, in the end, that the *inuksuk* would be great symbol, because it wasn't necessarily British Colombian, but it was all of Canada. And it's been very, very well-received and well-accepted, and you can find *inuksuk* all of over our country now. (C.ix)

Their final point resonated, as *inuksuit* were present on windowsills and shelves at the time of many of the interviews conducted in Ottawa that are cited in this book, and as statues and illustrations across the country (see Figure 5.2). On this reflection, one official explained that 'because of our kind of hybrid, mosaic identity as a country, [we're] able to see the local symbol of another region as a symbol of the whole and get behind it and associate with it' (C.v). In other words, the particular has come to symbolise the national – an Arctic stone figure to represent the Canadian.

In addition to its meaning for Canadian audiences – symbolising diversity and unity all at once – the *inuksuk* undoubtedly also flagged to international audiences Canada's Arctic state identity (and in this context perhaps winter sport traditions). Much as Icelandic citizens and state personnel above are reminded of their Arctic statehood through touristic branding, so too could the *inuksuk* reflect back an image to Canadians themselves.

Figure 5.2 The Inukshuk of Inukshuk Park in Toronto, Canada
(Source: Peter Broster, CC BY 2.0)

One interviewee described the event in 2010 as a grand show and
performance, with the *inuksuk* as 'our brand to the world. We use
it to make money, I guess, for tourism. That's – the Vancouver
Olympics thing, that wasn't done for Canadians, right, that was
done for the world. To the world, that's interesting, "oh look,
the, you know, the Inuit"' (C.xviii). Continuing, they further
explained that 'in my everyday, day-to-day life it means nothing,
but symbolically it means something to us' (C.xviii). And it most
certainly means something to the tourism industry, with *inuksuit*
and polar bears common across souvenir shops; and, in diplomacy,
the practice of gifting Inuit art has been common, an act of pro-
jecting Canadian sovereignty (Lennox, 2012). Not limited to the
specific service of the *inuksuk* for the Olympics, Inuit culture and
art have been invoked to construct a romanticised past for the
country, not unlike nation-building projects elsewhere, such as the
German *volk* movement (Pupchek, 2001) – co-opted and idealised
'in the service of a state dominated by non-indigenous southerners' (Arnold, 2010: 460). That being said, Inuit are today also

reclaiming their symbols in displays of own identity and agency (Graburn, 2004), including the *inuksuk* on the flag of Nunavut, the majority-Inuit territory that was created in 1999 as a result of a historic land-claim agreement. Guibernau (2013) explains that national symbols allow 'emotional creativity' for individuals to form their own subjective bonds and meanings, in turn allowing communities to come together around shared yet plural meanings. And with symbols linked to sporting events where national identity is felt and even experienced as an 'affective atmosphere' (Closs Stephens, 2016, 2022), the symbol of the *inuksuk* is re-signified in the south – ascribed new meanings of belonging and identity. Branding or banal, reminders of the North travel south, and the Arctic state becomes present in the everyday.

Arctic stories and national storytelling

Ideas of Arcticness travel not only through touristic images, symbols, and sports events but also through popular culture – through the stories told about self and other. With experience from the Norwegian Ministry of Foreign Affairs, one interviewee reflected on the relevance of the naming of Arctic statehood and identity, of telling the same story in the language of Arcticness (see Steinveg and Medby, 2023):

> [Y]ou can of course put a lot into the Arctic or High North identity, or inside that bubble, that would have been there regardless of us having those labels on it, right. Now we have a label; now we can say when we build a new ice-breaking research vessel that it is an Arctic investment, but [before] we would have just called it marine research. So, we didn't have – we had perhaps done it anyway, but we hadn't, sort of, had a 'hook' for it. (N.i)

However, the national narration of Arcticness was not only one of retelling existing practices with a new inflection but also required certain practices – 'filling the strategy with concrete content':

> Building an [Arctic] identity, you build a brand – that is, Norway: a brand – which requires that the state – the state administration, government and parliament – have to deliver something within it.

> So it drives development. And then, some might say that nothing has happened; and there's probably something to that, but I think less would have happened if one hadn't chosen to have this 'heading' (N,i)

In other words, the story of the Arctic state and its identity is not just one told in order to sell souvenirs or even convince voters but also frames the options available to politicians and state personnel themselves – here, what practices to follow the articulation of being Arctic.

The importance of language extends beyond the specific naming of the Arctic region too – a foreign label, as we have already seen in Chapter 1 – to ideas of national identity and selfhood. And language and language-use are, of course, deeply geopolitical – connecting place and power – and matter to understandings of Arctic identities too (see Jones, 2024; Medby, 2023; Medby and Thornton, 2023). In the example of Iceland, the role of language is significant in the previously discussed understandings of independence – and some would consider Iceland's contributions to Arctic cooperation to be cultural: 'since we are very well-known as the "country of books" or something, the land of the sagas' (I.ii). Literature and the famous sagas were important in the national movement for independence at the time, and the celebration of canonical texts such as the *Íslendingabók* and the *Landnámabók* is part of an identity that is arguably intimately tied to language and poeticism (Hastrup, 2010; Sizemore and Walker, 1996): 'Iceland is a proud nation, which is proud of its past, of its history, of its literature, and the culture. And even – it is proud of its language, which is isolating [it from] people from other areas' (I.iv). What could be seen as isolating is also what is celebrated as making a people stand apart and to be proud of: 'being this small nation with its own language on an island, that affects your outlook a little bit' (I.vii). As such, language and the meaning not of the words but of their *use* are interwoven in Icelandic stories of self, and in turn of actions to follow in the name of the Arctic state.

We have already seen the importance that education and history teaching can have, but also storytelling, fiction, art, and music can serve to disseminate ideas of Arctic identities in everyday life. Through shared stories and myths, the past and present mix, and their factuality matters less than the meaning they provide from childhood through adulthood (see Francis, 1997). Writing from the Canadian context, Emilie Cameron (2015: 12) shows that stories serve to make networks of people, ideas, and things become 'sensible, legible, and political' – and, whether or not they are true, stories of the past continue to order relations. Like her example of the 'Bloody Falls Massacre' story, they can order relations between North and south, Inuit and *Qablunaat* (non-Inuit), white and Indigenous, colonised and coloniser, territory and federal state. Through the telling and retelling of stories, in different ways and contexts, certain ways of seeing, relating, and knowing the Arctic are produced. As one of the interviewed Canadian state personnel reflected:

> [T]hese are definitely, I would say, nation-building stories ... that people like Pierre Burton and some of the great historical fiction writers in Canada have played up [...] They always become bestsellers in Canada, because people love to hear about these stories, about adventure in our past. (C.ii)

Adventure and enjoyment are, in this way, part of building the nation, of constructing a community as Arctic and Canadian. And stories can make unfamiliar spaces feel 'familiar', in turn guiding actions to follow, based on imaginaries as much as experiences. Grace (2001: xvii emphasis added) explains that, in Canada, the 'North is an *idea* as much as any physical region that can be mapped and measured for nordicity'. When, in turn, stories become something that unites nations across state space, they take on political power too – such as the example of the previously discussed lost ships of Sir John Franklin. Following the first discovery of one of the lost ships, the HMS *Erebus*, then-PM Harper also observed that 'For almost 200 years, the fate of the Franklin Expedition has captured our imaginations. Sir John Franklin's story has inspired historians, singers and writers' (Harper, 2014a: n.p.). And he continued that it was 'more than just a tragic story. It is also a key moment in our country's history' (Harper, 2014a: n.p.). But perhaps there is never 'just' a story – as with shared symbols, stories can take on a multitude of meanings, both subjective and collective, that shape understandings of identity.

Stories of the North, the Arctic, and its 'strangeness' clearly continue to have an appeal as popular themes in fiction. The world-famous Canadian author Margaret Atwood (2004) has traced such myths of the North, showing how they continue to influence literary tradition in the country. And while ideas of both national and state identity flow through popular culture, causality is not straightforward – one influences the other in mutually constitutive ways as they are 'read' by different people in different contexts, including by those in state offices (see Dittmer, 2010; Sharp, 1993). They too may encounter the North through TV programmes, paperbacks, and imagination – bringing what a senator called a 'land of mystery' (C.ix) to southern audiences (Chartier, 2006; Hulan, 2002; Moss, 1997). However, stories of Canadian north-ernness of course 'tell us virtually nothing about the north, while revealing a great deal about a society in which most people will never go there except in our collective imagination' (Arnold, 2010: 460). What some thought of as 'fascinating' and 'romantic stories of adventure [...] in our past' (C.ii) are, of course, no substitute for lived experience of the Arctic – yet they do offer a mode of imaginary travel to an otherwise often inaccessible space. And as with flexible symbols that can mean many things all at once, stories and ideas of 'the North draws together cultural value and identity to produce a metaphor for imperial grandeur, innocence, and sov-ereignty' (Baldwin et al., 2012a: 2). They are imaginaries then that tells us something *more* – again they are not 'just' stories, but part of the articulation of identity.

Having seen the role of stories, language, and fiction in under-standings of Arctic state identity, there is one final example that cannot go unmentioned, even more powerful and geopolitical than Sir Franklin's tragic fate: that of Santa Claus. Shared practices and customs work to unite a nation: 'common experiences, like Canadian winters and the things that you do in order to survive the Canadian winters, have fun in the Canadian winters' (C.v). Another interviewee explained that so-called 'northern activities' such as curling or hockey serve as a 'connection to the snow and the ice and the cold' (C.i) – which led them to the geopolitical debate of the Arctic: 'who really owns the North Pole' (C.i). Described with a smile, the topic came up in more than one interview:

Canadians believe that Santa Claus is Canadian. I think that tells you – I mean, it's silly, right, but I think that tells you something. We grew up believing that we own the North Pole. Like, that is – there's no question. You tell a Canadian that Santa Claus is Norwegian; they'll be like, 'no. You're wrong.' And that right there, from childhood – we see ourselves as an Arctic country, absolutely. I always did. (C.xviii)

And while the example is described tongue-in-cheek, it most fittingly connects familiar stories and childhood nostalgia with Arctic geopolitics and statehood – here, to deliberations about which state's continental shelf the North Pole can be claimed to be on under UNCLOS (Medby and Barnes, 2022). Arguably of more symbolic than commercial value, claiming the North Pole has been on the state's agenda for more than a decade – as illustrated with stunts such as issuing Santa and Mrs Claus with Canadian ePassports (Chase, 2013). Clearly arguments are also of strategic character: when Canadian leaders requested that the North Pole be included in their submission to the Commission on the Limits of the Continental Shelf, it was also likely a response to Russia's 2007 flag-planting on the polar seafloor. One official laughed, 'As you know the North Pole was already claimed by the Russians; they put a flag underneath the ocean!' (C.iii). This, in turn, no doubt raised Cold War-era worries, when 'there was a sincere feeling that the Russians were going to come over the North Pole and invade Canada' (C.viii). Whatever the likelihood of Russian activities there might be, both Russian and Denmark/Greenland's potential continental shelf claims may overlap with Canada's. This is, however, something to be resolved through the mechanisms of the Commission – while the citizenship of Santa remains an open question. But what this issue – mentioned by several Canadian state personnel – shows us is that Arctic statecraft and geopolitics intersect with other ideas of identity, childhood, and shared stories in often unexpected ways. And in that way, Arctic statehood becomes interwoven through the national and through everyday life, neither causal of the other but co-constitutive of identity.

States and their nations

In the end, even an externally articulated label reaches not only outwards to other states and the international community but also inwards to existing ideas about who 'we' are. For example, the practices and imaginaries of an Arctic state are also those of the Icelandic state, and the two cannot easily or obviously be disentangled. Articulating an Arctic state identity will always rely on the grammars of pre-existing state identities – and they will link to national identities too.

These identities can be simultaneously spectacular and mundane, something celebrated and something unnoticed; they can be implicit in school curricula and museum exhibitions – domesticating the Arctic also means that the domestic itself changes. In turn, people, communities, and national societies 'become' Arctic too – including state personnel. And while often not noticed or reflected on, normalised to the point of invisibility, there are reminders of their state across people's everyday: symbolic images of polar bears across southern capitals, polar brands and marketing, and statues frozen in time in town squares. In that way, the Arctic becomes a part of 'who we are' – but how this is felt is, again, relational and contextual, and certainly not the same for everyone everywhere, as the following chapter will show.

Notes

1 Anecdotally, the emotional was also material in this example: I left that particular interview with a stack of books, brochures, and official publications pertaining to polar Norway – state-level statements in material form that travelled with me, the researcher, outside the institution and outside the state.

2 The Indigenous peoples of Canada were largely excluded from this imaginary: 'Canadians' meant the white European settlers.

3 Except notably on the Icelandic coat of arms.

4 *Inuksuk* (pronounced and sometimes spelled *inukshuk;* plural *inuksuit*) is actually a misnomer for the humanoid stone structure that it is usually used to refer to. In Inuktitut, it means 'to act in the capacity of a human',

and tends to be piled stoned or boulders used for communication. In contrast, the clearly person-like figure that the Olympics used would correctly be called *inunnguaq*, meaning 'in the likeness of a human' (Hallendy, 2015). One interviewed official also pointed this out to me as an example of what he called 'Southern expropriation of Northern symbols': 'An *inuksuk* is just a pile of rocks! So, it's even funnier, it's even more ironic that not only did we poach a Northern symbol, we have used the word incorrectly, poached it incorrectly' (C.xv).

6

Identities within the Arctic state: domestic differences and diversity

Through the everyday, through symbols and stories, people may be reminded of their state and its identity. However, the ways in which these reminders are received and responded to are not universal. As we have seen so far, identities are always relational – and they are also always subjective and contextual (e.g. Mavroudi and Holt, 2015). The same aspects that may unite can also, at other times, be what highlight difference. For example, the stories of polar explorers that previous chapters introduced will inevitably mean something very different from the perspective of the former coloniser than it would from that of the colonised. By focusing on experiences of identity in and through the everyday, it soon becomes clear that it is contingent and complex – what may be 'banal' aspects of nationalism for some can be far from it for others (Jones and Merriman, 2009). And indeed, the power of many affective symbols – such as the flag or the previously mentioned *inuksuk* – is exactly their ambiguity and malleability, interpreted differently by different people in different places (Guibernau, 2013). No matter how homogeneous a group, such as a 'nation', may seem, there is always some level of diversity and difference. The so-called 'other' is not always other states or nationals, but can also at times be people within a people, subgroups within a group, or otherwise those who somehow disrupt a seemingly linear narrative of self.

However, differences within a state's borders are not necessarily a challenge to identity of course – in fact they can be integral to it. For example, ideas of multiculturalism can serve as key values of a perceived identity (Antonsich and Matejskova, 2015), again potentially uniting across some difference. In this context, difference might be articulated as diversity rather than deviation, and seen as a strength rather than threat. And in this way, a state's constituent parts can serve to reinforce the whole, and ultimately be instrumental to the state (see Mitchell, 2003). The institutionalisation and inculcation of diversity as part of an identity can, as such, also be a form of control, of defining 'acceptable' divergences; and drawing new lines between those 'inside' the plural nation-state and those 'outside' (Brown, 2008). In other words, whose difference is accepted and accommodated is also a question of power, which in turn orders relations within a group hierarchically and asymmetrically. Geography is one such ordering mechanism, whereby difference is articulated in spatial terms, 'here' and 'there'. In questions of state identity and domestic difference, this brings our attention to regions within states (as opposed to the circumpolar Arctic region per se), the urban and rural, coastal and inland – all of which are distinctions that take on (and off) meaning according to context and conversation.

Indigeneity and ethnicity are two further of lines of difference that may run through a state, and the former is of particular relevance in the context of Arctic statecraft. So-called inclusion of Indigenous peoples *within* a state – rather than *across* them – can thereby paradoxically work to strengthen state claims and identities (Medby, 2019b). And, while some may conceptualise Indigenous peoples as 'more Arctic' than their non-Indigenous compatriots, their inclusion in the larger whole seems to add weight to a state identity (Medby, 2014), as we will see below. In this way, domestic relations within a state can be instrumental in some contexts, if it is of the 'right' kind of difference, but can also produce hierarchies and uneven relations of power.

In short, to understand state identities we also need to look within its boundaries. This chapter seeks to do just that, starting by looking at geographical differences, north and south, before it turns to indigeneity, and finally, most relevant in the Icelandic context where there is no Indigenous population, the role of the local and traditional.

North and south

Thinking about differences within state borders – and having already considered the importance of geography in the articulation of Arctic state identities – the most obvious place to start is relations between north and south. At risk of stating the obvious, the further north you go, the 'more Arctic' it is seen to be. Considering domestic differences within the state, northernness therefore carries particular weigh when it comes to questions of Arctic identity. And on the basis of the latitudinal (and political) definition of the Arctic, it is actually only the northern parts of the eight Arctic states that grant them their Arctic title: In Norway, it is only North Norway[1] that is latitudinally located within the circumpolar region (see Figure 6.1). Although central to Arctic statehood, the three northernmost counties – Nordland, Troms, and Finnmark – were historically considered peripheral, and with many negative stereotypes attached to them.

Figure 6.1 'Gate' to North Norway (Nordland county) on the road from the south (Trøndelag county) (Source: Zairon, CC BY-SA 3.0)

Although much has changed today, some of these stereotypes may still persist – as one interviewee from North Norway explained it, some may still believe 'that not much is created here, there is a lot of whining, and a lot of people on benefits. Yes, I think that still persists a bit; that you, kind of, joke about it and that some also, perhaps, mean it' (N.xv). On the contrary, defined against Europe and great powers – as we have seen in previous chapters – Norway can be thought of as a country of peripheries (Aarebrot, 1982), where regional and local identities are seen as positive rather than negative. But paradoxically, as a collection of peripheries where local identities are celebrated, it can be even more challenging to not fit that traditional view of what an identity does or should look like: 'Norway is a very conformist society, everything from the media etc., which is very conformist; you have a very similar mindset' (N.xiv). Interestingly however, North Norway was the first recognised region of Norway in the nineteenth century (Niemi, 1993; Tjelmeland, 1996). And, from that time onwards, it has been and still is a construct with a dual meaning: expressing both difference and equality, a desire for both recognition and integration (Arbo, 2015; Fulsås, 1997). Today, this difference and its integration are key to the country's Arctic statehood and identity. Indeed, it is a process that is key to any country's statehood and identity – integration, assimilation, difference, and its limits.

As the north is increasingly re-labelled as 'Arctic' (N.MFA, 2021) – at least internationally – the connotation of belonging to a circumpolar region, not just a state, is clear. The importance of domestic politics, such as North Norwegian concerns, as part of an Arctic political approach is obvious to a state government too. This is something that Norway's Arctic policies explicitly recognise – for example:

> North Norway accounts for 35% of Norway's mainland territory, and 9% of Norway's population lives north of the Arctic Circle. Responsible economic growth and future-oriented jobs in the north are therefore a matter of national interest. Considering Norway's geopolitical location, this also has strategic significance beyond the demographics. Further developing North Norway as a strong, dynamic and highly competent region is the best way to safeguard Norwegian interests in the Arctic. (N.MFA, 2021: n.p.)

In other words, North Norway *matters* to the state writ large, and specifically for its interests in the Arctic; Norway is an Arctic state only because of the north. Perhaps unsurprisingly then, Norwegian state personnel also spoke highly of it, the 'region of opportunities' [*mulighetenes landsdel*]. Several reflected on the contrast between today's optimism and the previously mentioned negative stereotypes, for example it being a 'subsidy drain' (N.xvi; N.xi), 'outskirts', and 'outpost' (N.xvi). A former senior politician in the Conservative government of 2013–21 described the northern region in warm terms:

> [W]hen you are in North Norway, the first thing you notice is a strong optimism, a lot of vitality, many plans, a lot of discussion about opportunities that can be used. So, that makes me think that the North Norwegian self-perception is changing. This connects to how it has traditionally been: namely, a self-reliant and strong people in a robust region. (N.xii)

And, while critics point out that these promises, optimism, the 'Arctic euphoria' (Hønneland, 2017) have not come with many tangible benefits, it does undeniably give North Norway an elevated status and attention from the capital. This, in turn, means that an articulation of an Arctic state identity also requires some political action from those state officials, including investments in and considerations of the people in the north. Interestingly, several of the interviewed state personnel also described their professional engagement with the Arctic as linked to their own northernness or connection to the north: identity, authority, and legitimacy as a representatives of the Arctic state articulated through their own relative northernness.

The domestic hierarchy of Arctic identities within a state is clearly in part about geography, the above relative northernness conferring some kind of elevated status, but also maintains the north firmly as 'part of' or a sub-category of the state itself. In other words, hierarchical (and other) differences therefore remain within the agreed limits of acceptable diversity of the state – part of and even an advantageous level of domestic difference. Despite the local pride in each 'periphery' of the state, the level of heterogeneity in Norway is actually quite low – as the earlier quotation about a 'very conformist society' (N.xiv) pointed out. Researching perceptions of 'Norwegianness' among white-majority Norwegians in Oslo, Vassenden (2010) found that this is made up of a number of different components – citizenship, cultural traits such as language and religion, and ethnicity (particularly whiteness) – and that these will vary in importance according to context. And similarly, it has been found that 'ethno-racial origins and religious affiliations are major hurdles for acceptance' (Friberg, 2021: 21), suggesting that visible difference from that 'white majority' still matters. Moreover, values that Norwegians tend to prioritise include democracy, equality, and community (Larsen et al., 1995) – all of which seem to support the idea of a unified 'nation-state', with arguably less room for difference beyond these. All of this is to say that domestic hierarchies or not, Arctic policies and identities are, in the end, at the level of the state and state interests – as highlighted by the above policy excerpt too.

A decade earlier than that cited above, the 2011 White Paper on the High North (N.MFA, 2011: 9) also explicitly stated that 'This is not a "North Norway-paper" nor a regional policy treatise. The *High North Policy* is about strengthening Norway's position in the north by drawing on experiences, knowledge, and resources from the entire country.' While some northern politicians may feel that North Norway should have a bigger role to play in Arctic geopolitics, state personnel in the south were eager to praise the 'extremely active North Norway' (N.vi) for its work with state bodies. On the whole, northern politicians too recognised that 'there is very strong support for the High North policy being a *national* initiative, but [acceptance] that it demands, of course, extraordinary investment in North Norway' (N.xvi). In other words, elevated status or not, state personnel did not see competition between domestic regions. But, said with a smile, any competition might be on a more local level: 'between the cities in the north [...] competing for resources and entrepreneurism' (N.iv). In this way, Arctic state practices also become domestic ones, with discussions and considerations that are as much about international geopolitics as they are about local concerns, budgetary constraints, and regional responsibilities:

One says that, yes, there are a lot of exciting things in the north; it can become a very important region also in order to lift the whole Norway into the future, with everything that lies there. However, at the same time, there's the everyday reality. So, when it comes to tough prioritisation in budgets and other things it is often a fight for resources. (N.ii)

In the end, North Norway is a prefixed part of the state, even if it does hold a particular status in Arctic geopolitics. In return for increased attention and investment that might come with this role, all parts and people of Norway may claim belonging to an Arctic state of course. In short, Arctic state identities that firmly articulate the north as part of the larger whole are instrumental for the way the state is enacted as Arctic – and it requires certain political practices domestically too.

In contrast to other Arctic states, Iceland does not have a clear north/south divide or domestic hierarchy of Arcticness. In fact, when the Canadian chairmanship of the Arctic Council in 2013–15 named one of their priorities as 'development for Northerners', some Icelandic state personnel felt that this was 'foreign [...] it does not relate to us' (I.i). However, as we saw in Chapter 2, not having a distinct or distant north supports the idea that the state is therefore 'wholly' Arctic – as was reiterated in interviews too: 'there is an awareness [among the Arctic states] that you have different situations in different countries. And when it comes to Iceland, then we are the only one [...] completely *within* the Arctic' (I.i). Without distinct domestic differences of Arcticness, some of those interviewed speculated that perhaps this was why *norðurslóðir* might resonate more with the Icelandic public than 'the Arctic' (I.xii). This is a name closely related to Norwegian preferences for *nordområdene*,[2] which emphasises relative northernness more than the international and indeed foreign 'Arctic'. In other words, it allows the 'domestication' of an otherwise foreign denomination, and it highlights the relativity of north and south also there.

Although Iceland does not have the same domestic difference that you find, to varying degrees, in other Arctic states, the northern town Akureyri is home to a bit of an 'Arctic cluster' (I.viii). The town of approximately eighteen thousand people is the largest outside the capital region in the southwest, and hosts a number of Arctic institutions. As the website Arctic Akureyri (n.d.) promotes, institutions such as the secretariats of the International Arctic Science Committee and two of the Arctic Council's six Working Groups (CAFF and PAME), the Polar Law and the Stefansson Arctic Institute, and others are all based in the relatively small town. And this is also a deliberate policy from the state's side, as the last of their Arctic policy's nineteen priorities is to 'further strengthen the position of Akureyri as the centre of Arctic matters in Iceland, including by supporting education and research bodies and knowledge centres and by strengthening local consultation and cooperation on matters concerning the Arctic region' (I.MFA, 2021: 6). Perhaps especially the mention of the 'local' is worth taking note of here, suggesting that the state's Arctic title is one to be increasingly engaged with by the nation too, and particularly there in the northern Icelandic communities. And although average Akureyri residents might not necessarily see themselves as more 'Arctic' than other Icelanders (yet?), you might expect that local researchers and politicians are professionally more directly engaged with and aware of the country's Arctic statehood. If so, domestic differences within the Icelandic state might have less to do with latitude per se and more to do with professional contact and involvement. Some of those interviewed also reflected on how they felt that their sense of an Arctic identity was tied to their engagement with the state's title as such in their day-to-day work. We will return to the subjective and personal scale of state identity in the next chapter, but suffice it here to say that state identities are not uniformly experienced – but that differences are not always as straightforward as geographical distance or proximity, but about more complex connectedness.

Different levels of connection, connectedness, and even material connectivity are arguably felt even more across a federalised, large, and historically settler-colonial state such as the Canadian, where diversity in the form of multiculturalism has been promoted as one of the defining features of the country. In contrast to the above Icelandic example, Canada is a proudly heterogeneous society (see Harris, 2001; Kymlicka, 2003). Following the full start of non-Western immigration to Canada in the 1960s and the federal state officially becoming French–English bilingual, then PM

Pierre Trudeau introduced a policy of multiculturalism. Unlike the so-called 'melting pot' across its southern border, the Canadian state has sought to promote its celebration of diversity. Writing even before its official enactment through policy, Gibbon (1938) famously described the 'Canadian mosaic', whereby each different piece makes up a whole. Describing a concept by now enshrined not only in state policies but also in people's sense of community, Kymlicka and Banting (2006: 301–2) argue that 'It is "un-Canadian" to oppose multiculturalism, a betrayal of the national code. Opposing multiculturalism in Canada is not only or even primarily an attack on particular minorities, it is an attack on the symbol and substance of Canadian nationhood.' Needless to say, there is a level of conformism here too, not unlike what we have seen in other examples, although articulated along different lines. As Mackey (1999: 70) puts it, a policy of multiculturalism also serves to 'institutionalise, constitute, shape, manage, and control difference' (see also Brown, 2008). In effect, any difference needs to conform to the 'right kind' and acceptable level (Chung, 2007). As such, for those representing the Arctic state of Canada, they are representing diverse peoples and identities – all of whom, however, are expected to fit the mosaic.

Domestic differences within state identities can be about geography, contact, or culture – and they are also tied to histori-cal relations. Canada also has strong regional identities, which is perhaps not surprising given both geographical distances and historical recency of provincial incorporation within the federal state. Although there were of course peoples living in what we today call Canada long before, the state became such only after confederation in 1867, which unified some of the French and British colonies. Initially, it consisted of only four of today's provinces, Ontario, Québec, New Brunswick, and Nova Scotia, before an additional six joined, namely Manitoba (1870), British Columbia (1871), Prince Edwards Island (1873), Saskatchewan (1905), Alberta (1905), and Newfoundland and Labrador (as late as in 1949); as well as the three territories in the North (Ajzenstat, 2003: 3–4). What this highlights is the relative recency of the state itself, which in turn undoubtedly has implications for discourses of state identity. However, the implications need not be negative, but rather again a defining feature: 'Canada is often described as being a very "hybrid" country [...] we are strangely comfortable with multiple identity categories. [...] You know, friends of mine can be Aboriginal Canadian, they can be Cree, they can be Canadian, and they can be Albertan, and – we navigate' (C.v). How and when identities are articulated are, again, contextual and relational – even navigational – and all identities are always plural, also that of the state.

With the above in mind, it follows that the north–south differences we saw in the Norwegian example are even more pronounced in a country of Canada's 'vastness' (C.vii), or indeed in some of the other Arctic states such as Russia and the USA. In Canada, differences between north and south are not only cultural but also economic and political, which unsurprisingly influences how identities come to be understood too. And again unlike the other two states, physical connections in the form of infrastructure, transport, and communication are all limiting more contact between regions – and with that, direct contact with the 'Arctic' of the 'Arctic state'.

> It's prohibitively expensive to travel within Canada, especially up North. So, I think that also kind of puts limits on identity with the North, and kind of, maybe, creates perceptions that may be inaccurate within Canada itself. Just because there isn't – it's very hard for people to explore that part of our own country. (C.xix)

The North has been referred to as a 'place on the margin' (Shields, 1991), not only geographically but also mentally so – as the periphery of the state's 'body', its territory, where its centre and core lie in the south. Recalling the 'strangeness' that was discussed in the previous chapter, a popular theme in fiction and entertainment, for many the North remains inaccessible through other means than screens, books, and imagination:

> [I]n our national identity, our imagination includes the North. We see it on the maps, our national broadcaster; there's lots of documentaries and news-stories about life in the North, and what's happening there ... But ... so at the level of our mental imagination I think it has a place, but generally speaking it's pretty far away and it's not part of our day-to-day. (C.xiv)

And to be clear, another state official explained the physical challenges of a unitary state identity:

> [W]e are conscious of that vast expanse of territory that we have above the top of the provinces. And we do think about it as being part of Canada and an important part of Canada, but on the cultural side I think that, you know, the infrastructure challenges and sometimes the communications challenges mean that the usual conversations between regional identities that we have are just a little bit more difficult with the North. (C.v)

If such 'conversations' are made more difficult with the North, the role of state personnel in mediating across a divide becomes even more impactful. And, importantly, the recognition of not just diversity but disparity and inequity within the state's borders is a responsibility and should be tackled through political means. As such, the title of Arctic statehood requires certain political practices that are also of domestic nature. It is not enough to have 'boots on the ground' and an international position in global geopolitics: being and representing an Arctic state also means investments in roads, schools, and healthcare – and at home too state identities have many facets.

Indigeneity

As we have seen above, domestic differences, even hierarchies, of Arcticness can be about relative geographical northernness, professional engagement, culture, and historical and political ties. This section turns to the role of Indigenous peoples and indigeneity – and political questions that matter to all eight Arctic states: unquestionably important and always part of ideas of Arctic identities. However, Iceland is the only among the eight states which is not home to an Indigenous population – hence the noted feeling Icelanders had of not being included among 'Northerners' – and so is not included here, but we return to it in the final section of the chapter.

Some of the differences between Norway and Canada as two Arctic states, including their relationships with Indigenous peoples within the countries' borders, have already been mentioned. What is relevant here, however, is the recognition that their different histories of settlement clearly have led to different state–Indigenous relations today; and yet, in spite of these, there are also more similarities than many might care to admit. Only one section in one chapter of the book feels perhaps too little to do the topic full justice, but this might unfortunately be a reflection of the still limited role of Indigenous peoples within state (geo)politics. Despite this undeniably limited role, there *is* more scope for Indigenous voices in Arctic geopolitics than elsewhere, for example through the Permanent Participants' seat at the table of the Arctic Council. And, as we saw in Chapter 5, there is symbolic power in Indigenous recognition and identity – as with the *inuksuk*, appropriated but also reclaimed. For the Arctic states, there is no denying that the recognition, respect for, and partnering with Indigenous peoples are key to the enactment of Arctic statehood. And, in fact, also non-Arctic states and organisations wishing to become observers in the Council are required to 'respect' and to demonstrate 'a political willingness as well as financial ability to contribute to the work of the Permanent Participants and other Arctic indigenous peoples' (Arctic Council, 2013: 14). In other words, indigeneity holds a particular role in circumpolar state relations, and to state identities.

Among the Indigenous peoples of the Arctic, the Sámi people live across today's states Norway, Sweden, Finland, and Russia. Roughly half of Norway's territory lies within Sápmi, the traditional Sámi homelands. The 2014 Norwegian *Arctic Policy* summarised that the Norwegian state estimated that there are around eighty to a hundred thousand Sámi people across the four states, but that the largest portion live within Norway's borders – illustrated in the White Paper by a reindeer and *lavvos* (N.MFA, 2014a: 42). However, an exact number is difficult to produce, as Statistics Norway explains 'there is no collective register' (Statistics Norway, 2022: n.p.), and defining who is and is not Sámi is problematic after centuries of interaction and assimilation policies (Larsson and Buljo, 2013). In order to vote in the Sámi Parliament in Norway (see Figure 6.2), a person has to self-declare that they fulfil one of three criteria: that they speak Sámi as their first language at home; that a parent, grandparent, or great-grandparent does or did; or that they have a parent who is or was registered on the electoral roll. Prior to the

Figure 6.2 *Sámediggi,* The Sámi Parliament in Karasjok/Kárášjohka, Norway (Source: Sara Márja Magga/Sametinget, CC BY-SA 2.0)

2021 election, there were more than twenty thouand people registered (Berg-Nordlie and Skogvang, 2022) – however, it is of course difficult to ascertain whether an actual Sámi identity and a name on the self-defined electoral roll match. Some point to the subjective nature of the electoral criteria, and argue that being Sámi is about belonging in a community and people. Others, in contrast, suggest that many more North Norwegians have some Sámi heritage, likely silenced as part of the state's historical Norwegianisation processes; and they see this as part of a proudly 'diverse population' (N.ii) that they are both part of and represent. Also the Norwegian state highlights that 'Sami culture is a valuable part of our national historical heritage in the north and an important component in our Arctic policy' (N.MFA, 2021: 2). And, it is of course no coincidence that this is stated already in the Policy's preface – again, indigeneity is an 'important component' of Arctic statehood.

Despite the value and importance that current Arctic state documents speak of, indigeneity was seen in a very different light not long ago. Recalling that Norwegian identity is often premised on whiteness, and that the linguistic variations most often discussed are the idiosyncratically similar *bokmål* and *nynorsk*, Sámi and other minorities' identities have not always been welcomed as part of the state's identity. On the contrary, the Norwegian nation-building project from the 1800s onwards involved a deliberate and at times violent Norwegianisation policy, which sought to assimilate minorities including the Sámi. For example, rights to citizenship and property were tied to Norwegian language abilities, and traditions, cultures, and practices were suppressed in what can only be described as a colonial approach. Following the Second World War, state policies gradually started to change, but many date the true political awakening of a Sámi identity to the 'Alta case' in the late 1970s and 1980s. In brief, the conflict that centred on Sámi and environmental opposition to hydropower development in the Alta-Kautokeino river stretch eventually led to the establishment of the Sámi Parliament in 1989. In the decades since, the rights and recognition of Sámi people in Norway have thankfully improved, but there is also no denying that discrimination and prejudices still persist. Brought to light in the culmination of a five-year-long process, the 2023 Truth and Reconciliation report made for hard but long overdue reading for state personnel as well as the wider Norwegian public, detailing experiences of the Norwegianisation assimilation policies among Sámi, Kven, and Forest Finns (Sannhet- og forsoningskommis-jonen, 2023). Through personal stories, research, and mapping, the seven-hundred-page report leaves it clear not only that there are historical injustices yet to be dealt with but also that there is much still to be done for a just present. As a recent example, it was as if pre-empting the backlash that too often accompanies the celebration of the Sámi National Day on 6 February (unlike Norway's on 17 May), that then president of the Sámi Parliament Aili Keskitalo explained that they are 'a people without its own state. [...] The term "nation" refers to the perception of community; that we see ourselves as one people', and not a nation-*alist* expression (Keskitalo, 2015). Instead, the Sámi celebrate unity, not exclusion and division (Keskitalo, 2015) – being part of a state-crossing people, and not simply a component of a state identity.

The relation between an Indigenous and a state identity is no doubt complex and contested, and a topic of books in their own right (see e.g. Gaski, 1998). But specifically Arctic state identities also cannot be understood without some consideration of indigeneity – and more than one of the state personnel cited in this book also identified personally as Indigenous, as we return to in Chapter 7. When it comes to circumpolar politics in the Arctic Council, the Sámi across all four states are represented by the Saami Council, one of the six Permanent Participants (Knecht, 2013). However, again, it is only the state representatives who have voting rights on any decisions – while the Permanent Participants, such as the Saami Council, are to be consulted prior to this. That means that for example the Sámi people residing in Norway are, in the end, formally reliant on the vote of a Norwegian state representative. The Norwegian state, in turn, recognises the particular standing of the Sámi in Arctic affairs. As explained by an employee in the Ministry of Foreign Affairs, they 'have a close cooperation with them [...] And it is clear that it is extremely important to get their experience and have concern for the Indigenous interests' (N.vi). And according to another in the Ministry of Justice and Public Security, the Sámi play a 'phenomenally important role, of course' (N.vii). For some, this also presented one of the main challenges of Arctic politics: 'the conflicts of interest that can arise from the meeting of desire for economic development and for maintaining Indigenous traditions and knowledge; traditions, knowledge, language, and culture' (N.viii). As the 'local democracy in the Arctic' and 'important voices that means a lot, perhaps, for each nation's development of policy' (N.ii), it is the Indigenous peoples of the Arctic who would (or should) potentially be 'left with the positive – that is, part of the positive things, hopefully, if we do this well – but also the negative consequences if we do this badly' (N.vii). The 'we' in these statements are, however, seemingly not inclusive of the Indigenous peoples themselves; instead they are given a defined role as consultative, but not decisive in Arctic geopolitics and statecraft.

The Canadian constitution names three groups of Indigenous peoples: First Nations, Inuit, and Métis. According to the government's census, five per cent of the country's current population identify as Indigenous, with more than fifty distinct nations and languages (Government of Canada, 2022). In the Arctic context, Inuit are perhaps the best known, but all three groups are present in the North – and in the Arctic Council also the Gwich'in and Athabaskan peoples' organisations are among the six Permanent Participants. Indeed, according to one interviewee, 'you can't talk about the North in Canada without talking about aboriginal[3] peoples, because Northern issues are aboriginal issues in Canada' (C.ii). As in Norway, the Canadian state has a legacy of assimilation policies and racism that continue to affect people and communities. While many would say Canada has come further in its Truth and Reconciliation processes, the settler–colonial histories that the state is built upon are not straightforwardly (or uncontroversially) dismantled. And the asymmetrical relationship between the North and the capital centre in the south continue to order politics – and it continues to influence perceptions of self and other.

A paternalistic view of what the state should do dates back to colonial times, has persisted through the 1950s 'Eskimo problem' (Marcus, 1995), to being seen similarly today as an issue for the state to deal with. The view that the federal government is required to somehow 'support' the North through subsidies and decision-making often remains close to the surface, even if many important and powerful steps in the right direction have been made in recent years:

> [T]here's a civilisational narrative that I think persists, a sort of backwardness of the northern area [...] I think [through] a lot of Canadian history probably the Arctic and the North was considered places to conquer and to tame and to visit bravely as, you know, this kind of more backwards population that needed, sort of, you know, integration into our 'advanced'. (C.vi)

The above state representative explained the historical coloniality and assimilation stories, reflecting on the evolution of today's federal relationship with the northern territories. Remembering also the limited connectivity and travel opportunities between North and south, another explained that some might still think that the North is 'poor or somehow a second-class part of the country [...] I think it is sometimes naive rather than, you know, in any way malicious' (C.v). A Canadian foreign policy employee more critically described some fellow state personnel's views on the North: 'Most people […], they don't perceive that there's much intelligentsia going on there, but you see, like, "good people with a good heart"' (C.xii). This seemingly patronising perception bears unfortunate resonances with that so-called 'civilisational narrative'.

With multiculturalism having become so firmly embedded within ideas of Canadianness, as both policy and value, there is today celebration of Indigenous cultures – and most would agree much remains to be done, which is less about integration and more about empowerment. The comparison is often made with the southern neighbour – as with much of Canadian perceptions of self, the US is often the nearest 'other' to distinguish yourself from – to present a different 'frontier' settlement, which was ostensibly marked by generosity and even benevolence towards the Indigenous populations (Dodds, 2012: 1000; Winter, 2007). And today, linked once more to ideas of stewardship and responsibility, Arctic statehood carries with it a requirement for political practice, which in the Canadian (and perhaps most others') case should lead to an honest reassessment of state–Indigenous relations. That is arguably less a matter of change in the North, but rather about changing perceptions, prejudice, and ignorance in the south – even if intentions are not 'malicious', their effects may still be. In other words, an Arctic state identity of course involves political involvement in the Arctic, but, as we have seen here, it might have an important political component to play out further south too.

Perhaps there is growing awareness of disparities and inequities within the state's borders, however, and perhaps this jars with ideas of Canadian identity as moral and just:

> I would say, because of the social disparity – I don't know if that's the right term, but – between the North and the south, I think that most Canadians feel that it's necessary to focus on Northerners. […] There's been an injustice in the past, and we need to do what we can to support development in the North. (C.iv)

And so, state investments and focus on the North could be seen as a 'safe priority' (C.iv), something that neither voters nor the political opposition would likely disagree with. Again, this is the enactment of an Arctic state identity also in the south, for the south – and enacting the North as both different and 'part of' the national whole. The importance of domestic politics in fact also goes beyond domestic audiences, as the international performance of Arctic statehood involves and requires working with Indigenous peoples within the state's borders. In the more cynical view of one interviewed state employee, there is a trace of coloniality in the international dynamic between Indigenous peoples and the government: 'the Canadian government wants to be able to show that [it] cares' (C.xii). Whatever the motivation, any Arctic state identity requires political actions – not once, but ongoing – as identity is a process.

> [T]here's nothing worse for a government than giving the impression that they haven't done anything new, or they don't have promising projects and all that, so ... when they come up North once a year it's always to show how they've got a position and continuity from the line of developing the North and making it Canadian. (C.xii)

These performances of the state's Arcticness are not dissimilar to those discussed by their Norwegian colleagues, of 'filling' policies and strategies with meaningful actions. Among these initiatives, governance in the North has increasingly been devolved. This is a process that was set in motion half a century ago, and the creation of the territory of Nunavut in 1999 has been considered a sign of its progress (see Doubleday, 2003). Unlike in a province, however, constitutional powers are delegated from the federal government in Ottawa (Government of Canada, 2010). Seen as part of an active display of the state's Arctic identity, an act of gradual devolution can thereby, paradoxically, be seen as strengthening Canada's previously discussed 'sovereignty' in the Arctic.

What the above shows is the importance of the 'part' for the 'whole', and domestic politics that bolster foreign affairs and geopolitics. Seemingly unaware of the connotations of forced displacements of Inuit families in the past (see Marcus, 1995), this point was made also in the following: 'We started realising – what does the sovereignty in the Arctic mean for Canada? Is it a military presence there, or is the resource extraction, or is just having people live there? And it's beginning to look like it's having people live there' (C.xx). People, therefore, are and have been a key part of

Arctic statecraft limited not to military enactments of sovereignty
but also to claims of both historical and ongoing use of lands and
seas. It was also a deliberate security priority for the Canadian
Government in its 2009 *Northern Strategy* to ensure 'putting more
boots on the Arctic tundra, more ships in the icy water and a better
eye-in-the-sky' (C.DIAND, 2009: 9). An official in the Department
of National Defence similarly praised Inuit Canadian Rangers as
the state's 'eyes and ears in the North' (C.xi). From simply living
there to actively taking part in state employment, Inuit and other
Indigenous peoples in the North do play a particular role in the
state's Arctic identity. That is, even though Arctic identities might
primarily be felt by those living in the region (though whether they
would use those words is perhaps less likely, as we have seen), an
Arctic *state* identity is just as much about enacting partnerships,
responsibilities, and recognition of Indigenous peoples. And so,
state personnel speak of Arctic identities as relative: they may be
'Arctic' when faced with non-Arctic others, but domestically there
are nuances, complexities, and hierarchies that will vary according
to the contextual self and other.

The local and traditional

Although Iceland does not have an Indigenous population, you
might sometimes hear mention of 'local and traditional' issues and
knowledges. There are real political risks of conflating Indigenous
with local and traditional – e.g. in discussions of Indigenous knowledges (and related terms) – which have to do with the specific legal
rights of Indigenous peoples. For Iceland, there has not been an
attempt to present local concerns as equal to Indigenous such, but it
is for these reasons that the previously mentioned discomfort arose
around the Canadian focus on 'Northerners' as excluding Iceland.

As with the 'hierarchies' of Arcticness we have seen above, it is
perhaps not surprising that some felt 'less' Arctic than those from
the other seven states – in spite of the official reassurances that
Iceland is the only country 'wholly' within the region. The absence
of any Indigenous population was mentioned by most of the interviewed Icelandic state personnel as something that set them apart

in Arctic geopolitical contexts, and which sometimes made some deliberations less relevant for them: 'we try to be informed on this Arctic [Council Working] Group that we are in. But it is very much [focused] on the Inuit population, on populations that we don't have, on problems that we don't have' (I.x). As such, relative national homogeneity – seemingly presenting a textbook example of a hyphenated 'nation-state' (Pálsson and Durrenberger, 1996: 1) – can actually be a hindrance to 'taking part' in all Arctic matters, and as such to performing an Arctic state identity. For an employee in the Ministry of the Environment and Natural Resources, Iceland's Arctic state identity was based on maritime activities, and offered a qualitative differentiation in Arctic statehood:

> But we are not an Arctic nation as the Indigenous people in Alaska or in Canada or the Sámi people in Norway and in Scandinavia [...] That's my view on that, because if you look around you here in Iceland it's more Western-style living, and we are not dealing with these different kinds of groups, Indigenous groups, or Indigenous rights and things like that. One nation in the country. (I.viii)

But even though some see Iceland's lack of Indigenous peoples as leading to less involvement with certain Arctic politics – and perhaps a lesser Arctic identity – others saw different ways of relating to the political struggles of Indigenous groups, based on their own history as a Danish dependency:

> Because [Icelanders] see [Indigenous peoples] perhaps in a similar situation to what Iceland was once in, and also, their livelihood is very much tied to fishing and hunting, so ... [...] And like, Iceland is very supportive of Greenland having independence, and that is based on this historical experience of Iceland, [and] this notion of language, preserving the language, which has been very much the case here in Iceland [...] That is also very important about how you develop your own identity, with a distinct culture and language and history and things like that. [...] That is very important in this Arctic cooperation if it is to be of benefit to everyone. (I.iii)

In other words, the Icelandic state's contributions to Arctic political relations might be different but potentially valuable in another way. Many of the interviewed Icelandic state personnel cited their close cooperation with Greenland and the Faroe Islands, for example through the West Nordic Council, as complementary to the work within the wider Arctic Council (see Konradsdóttir and Nielsson, 2014): 'There is a special cooperation between these countries; you could call this cooperation a smaller Arctic cooperation' (I.vi). And, moreover, the contributions of local knowledges were highlighted as adding to the work of Arctic Council Working Groups, however challenging that is in practice (I.viii). Some related challenges were also mentioned, such as sparse and distant populations, vast distances in need of better infrastructure, and tough climatic conditions (I.xi) – all of which serve to bridge circumpolar differences in domestic contexts. As this clearly illustrates, Arctic state identities are multifaceted, and which elements come into play at different times are contingent on setting and relation. But what should also be clear in all of the above is that the experiences of state identity are not only contextual but also domestically diverse – the state will always, of course, be as plural as the people who enact it.

State identities as seen from the inside

Despite the seeming singularity of 'the state', it is always inevitably made up of numerous peoples, practices, and perceptions – all of which are *different*, and relationally defined in specific contexts. While the previous chapter showed us how shared values, features, and symbols can serve as reminders of a national whole, this chapter has gone on to show that those same things can also at different times highlight domestic differences. To again take the example of the *inuksuk*, the stone figure most likely means something very different for a senator from the south who might have picked it up as a souvenir from the North or the 2010 Olympics, from what it does for an Inuk representing Inuit in the capital.

Distances and (dis)connections across geographies, cultures, and communities within a state's borders all contribute to different identifications and attachments. Even if the entire country is considered an Arctic state, what that means for groups across it will depend on a number of factors. Northernness is one such factor, and it is perhaps reassuring that many state personnel also recognised that the people from and in the north are those with a primary claim to Arcticness. However, the relationships between geographical regions – north and south, or urban and rural – are often characterised by asymmetric powers, which also has implications for the ways state identity is understood.

The seeming hierarchy of northernness as 'more Arctic' is also often linked to indigeneity, where Indigenous peoples from the circumpolar north are seen to have an added and different claim to identity. Again, that people within the state recognise this, and that some of them identify as Indigenous themselves, is positive, potentially a sign of long overdue changes to state–Indigenous relations. However, it is also clear that states' legitimacy is strengthened by their performance of these relations, where Indigenous peoples' histories and cultures become appropriated in the service of state geopolitics. As with Canada's emphasis on its multiculturalism, diversity itself can become co-opted for political gains – while, at the same time, having more just outcomes than had it not been the case.

As should be clear, state identities – like any identity – are complex, and the above only touches on some of the many domestic differences that come to influence its enactment. 'Peopling' the state and geopolitics means paying attention to these differences, recognising and even celebrating the nuances that exist. Beyond groups and regions within the state's borders, however, there are also individual, subjective, and personal differences among the numerous people performing the state on a day-to-day basis. The next chapter turns to our final scale of relationality, the person within and as the state.

Notes

1 As we saw in Chapter 2, other scientific definitions of the Arctic actually leaves out most of mainland North Norway too. Perhaps surprisingly, Svalbard – the northernmost archipelago which unquestionably *does* lie in the Arctic – features less in discussions about state identity, possibly due to its particular governance and habitation mechanisms; it is both undeniably Norwegian and yet far from most Norwegians (see Pedersen, 2017).

2 Also literally 'the northern areas', or in English usually translated to 'the High North'.

3 Although I use the term Indigenous, some interview participants used the term aboriginal interchangeably – this was more common in Canada.

7

The Arctic state as personal and professional: identities of state personnel

It is not only various constituent 'subgroups' within a group that simultaneously produce and may challenge the collective and collective imaginaries, but the same can be said for each identifying individual – the person within the state. And this is also an additional reason for focusing on the everyday aspects of state identities, as the 'everyday' will vary according to each person's lived experiences. Judith Butler argues that 'identity' in the singular case is a misnomer, as it is always made and remade along the 'axes of power relations', including gender, race, class, etc. (Butler, 1999: 7). I would suggest the same goes for state identity too, that the reality of how it is experienced is always made up of numerous subject-positions: No one is ever 'only' their professional position, thankfully. It is the combination of numerous or even innumerable subject-positions that produces the self, subjectivity: a recognition that also points to its ongoing production as new combinations are made, new encounters unfold, as life does. It is this process of identity, of identi*fying*, as someone working for and as the Arctic state that this chapter turns to, focusing on the person, professional and personal.

Theories of identity tend to focus on either personal or collective identity; and while the former has been increasingly recognised as socially produced, less has been written on what it would mean to consider the collective as a *collection* of complex subjectivities (see Brubaker, 2006). In other words, how do state personnel's subjectivities – based on multiple subject-positions – filter into the enactment of a collective; and, vice versa, how does a collective filter into the enactment of the subject itself? Rather than seeing the individual as autonomous from the groups that they see themselves belonging to, the point is rather that these cannot be simply disentangled. For example, identifying as a woman, daughter, aunt, writer, dog-lover, European, Norwegian, and so on are social categories that all play into how the self *and* how other social groups come to be understood, and subsequently performed through words and actions. And if our aim is 'peopling' concepts and their production, such as the state (see Jones, 2007; Kuus, 2014), the idea of 'people' too must be conceptually deconstructed into its parts: the person, however socially defined. And again, if we recognise 'the state' as not an actor itself, but rather the illusion of one, produced by the many actions in its name (Abrams, 1988; Mitchell, 1991), it should follow that the focus needs to be on those many individuals enacting those actions, enacting the state: What guides them, and how do they make sense of their roles?

In short, state identities are made up of relations at all scales – from the micro to the macro – and in order to understand the functioning of the whole, there is a need to understand its components, namely the complex subjectivities of state personnel. It is this that this chapter seeks to do, focusing on, professional identities as state personnel, particular roles within the state, private and familial identities, and finally, the role of certain individuals within the state.

Identifying as an Arctic state professional

Much has been written about national identity, but as is hopefully clear by now this book sets out to discuss state identity as something different from that: a perceived identity of a *state*, which in turn is performed into being by state personnel. The reason for reiterating this here is that, when it comes to state personnel's reflections on their individual senses of Arctic identities, they were often articulated as a result of their professional positions. Of course, a politician, civil servant, political adviser, or diplomat is also a member of the nation – but what is interesting here is that a distinction was frequently made between feeling belonging to a state that is Arctic and belonging to a nation that is much less clearly so.

As most of the interviews for this study were conducted in capital cities, it is perhaps not surprising that many of the participants were not from the latitudinal Arctic themselves (with some exceptions), yet it is a challenge for the region if decision-makers see themselves as somehow apart.

In spite of governmental rhetoric about the importance of including the public, youth, and local voices, it is still likely the case that many people in the more southern regions of the eight Arctic states do not necessarily identify themselves as Arctic (see Medby, 2014). A Norwegian parliamentarian jokingly described Norway's Arctic statehood as 'a politician-thing' (N.ix), implying it is something that remains irrelevant to most (other) Norwegians. Whether or not they are right, another parliamentarian assured me it was something that 'many politicians care about and relate to' (N.xv). Recognising the difference between those whose work involves thinking about Arctic politics and those whose work does not, another Norwegian state employee agreed: 'we at the authority level are very aware' of current interest in and the significance of Norway's Arctic statehood, but 'most people are not particularly concerned with what big newspapers or big central think-tanks in the UK or Belgium write about the Arctic' (N.vi). On the topic of Arctic identity, they also said that 'It depends on who defines the Norwegian self-perception: Is it the "elite" in Oslo, like me, or is it most people?' (N.vi). This implies that there is different awareness of the Arctic, and different meanings attached to it, according to your role. And further, while interviewees held a range of different positions, the following reflection on professional identity was offered by a Norwegian Conservative Party parliamentarian: 'As a politician, and often in central positions in the state administration, you know that you have a position that is bigger than yourself; and then that requires you to lift your gaze, and not just be self-centred in the decisions and judgements you make' (N.ii). As their words indicate, professional roles can feel meaningful and important, 'bigger than yourself', which might allow a different perspective from 'most people' as above. And not being 'self-centred' also suggests a view on identity that may transcend your own personal experiences, to encompass the responsibility that comes with representing others. This was a point reflected on by others too, articulating what they saw their role requiring of them: 'I think that politicians have [...] sort of a bit bigger overview, perhaps, than the population. That sort of goes for all issues, but also typically on topics like this, where the population is more concerned with the concrete, singular issues that, perhaps, also affect them, but politicians to a larger degree see the whole picture on those types of things' (N.xiv). These reflections highlight the relevance of looking at state identities as distinct from national such, encompassing an awareness of the state and what it entails to hold a professional position. And considering the many subject-positions we all find ourselves in, it also implies that state identities can exist alongside other, regional, local, or otherwise identifications that come in and out of view.

How close or distant state personnel are to 'most people', as above, will vary from person to person, and from country to country. In a small country such as Iceland, with fewer than half a million inhabitants, it is perhaps not surprising that there is not such a clear distinction between 'elites' and others as you might find in larger countries. So, unlike the Norwegian person who reflected on themselves as part of an 'elite', several of the interviewed Icelandic state personnel did not identify as such even if they were involved with government – rather, the elite might be bankers or the extremely wealthy: 'when Iceland was booming, the elite here got very self-confident and arrogant' (I.iii), referring to the time prior to the financial crash in 2008. This particular interviewee was involved with research and science, and described how their interest and involvement in Arctic issues had gone from being referred to by colleagues as their 'pet project' to now being a priority for the state (I.iii). A former Icelandic minister reflected on their own identity, and how it differed across generations with notable societal changes since the end of the Second World War 'also changing the perception of who we are and all of that' (I.vi). As such, the relatively new title of Arctic statehood is one of several changes that influence identity as well as what it means to represent a state. The same former minister reflected on the differences between their parents, themselves, and their children – three generations with very different experiences of what Iceland and the Icelandic state are. In particular, the younger generation, they speculated, who grow up with the internet might have a more global perception of Iceland as Arctic. How these wider societal and cultural relations affect your professional role was something others reflected on as well. For example, a parliamentarian described how it was a period of living abroad in their youth that had made them aware of the Icelandic, Nordic, and even Arctic 'energy', as they called it (I.ii). These are all illustrative of how state personnel may both see themselves as part of a nation – even if recognising that their particular job is different, as we saw in the Norwegian example – and bring with them their personal experiences and reflections from elsewhere into the job and its performance.

Just as experiences and reflections from elsewhere can be brought to the role of politician or civil servant, so too can a lack of personal experience be something you are conscious of. For those who feel distant from the Arctic, both geographically and culturally, that too will influence the job – and inevitably how you perceive an Arctic state identity: 'I associate [the Arctic] with certain Indigenous populations, Inuit populations, but it's not something that I feel … as deeply … It doesn't … I sort of see it as a, sort of, a separate place; that it is part of Canada, and Canada is an Arctic nation, and it's very much an important theme at work' (C.vi). In this example, Arctic state identity is limited to the professional – an identity within a department, a context, and certain relationships, but not necessarily beyond the office (see Neumann, 2007). Among the interviewed officials in Ottawa, several talked about their conceptualisation of Arctic identity as distinctly professional: an awareness of the state's Arcticness without their own everyday life being so. One explained that: '[Northerners/Inuit] they're different from me, but they're part of Canada' (C.xviii) – and, as such, resonating with ideas of the multicultural 'mosaic' we saw previously. And many if not most of the Canadian state personnel were careful not to speak for Northerners, but instead to show sensitivity and respect: 'there's a huge focus – and rightfully so! – on the people and the impact that your policies and programmes may have on the people, their culture, their way of life' (C.xxi). Especially topics of inequality and social problems were sometimes avoided as 'controversial' (C.xviii) or skirted around. While the care taken not to speak *for* others is important – and perhaps long overdue within some state institutions – it should not mean silencing of political issues, but rather the need to *listen*. Either way, what is clear here is a distinct awareness of one's own professional role, professional identity, which comes with certain responsibilities – but also certain limits and humility, however those are dealt with in practice.

Contact with Arctic statehood

As we have seen so far, state identities can sometimes be distinguished from national identities as professional roles and contact with the idea of a state's specifically Arctic statehood. As such, the frequency with which state personnel engage with Arctic policies or geopolitics influences how they think of the state's identity. Unsurprisingly, inviting interviewees to speak about Arctic statehood and identity may attract responses that do not represent everyone working within state institutions but rather those who have a particular interest in the topic. We have already seen how one's interest had been referred to as a 'pet project' before, and, interestingly, several made similar comments. Not only may identities look different from the vantage point within the state, as in the above section, but also within state institutions can we find differences based on specific roles and daily responsibilities. A Norwegian employee in the Ministry of Climate and Environment reflected on the relationship between Arctic and national identity:

> Everyone has a relationship to this [the Arctic], but I don't think, like, that it is, sort of, a central part of the national identity. I'm very unsure of it being that any more. Perhaps that I – for us working with the Arctic, perhaps it can [be]. We are of course interested in it. We have read all these books and, like, know this history and such because it is a field that interests us. (N.x)

Their view was that, although the Arctic had mattered more to Norwegian *national* identity during the time of explorers and nationalism, when Nansen and Amundsen became international celebrities, it still might do for those working with it – what I call a *state* identity.

Appreciating that a state is actually made up of numerous actions and performances that make it 'real', and that these are all enacted by different people with complex subjectivities, it is clear that we cannot talk about states as unitary actors. And a sense of state identity depends not only on what your specific role is – for example, working with climate and environmental policies as above – but also on the current political situation. For some of the Icelandic state personnel, the focus on the Arctic came with a change of government in 2013 when the bid of EU membership was abandoned, which meant 'turning the ship towards the Arctic, away from the EU' (I.ii). For others, it was the financial crisis in 2008 that had led to a change of focus towards nearer, neighbouring countries and 'looking inward [...] the attention went from conquering the financial markets to cultivate your garden' (I.iii). And for others still, it had come about as a tactical move by the former president Grímsson: 'after the collapse of the Icelandic banks, he changed the compass; he changed the navigation, and began these Arctic issues!' (I.iv). Regardless of what the origin of the Arctic geopolitical attention is, these quotations highlight both the recency of an Arctic state identity and how it is seen as part of a wider political and professional picture. Just as state identities are understood through relations to international and national communities, so too do other political issues, communities, and even colleagues influence how they are experienced.

Possibly again a result of Canada's larger size, the differences within the state are even more easily distinguishable there. Some of those who were indeed directly involved in Arctic issues and policy explained that their sense of identity might be unusual within the federal state administration: 'most of the work that [my] department is responsible for is based in the south, not everyone [here] is conscious of or aware of or would see ourselves as an Arctic state' (C.xiv). And this was something felt even more by those who spend or have spent significant amounts of time in the North themselves. Interestingly, one interviewed state official reflected on how living and working in the North as a non-Indigenous person had made them suddenly aware of their own Canadian identity; and another reflected on the added perspective it had given them on their own region as well: 'They talk about going down south like it's going to another country!' (C.x). In this way, going North or at least working with Arctic issues makes you aware of the state and your own identity – even if this is a feeling of otherness vis-à-vis colleagues within the federal state. Reflecting on how they experienced themselves being seen in the North, this too will undoubtedly influence the ways that state identity is viewed:

> It's been a perennial problem in Canada that the further away you are from the central government, it's easy to always point to the central government as the 'bad guys'. And because of our geography, you know, a lot of people in the North feel that people in the south don't pay attention to their issues, or that what we think is important is probably not what they think is important. (C.xiv)

The North–south divide that we saw in the previous chapter is therefore clearly also felt in state offices, influencing sense of self and community, belonging, and otherness. Representing an Arctic state might, in other words, involve a sensitivity to how that state identity is experienced very differently across state departments and institutions, as well as across regions and communities.

Beyond professional positions

Although the above shows how state identities differ from national identities, and how they are tied to professional roles and responsibilities, it should also be clear that disentangling singular aspects of people's identities – subject-positions from subjectivities – is always somewhat reductive, each influencing the others. We can talk about 'state identities' as identities people ascribe to a state, but, when we start exploring the 'person' in 'state personnel', they are of course always, inevitably, people with complex backgrounds, hopes, dreams, and feelings that far exceed professional titles. In this section, we see how some of these other aspects also influence people in their jobs – and how these wider realities and rich experiences also influence state identities.

Perhaps it should not come as such a surprise that asking state personnel about their sense of Arctic identity might lead to some more personal reflections – and yet, it *did* surprise me. It was in part the thoughtful and emotive answers some of them gave that made me realise that much existing scholarship on the state, national identity, and even nationalism tend to underestimate the fact that all of these abstract concepts are the outcome of people and their actions. This is what I mean by 'peopling' concepts, namely adding back in the humanity, subjectivities, emotions, and everything else that comes with being alive and doing a job (see Jones, 2007). We have already seen above how some people's personal interests and passions influenced their jobs, and how they reflect on their own role within a state institution. And, more than this, state personnel are also part of nations – watching TV, listening to music, and influenced by the media (Sharp, 1993). In some of the interviews, they spoke about inheriting a keen interest in the polar regions from parents and grandparents. For example, one of the Norwegian interviewees described how their grandmother had worked in a can-factory where Roald Amundsen 'was one of the heroes' (N.vi) (see Figure 7.1). And such familial and personal background were recurring themes when reflecting on identity: 'Because I am born, have family, and have spent a lot of time in North Norway, I have a completely different identity and emotional attachment to North Norway and to the Arctic than people who do not have that background; of that I am completely sure' (N.xii).

Another senior politician also reflected on how professional and personal identities, regional and Indigenous, can be co-constitutive of each other:

> [M]y identity is very tied to being a *Finnmarking* and having a multicultural background; that is, I am both Norwegian and Sámi, and have always lived in that tension. And I am, of course, also now a representative for the state, the country, Norway. And obviously that influences my mind-set and my approach to very many of the High North questions that I have been part of dealing with in some way or another. (N.xvi)

Both of these reflections illustrate how identity is always made up of numerous aspects of the self – of which being a state representative is only one that will always be experienced in light of the others. And so, when it comes to performing Arctic statehood, enacting

Figure 7.1 The Norwegian polar explorer Roald Amundsen
(Source: Wikimedia Commons)

the state through policies and practices, these other aspects are also there, also part of how the state comes into being.

It is not only family and personal backgrounds that come to define who you see yourself as, but also the environments and nature that were discussed in Chapter 2. Several interviewees spoke about how the spaces they grew up and felt attached to mattered for their sense of identity. For some, this awareness and attachment had become clear to them after spending time abroad, away from 'home'. For others, it was the daily reminders of the weather that reminded them of wider climates and currents that connected them to the Arctic. In other words, these are not just descriptions but embodied experiences of environments – even if they took place south of the Arctic Circle, the feelings of cold or wind could help people connect personally to distant spaces. As one of the Icelandic parliamentarians matter-of-factly explained:

> You come from a certain place, and you are influenced when you grow up and when you live here; you are influenced by media, of course, and by nature, and by just being here. [...] When you become a politician you are a person with your experience and your education; of course you put it all together and you reflect what you are. You can't be anything else. So, I think that yeah, your identity and who you are and what you are, it [influences] how you play the politics and your views on the world, of course. (I.ii)

As the above also highlights, this sense of identity – tied to where you are from – influences the political actions you go on to do, 'how you play the politics'. These are, again, insights that are easy to relate to, and yet also insights that are often left out of traditional attempts to understand state geopolitics.

It is well known that interviewing officials in a professional capacity has limitations (Kuus, 2013) – it is, after all, their job to represent the state also when speaking to researchers. Iver Neumann (2005) writes about diplomats' 'techniques of the self' that involve separating the private from the personal and professional. No doubt the stories and reflections that were shared by state personnel were selective, but I do not think they were 'strategic'. Instead, many were willing to reflect openly on what it means for a state to have the title of Arctic statehood, and what it means for identity. For Canadian state personnel, the role of stories came up several times – reading and learning about the Arctic from afar, which in turn had led to where they are today:

> [T]hinking about my own childhood [...] it's not like they [their parents] have any close connections to the Arctic, but I've always been drawn to it; it's always been something that's just been fascinating. I didn't even realise until I took this job just how much I'd already read about the North because I was so attracted to it! (C.ii)

And, for some, the stories were even more personal, linked to love and childhood imaginaries – and as the researcher across the table, I felt privileged to listen to their retelling in turn:

> And I think, when I started thinking about it, I do have an identity with the Arctic for a number of reasons ... why? My father spent thirty years in the Arctic as a naval officer during the Cold War. So all his work in the Arctic was top secret, and he would come back

with all these stories – well, the stories he could talk about! – about the Arctic. And he lived with the Inuit, travelled with the Inuit. So I grew up with these stores about the Arctic. So I knew my dad as an Arctic person; and in some ways, I'm trying to maybe follow in his footsteps a little bit, you know. [...] To keep his work alive a little bit, and learn about the Arctic the way he saw it. [...] I identify with my father and the Arctic, they go together. (C.viii)

In this way, we see how the deeply personal sometimes can and does become part of professional roles, and more importantly how the state as employer comes to be conceptualised. Tracing these long lines of past moments and memories, state personnel themselves articulate what the Arctic state means to them.

The role of influential individuals

With the recognition that the people 'within' a state matter, those enacting and performing the state into being on a daily basis, it also follows that certain influential individuals have played a particular role when it comes to Arctic statehood and identity in each of these countries. These were people who have held positions that have allowed them to shape narratives and policies, and to shape how each state's Arcticness comes to be represented.

It is not new that famous individuals can influence political perceptions, and this is also true in the Arctic; we have already seen how the explorers of the late nineteenth and early twentieth centuries become 'heroes'. In Norway, Nansen and Amundsen continue to be mentioned in Arctic contexts – and, as above, they may even influence today's state employees via their grandmothers' past ... More recently, however, the former Minister of Foreign Affairs – and, at the time of writing in 2024, PM – Jonas Gahr Støre (Labour) has played a pivotal role in Norway's High North, later Arctic, political engagement (even though this was less a topic among interviewees per se). As minister, he had ambitions for the High North (Gjerde and Fjæstad, 2013) – and was part of the optimism that some have referred to as a 'High North euphoria' (Hønneland and Jensen, 2008). One senior Norwegian representative highlighted how Norway had 'sharpened' its identity as Arctic, and that Støre, and the Minister of Foreign Affairs after him, Espen Barth Eide (also Labour), both very deliberately 'spent a lot of time and energy travelling around and talking about the High North' (N.i). Gjerde and Fjæstad (2013) write about Støre's legacy, concluding that the Arctic was lifted during his time as Minister of Foreign Affairs – but primarily it became a foreign policy issue, rather than necessarily leading to the improvements that some envisioned in and for North Norway. Nevertheless, the story of Norway as Arctic cannot be told without mention of the person who was most directly involved at a time when people around the world became aware of the so-called 'age of the Arctic' too.

If Jonas Gahr Støre is a necessary name to mention in the Norwegian case, Ólafur Ragnar Grímsson is even more influential in Iceland's (see Figure 7.2). We have already seen how some referred to him changing the compass and navigation, directing the country towards the Arctic (and away from Europe). Ólafur Ragnar Grímsson is Iceland's longest-serving head of state as

Figure 7.2 The former President of Iceland and founder of the Arctic Circle Assembly Ólafur Ragnar Grímsson (Source: Arctic Circle Assembly, CC-BY 2.0)

President between 1996 and 2016; and, interestingly, he holds a PhD in Political Science from the University of Manchester,[1] specialising in how inherited ideas from the nationalist independence movement continued to matter in Icelandic state discourse (Grímsson, 1978). In more recent years and relevant here, however, he is a founder of the Arctic Circle Assembly in Iceland: an annual, international event that brings hundreds of foreign delegates, businesspeople, Indigenous peoples, and academics to Reykjavík to discuss Arctic matters. As a result, the Icelandic capital has become a focal point for Arctic geopolitics and meetings every late autumn (Steinveg, 2023). A skilful orator, Grímsson has talked publicly about Arctic identity – linking the country's history with personal stories, such as in this example on the topic of glaciers and global ice loss:

> My father was still a young shepherd chasing sheep in Icelandic valleys when the famous Norwegian discoverers, Amundsen and Nansen, made their pioneering Arctic journeys. Together with their Icelandic-Canadian colleague Vilhjálmur Stefánsson, they embodied, in the early decades of the twentieth century, a spirit of discovery that was widely admired. So fresh in living memory were their explorations that the generations which celebrated the independence of Norway and Iceland saw them as their respective national heroes. (Grímsson, 2014b)

In the example above, he draws lines of similarity between two Arctic states, of past experiences of both nationalism and exploration, and even to his own personal background. While some might be critical of his political involvement, in particular during his time as President (which before had been more of a ceremonial role), one explained that he is 'a politician, really' and that the Arctic had been one of his own projects (I.xii). Another parliamentarian suspected that he was 'looking towards his legacy' (I.ix). And whether or not that is the case, the Assembly is a fantastic success if the aim was to create a new image not just for himself but for Iceland after the financial crisis. To domestic audiences, 'this conference – it's a big conference – it sends a very powerful message to the Icelandic people: that we get all these visitors and guests, participants, to the conference because we are an Arctic nation' (I.iii). Others still see it more as an activity reaching outwards, promoting Iceland to international audiences (I.xii). Either way, the fact that Ólafur Ragnar Grímsson's name was mentioned by most Icelandic state personnel cited in the book shows clearly the role of an individual. Even though he does not define what an Arctic state identity for Iceland is, others' reflections often referenced this particular performance of it as something they either agreed or disagreed with, in turn leading them to their own views on the topic.

Also in the Canadian context, powerful men in high offices were mentioned. However, we have already noted one example of these, the former PM Stephen Harper (Conservative), who did indeed play a role in bringing Arctic geopolitics to southern Canadian people. His annual media tours to the North serve as one illustrative example of a performance that was both political and influential in constructing an image of the Arctic that enables and even requires political actions (see Dodds, 2012). More interestingly in the context of this section, then, is the frequent mention of Leona Aglukkaq (Conservative), the first ever Inuk appointed to the Canadian cabinet, who served as Canada's Minister of Environment and Chair of the Arctic Council during their chairmanship in 2013–15 (Exner-Pirot, 2016). Her background as both Inuk and Northerner gave her authority to speak about Canada and the Arctic in ways that others could not:

> [M]any officials haven't spent much time there [...] You can't say, 'well I grew up on the farm, and this is our experiences back then'. Minister Aglukkaq can talk like that, because she is from the North, but most of our government, our senior officials who talk about the Arctic are not Northerners. So there's a challenge. (C.iv)

And some saw her appointment as having had notable effects on policy and political practice:

> [The] Minister is an Inuit Minister and has a strong interest in the North herself, and it's an important part of her mandate. I think you'd be able to trace the increasing attention, orientation of the North in Canada and in government more generally through new institutions that have been created. (C.vi)

As we can see, individuals within institutions, the people of the state, can influence the ways in which statehood is enacted, practically as well as symbolically. And that is true not only for those in high positions and the media spotlight such as Støre, Grímsson, and Aglukkaq but also for those who perform the state into being every day. By paying attention to *people* and all their actions, spectacular and mundane, the Arctic state comes into view.

The people of the state

Exploring state identities across different scales, we see how they are understood in relation to others – be they other states, nations, groups within the state, and, in this chapter, individual people. To pay more attention to the people within institutions is what is meant by 'peopling' the concept of the state and geopolitics. It means considering the humanity – emotions, backgrounds, and embodied experiences – that influences the performance of statehood. As we have seen in the examples above, state personnel's identities are as multifaceted as everyone else's, and certainly not only a matter of professional titles. How you come to understand the state you are employed to represent, in other words, depends also on factors beyond your job contract. This should not be a particularly controversial statement, and yet it is often overlooked in discussions of the state and state practices.

Through the reflections and stories that state personnel chose to share, we have seen how, firstly, they do have a sense of professional identity that is often different from the nation in general. Secondly, state personnel who have more frequent contact with a state's Arctic title, that is its Arctic policies and priorities, have a stronger sense of such an identity. And, thirdy, state identities are understood as part of and influenced by wider, personal identities (or subject positions), drawing on personal experiences, familial ties, love and friendship. Considering what some said in Chapter 2 about embodied experiences of weather and climate as a way of connecting with Arctic geographies, this once again shows the 'person' among personnel. Lines on maps and letters in books become known through experiences, including childhood stories and parents' tales. Finally, the roles of individual actors with a particular role, passion, or platform – leaders in a way, if not necessarily heads of state – also tell us that state identities are social as well as political, and always again 'peopled'. Stories of the state become also personal stories (and vice versa), and the actions of the state are enacted by personnel. In short, the Arctic state bears traces, is even made up of, relations that far exceed it; a state identity is always about relating to others.

Note

1 As pointed out by a peer-reviewer (thank you!), Grímsson having studied for his PhD at Manchester might speak to his support for the UK and Scotland as near-Arctic partners and neighbours.

Conclusion: pluralities of state identities and ongoing geopolitical practices

'Do *you* have an Arctic identity then?' is a question I have been asked more than once, including by some of the interviewees cited in this book. Briefly turning the roles of interviewee and interviewer, this is of course an example of what this book has so far been all about: the numerous relations, and acts of relating, that make up any identity.

It is not an easy question to answer, and neither should it be. Like many state personnel, the researcher that I am finds it difficult to articulate 'who I am' in a single sentence, but what I can say confidently is that I am a citizen of one of the Arctic states. And that is what the point of this personal interlude is, namely that state identities are both relationally defined and based on statehood rather than necessarily a nation.[1] The headline issues that opened this book – the Arctic's low sea-ice extent, starving polar bears, natural resources, and so on – bring the region into many people's lives in new ways, and so too will a sense of 'the state' change accordingly. This book charts both the changing ways in which state identities are articulated in general, and how Arctic geopolitics are influenced by this in particular.

Seven chapters later, this book has itself become a written manifestation of state identities, a representation that not only describes but is *part of* the discourses that were explained in the introduction. Tracing stories and quotations back through the pages, we see the outline of Arctic states and their personnel. Not 'fixed' on paper but mediated by their telling and retelling across the years that have passed since their first articulation in interviews. We see, hopefully, the structure of state identities – space and time – and we see how they differ and change according to context and relation.

Although the aim of the book is first and foremost to present the conceptual framework of state identity and to discuss it in relation to Arctic geopolitics, it also seeks to share the stories and reflections by the anonymous state personnel who took the time to answer my questions. Hopefully the preceding chapters have done justice to the diversity within the state(s), demonstrating the need to 'people' our academic understandings of state practices and geopolitics. And, importantly, it has never been intended to describe and diagnose an identity 'out there', but to highlight commonalities and differences, what is shared and what is not, to generate further relationalities. That is, the relations of previous chapters are not the only ones of course, but instead the Arctic state is always an outcome of people and practices, of which we are all somehow implicated. Who we are (and who the 'we' is) shapes also what we become – which has profound importance for not just Arctic but global geopolitics in a time of change.

In what follows, this final brief concluding chapter draws together the insights from those preceding it, starting with the conceptual foundations of 'state identity' as a performative discourse, rooted in critical and feminist scholarship. It then turns to the specific aspects explored in the articulations of Arctic state identities: firstly, the spatio-temporal structure according to which the state emerges, and, secondly, the relations that we have explored along different scales; from the system of states, to the national, domestic, and finally the personal. It will summarise, rather than repeat, in order to show the wider implications of the insights across the book: for the empirical study of Arctic geopolitics specifically, as well as for conceptual and scholarly work more generally. Finally, the book closes as it opens: with questions and opportunities to explore, to learn more about people, politics, and power.

The conceptual foundations of state identity

It seems fitting to circle back to take another look at some of the conceptual foundations of 'state identity' in order to draw up some concluding remarks. First of all, state identities are 'discourses' – they are, again, 'specific series of representations and practices' (Campbell, 2009: 166), which in turn guide and shape how we understand the world and our role in it, what is possible and impossible. Although this is a simplified way of explaining discourses and their power, the key point is that discourses of state identity are closely related to the political practices that both precede and follow it. Such discourses are not manufactured or curated by individuals, but are a product of the above representations and practices across a range of modes that permeate society. For the Arctic state personnel cited in this book, a sense of their state's identity, and themselves in relation to that, undoubtedly influence how they do their jobs, even live their daily lives; but also vice versa, how they do their jobs and live their lives also produces and reinforces discourses. In short, who we think that we, and our state, simultaneously shapes us as we shape it.

Following a view of discourses as practices, produced and reproduced through actions, the concept of 'performativity' has been helpful throughout in allowing us to highlight their ongoing and processual nature. In simpler terms, it helps us see that state identities are based on innumerable actions, which are based on norms and habits, repeated and resisted, tweaked and changed, reiterated and uttered. For Butler (1999) it is through their performance that discourses become material reality. In our context, it is through the many performances in the name of the Arctic state that it becomes real. And, as such, it is the many people enacting these that produce the reality that in turn is their employer and societal structure, the state. This is the seeming paradox that Mitchell (1991) describes when he writes that the state is constructed through the same practices that it claims to have produced (see also Abrams, 1988). In other words, rather than the Arctic state *doing* something, it is the very act of 'doing something' that itself produces the Arctic state – the subject is produced through actions and relations of the many people employed in its name. And this is also where Butler's concept is particularly useful in showing the potential agency within discourses, how they may change and shift: While all practices are framed within discourses, performing otherwise is where there is also potential for disruption and change. It is not only ministers on podia, speaking lofty words of Arctic identity, who have the agency to define it, but rather it is in the many times that words are told and retold, actions done, redone, undone, that an Arctic state identity becomes real.

State identities in general, and here Arctic state identities specifically, are the perceived identities of the state – that is importantly different from a national identity. Although it is common to conflate 'state' and 'nation' in everyday speech, the distinction is significant, the former referring to the idea of a political organisation with territory and power[2] and the latter to an imagined community of people (Anderson, 1983). In other words, this book does not directly address national identity, though obliquely this features around the blurry edges of the state's identity. Although an illusion, the ideal of a nation-state – corresponding governments, territories, and peoples – is powerful, also among those employed to represent the state. All of this is to make clear once more that, when we talk about state identities, we refer to the sense of 'self' ascribed to that political organisation, perceived characteristics, and constant features (however illusory constancy is). And state personnel then are here used as shorthand for those whose employer is the state institution, whose job it is to represent and 'perform' the state – be they ministers, politicians, diplomats, civil servants, policy advisers, or parliamentarians. The book deliberately interweaves and places alongside each other statements from people of a variety of roles – the point is less personnel's position within a professional hierarchy and more their shared sense of own state.

With these particular foundations and clarifications in place, the book and concept of 'state identity' are positioned in a tradition of critical scholarship, and are particularly inspired by critical and feminist geopolitics. Without repeating the introduction, the aim throughout has been to challenge what we tend to take for granted, to highlight the things that we do not even consider that we needed to 'accept' in the first place – such as Arctic statehood and identity. Critical geopolitics provides tools to explore how politics become 'spatialised' and scripted (Ó Tuathail, 1996; Ó Tuathail and Agnew, 1992), and feminist geopolitics demonstrates the many scales this takes place at, not least the personal and intimate (Massaro and Williams, 2013; Smith, 2020). This book argues for a 'peopled' account of geopolitics, which similarly shifts the focus away from key terms such as 'the state' itself to look instead at those many 'performers', practitioners of statecraft (see Jones, 2007; Kuus, 2014; Woon, 2015). So, asking the question of what an Arctic state identity might be is really a question of how all of those state personnel imagine and perform it.

The question might seem fairly straightforward, and yet after all these pages there is still no answer that can summarise it in a similarly singular sentence. In contrast, what should be clear from previous discussions, citations, and examples is that a state identity is always plural, never unitary and universal. What we have seen are the rich stories and experiences, reflections and thoughts of different people who all in one way or another work for a state. The way that this state is perceived is influenced by not only formal facts but also personal background, histories, environments, and the many relations that we all find ourselves going in and out of throughout our daily lives. This is, once more, what it entails to add people back into geopolitical concepts, to look for the nuances and inconsistences rather than neat definitions and theories. Instead, we can look for some of the shared aspects of state identities, and we can consider these the frames (or 'discursive boundaries') within which the discourse comes to be performed relationally and contextually.

A framework of state identity

The frames mentioned above can be understood as a conceptual framework made up of the aspects detailed in each of the chapters: spatio-temporal structures, seen through the lenses of socio-political and geopolitical relations across different scales. But, once again, the framework should be read with an implicit recognition that there is a lot of diversity and even disagreement inherent in any state identity.

Although diverse, state identities tend to be articulated as structured by space and time, or geographies and histories – including a vision of how these will lead to a state future. If we call the first of these structuring axes of state identity its *geography*, we can start unpacking how not only formal maps and borders matter for how people think of its identity but also environments, climates, landscapes, and other spatial aspects. As we saw in Chapter 2, state personnel spoke about their own relations with and imaginations of Arctic spaces – and how these in turn were fundamental to an Arctic state identity. Or phrased differently, Arctic statehood is explained as a geographical title as much as political, and so the state's identity is rooted in spatiality.

We can call the second structuring axis of state identity its *temporality* – that includes history, but also perceptions of the present and future of the state. In all examples, people talked about the past as important for an identity, including formal history teaching as well as more informal stories and myths of the past. Across these Arctic states, the tales of explorers and polar adventurers feature prominently, but so does also an appreciation of Indigenous cultures that far preceded these.

Even with a shared structure of geography and history underpinning state identities, they are always understood and articulated relationally – that is, in relation to a contextual 'other'. The many relations that affect views of state identities are perhaps innumerable, and certainly not neatly stacked in anyone's minds; but in order to organise the discussion we have looked at them from the international, to the national, domestic, and finally personal scales.

The first of these scales involves state identities being articulated as a state among states, as a member of an international community. In the Arctic context, this includes the circumpolar north and the associated intergovernmental Arctic Council; but it also involves the many other international relations that a state will always be part of, such as organisations and collaborations. It also involves the role that state personnel think of their own state having within these relations, for example as leaders, pioneers, stewards, or otherwise. At times, international relations may be those between similar states, and at other times may be between 'us' and 'them'.

The second scale is the national, and this is where state identities are seen to intersect with national identities too. Like the previous focus on the international community, the national sense of state identities is also to an extent premised on what makes 'us' different from others, but the emphasis is on that internal cohesion and belonging. State personnel frequently spoke about characteristics that they associated with their country, and how this in turn was something they brought also to the political table. And it tied in with patriotic sentiments and emotions, imaginations, and even banal and everyday reminders of the state's identity.

The diversity of a state's identities has already been mentioned, but the third scale highlights in particular the intra-national differences that any country will inevitably have. Following the chapter on the national, this scale highlighted the differences also within this. Perhaps most obviously, there is a clear difference in Arctic state perceptions between north and south in any of these states. Their respective norths are seen as 'more Arctic', and with an additional role when it comes to policies. Despite local political issues, however, Arctic geopolitics is often defined by the south, 'for' the north. And equally if not more importantly, Indigenous peoples and indigeneity have a particular position within questions of both Arctic identities and politics. Even for Iceland, which does not have an Indigenous population itself, respect and partnering with Indigenous peoples are seen as important – and it is a required element of Arctic Council work. However, again, these recognitions and efforts do not always translate to equal participation. Instead, being 'part of' and included in state politics can paradoxically serve to reinforce the state's legitimacy and identity discourses.

Fourth and final of the relational scales, state identities will always inherently be articulated through the lens of the personal: the state person among state personnel, and their many subject-positions. Even though state practitioners are professionals, no one is ever only their title – and each of innumerable subject-positions influences the others. This means that their roles influence their sense of Arctic identities, and as does the frequency of contact with Arctic policy issues. But more than this, also their personal identities, backgrounds, familial ties, and childhood memories matter – all external to their day-jobs, yet intrinsic to their views on Arctic identities. The previously discussed environmental experiences, such as the cold, serving as connections to the Arctic are also examples of more intimate scales, involving state personnel's own bodily encounters with the world. And focusing on the personal, it is also relevant to note the role played by specific, often high-profile individuals in articulating the state's Arctic identities.

Chapter 7 therefore included examples of people whose platforms and positions have allowed them to have a particular voice. Whether or not others agree with their views on Arctic state identities, they can serve as a basis from which you articulate your own.

In summary then, state identities are always plural – but they share structures of geography and temporality, and they are articulated through relations. What this recognition means for the Arctic region and geopolitics is what the next section turns to, before a wider discussion of how the conceptual framework above should also be useful beyond the Arctic, potentially applied to states elsewhere and in different contexts.

State identities in, and implications for, the Arctic

From the outset I have contended that we ought to look more closely at discourses of state identities and state personnel in order to understand Arctic geopolitics more fully. Here, at the end of the book, it is worth returning to this once more. As is hopefully clear by now, statements of Arctic states' identities are frequent across political rhetoric in the region, and they certainly tell us something about how state representatives wish to position their country and themselves. However, what we might miss by brushing it off as 'just' rhetoric, 'just' lofty words, is how it may also play a powerful role in the understandings that state personnel have of their own jobs, own state, and themselves. And this, in turn, matters for how they come to enact their roles, and so the political actions of their state. To cite again a Norwegian official we met in Chapter 2: 'It defines us in terms of foreign policy, security policy, and implicitly also defence policy, that we – our geography – it is our identity' (N.i). In short, paying attention to discourses of state identities adds an otherwise often overlooked aspect of geopolitical practice and decision-making.

With attention to such concepts, we can add to the efforts seeking to challenge popular representations of the Arctic as a space to 'conquer', great powers' competition, and numerical quantities of undiscovered resources, shipping distances, or temperature rises. Rather than looking at numbers, even adding *more* numbers and more data, there is a need to look at people, behaviours, beliefs, and imaginaries. Not least if the topic is climate change, as it often is in the region, we have the data – the challenge is what people do with them. As we saw in the first two chapters, the growing subfield of critical polar geopolitics has offered such a counterweight to the prophecies of a 'new scramble' and so on (e.g. Dodds and Nuttall, 2015; Powell and Dodds, 2014), but the role of 'the state' and its personnel is what more direct engagement with discourses of state identity offers. Work on Arctic identity per se is limited (e.g. Burnasheva, 2019), and even more so if it is the Arctic state we are interested in. And yet, it is often state personnel who are tasked with making decisions that may determine the future of the region, and frequently do so from afar. This is so despite long-running arguments for the inclusion of Indigenous and other local peoples in decision-making (Medby, 2019b), and despite the broader academic warnings of methodological nationalism and state-centrism. It is undeniable that the Arctic region remains a state-governed region, and the Arctic Council's structure only further exemplifies this, however inclusive and unique it may be. And so, to understand, and potentially even change, future relations in the region, we need to look to the state, not as an autonomous actor, but at its practitioners – to 'people' our concepts and tools for understanding.

The book is written in the hope that it will be recognised that the future of Arctic relations and geopolitics matters well beyond regional latitudes: To cite a clichéd saying popular among high-level speakers on international podia, 'what happens in the Arctic does not stay in the Arctic' (see Lempinen, 2016). As with the region's climatic changes and connected global systems, so do geopolitical relations in the Arctic influence those elsewhere. And, for arguably the main global challenge of all our lifetimes, the climate crisis, attention to and knowledge about the Arctic is paramount. Frequently referred to as a 'bellwether' of climate change (e.g. Huebert et al., 2012), the region matters to us all at a global and planetary level. It is of course for this reason that non-Arctic states and actors – from China and India to big resource and shipping companies – are all interested in taking part in discussions of the region. In the words of an Icelandic parliamentarian from Chapter 3, it matters 'to be part of it, the making of the future of the Arctic' (I.ii). And the future of the Arctic is one that will affect us all. So, once more, understanding these ideas of state identities will help us make sense of not only Arctic realities and relationships but also how they affect and will be affected by global geopolitics – both empirically and theoretically.

'State identity' and scholarly attention

As this particular focus on the Arctic has shown, state identity discourses matter not only for politicians but also in diplomacy, international relations, and governance. As such, the relevance of the concept extends beyond not just the empirical region but also beyond theoretical and disciplinary boundaries. Relations between states and the symbolic value of cultural aspects of such identities are clearly important in the interpersonal encounters between diplomats and politicians, as well as civil servants and others. As we saw in the introduction, some excellent works on the state, diplomacy, and national identity exist, but these are rarely brought together. With a lens of state identity discourses we can therefore add to work in international relations and political sociology that explores, for example, professional and institutional identities of diplomats (Neumann, 2005, 2007); to work in political geography and critical geopolitics on everyday statecraft, nationhood, and assemblages (Closs Stephens, 2022; Dittmer, 2017; Painter, 2006); and political science and political anthropology on nationalism and national identities to mention just a few. With this transdisciplinary relevance, the application of the concept can hopefully extend beyond these case studies, not just to other Arctic states (Ferdoush and Väätänen, 2022; Sumarliðason, 2021) but also to wider scholarship seeking to understand some of the same underlying dynamics.

In addition to the specific concept of state identity, broader arguments about 'peopling' analytical concepts clearly also apply beyond the confines of the focus in the book. As mentioned above, authors such as Jones (2007), Kuus (2014), and Woon (2015) have all argued for a 'peopling' of geopolitical concepts, and this work adds further to that. And, as we have seen in the example of the climate emergency above, it is not scientific data on the climate per se we are lacking but an understanding of how and why people act (or do not act) the way that they do. While this is perhaps the most stark example of the discrepancy between scientific knowledge and behaviour, the same applies to other too-neat models and theories of geopolitics – missing out the 'noise' that is the messiness of any human reality. A call for 'peopling' our analyses is therefore a call to bring back in the messiness, to embrace the noise of human emotions, embodiment, subjectivities, and changeability that make up our shared realities. Tidy theories too often end up being reductive, and so the framework that I have offered here is one that is deliberately open in order to explore rather than 'fix'. In the end, the hope is that scholarship – whatever the discipline or field – is not an end point and final answer, but instead an opening to further questions and curiosity.

State identity futures

It is difficult to write an end to a story that does not really have one – state identities are ongoing and continual, and will always be changing according to time and place, people and peoples. For the three Arctic states that the book has mostly focused on, new state personnel will undoubtedly have taken over from some of those cited here before the book goes to print, and some of the storylines will have moved on from where we leave them. And, for sure, both day-to-day political work and geopolitical relations will be in constant movement, but, still, the framework of state identity remains valid across them. The issue is not whether geography and history still matter, nor whether the international, national, intra-national, and personal still do; but rather *how* these are understood, related to, sensed, and made sense of by the numerous people who represent the state on a daily basis. Fortunately, this means that state futures are still open and undecided, identities are yet being storied, and there is always more to tell.

At the time of writing, Arctic statecraft and geopolitics look different from how they did when the cited interviews were conducted, now marked by Russia's war in Ukraine. While the war's events to date are far south of the Arctic (both in latitudinal and in political terms), its effects reach northwards too – proving that the Arctic is not and never has been insulated from the rest of the world. The 'Arctic exceptionalism' – exceptional peacefulness and international cooperation – that has long been critiqued has now well and truly been disproved, with most notably the Arctic Council's work affected. And with that meeting forum, so too have the regular meetings between Arctic state, Indigenous, and other representatives been deeply affected (Alexander and Bloom, 2023) – no doubt affecting relations elsewhere in turn. That being said, there is clearly a will for the Arctic Council, and more broadly Arctic relations, to return to its prewar and pre-pandemic character among many if not most, so the current status is not a reflection of either past work or future relations. One can only speculate what this means for Arctic state identities of course, but it might include more emphasis on aspects of security, bilateral, and neighbourly relations, and so on for example – a topic for future scholarship, I hope.

With this, there is no doubt that the concept of state identity – and geopolitics more generally – will continue to evolve. And that is, of course, ever more reason not just to pay attention to the numerous relations that make political change happen but to *take part*. If state identities are the result of people's actions, then we all have a role to play in ensuring that the future – or futures plural – come about in the best possible ways. State or otherwise, identities matter. So, do *you* have an Arctic identity then – and why might the answer matter now and in the future?

Notes

1 Whether or not we see the Arctic *states* as Arctic *nations* is a different conversation, perhaps one for a different book by a different author!
2 This is of course a *very* simplified definition derived from literature discussed in the introduction.

References

Aarebrot, F.H. (1982) 'Norway: Centre and Periphery in a Peripheral State', in S. Rokkan and D.W. Urwin (eds) *The Politics of Territorial Identity: Studies in European Regionalism*. London: SAGE Publications Ltd, pp. 75–111.

Abrams, P. (1988) 'Notes on the Difficulty of Studying the State [1977]', *Journal of Historical Sociology*, 1(1), pp. 58–89.

Adler-Nissen, R. and Gad, U.P. (2014) 'Introduction: Postimperial Sovereignty Games in the Nordic Region', *Cooperation and Conflict*, 49(1), pp. 3–32. Available at: https://doi.org/10.1177/0010836713514148.

Agnew, J. (1994) 'The Territorial Trap: The Geographical Assumptions of International Relations Theory', *Review of International Political Economy*, 1(1), pp. 53–80. Available at: https://doi.org/10.2307/4177090.

Agnew, J. (2013) 'The Origins of Critical Geopolitics', in K. Dodds, M. Kuus, and J.P. Sharp (eds) *The Ashgate Research Companion to Critical Geopolitics*. Farnham: Ashgate, pp. 19–32.

Agnew, J. and Corbridge, S. (1995) *Mastering Space: Hegemony, Territory and International Political Economy*. London: Routledge.

Agnew, J. and Muscarà, L. (2012) *Making Political Geography*. Lanham: Rowman & Littlefield.

AHDR (2004) *Arctic Human Development Report*. Copenhagen: Nordic Council of Ministers.

AHDR-II (2015) *Arctic Human Development Report: Regional Processes and Global Linkages*. Copenhagen: Nordic Council of Ministers. Available at: http://urn.kb.se/resolve?urn=urn:nbn:se:norden:org:diva-3 809 (Accessed: 27 February 2015).

Ahmed, S. (2004) 'Collective Feelings: Or, the Impressions Left by Others', *Theory, Culture & Society*, 21(2), pp. 25–42. Available at: https://doi.org/10.1177/0263276404042133.

Ajzenstat, J. (2003) *Canada's Founding Debates*. Toronto: University of Toronto Press.

Alexander, E. and Bloom, E.T. (2023) 'The Arctic Council and the Crucial Partnership Between Indigenous Peoples and States in the Arctic', *Wilson Center, Polar Institute: Polar Points*, 27 July. Available at: https://www.wilsoncenter.org/blog-post/no-21-arctic-council-and-crucial-partnership-between-indigenous-peoples-and-states-arctic (Accessed: 28 July 2023).

Alexandrov, M. (2003) 'The Concept of State Identity in International Relations: A Theoretical Analysis', *Journal of International Development and Cooperation*, 10(1), pp. 33–46.

Anderson, B. (1983) *Imagined Communities: Reflections on the Origin and Spread of Nationalism*. London: Verso.

Anderson, B. (2015) 'Boredom, Excitement and Other Security Affects', *Dialogues in Human Geography*, 5(3), pp. 271–274. Available at: https://doi.org/10.1177/2043820615607759.

Antonsich, M. (2009) 'On Territory, the Nation-State and the Crisis of the Hyphen', *Progress in Human Geography*, 33(6), pp. 789–806. Available at: https://doi.org/10.1177/0309132508104996.

Antonsich, M. and Matejskova, T. (2015) 'Conclusion: Nation and Diversity – A False Conundrum', in T. Matejskova and M. Antonsich (eds) *Governing through Diversity: Migration Societies in Post-Multiculturalist Times*. Houndsmills: Palgrave Macmillan (Global diversities), pp. 201–209.

Aporta, C. (2011) 'Shifting Perspectives on Shifting Ice: Documenting and Representing Inuit Use of the Sea Ice', *Canadian Geographer / Le Géographe canadien*, 55(1), pp. 6–19. Available at: https://doi.org/10.1111/j.1541-0064.2010.00340.x.

Aporta, C., Taylor, D.R.F. and Laidler, G.J. (2011) 'Geographies of Inuit Sea Ice Use: Introduction', *Canadian Geographer / Le Géographe canadien*, 55(1), pp. 1–5. Available at: https://doi.org/10.1111/j.1541-0064.2010.00339.x.

Arbo, P. (2015) 'Integrated Modernisation', in N.MTIF, *Future North: Final report from 'Knowledge Gathering - Value Creation in the North'*. Oslo: Norwegian Ministry of Trade, Industry and Fisheries, pp. 25–32. Available at: https://www.regjeringen.no/contentassets/8aa6fc353593499ea9e1a343fcb19600/final-report_future-north.pdf (Accessed: 20 July 2015).

Arctic Akureyri (no date) *Arctic Akureyri*, Arctic Akureyri. Available at: https://www.arcticakureyri.is/ (Accessed: 1 July 2023).

Arctic Council (1996) *Declaration on the Establishment of the Arctic Council* [Ottawa Declaration]. Ottawa: Arctic Council. Available at: https://oaarchive.arctic-council.org/handle/11374/85 (Accessed: 26 February 2017).

Arctic Council (2013) 'Arctic Council Rules of Procedure'. Available at: https://oaarchive.arctic-council.org/handle/11374/940 (Accessed: 3 July 2023).

Arctic Council (2018) *The Arctic Council: A backgrounder, Arctic Council.* Available at: http://www.arctic-council.org/index.php/en/about-us (Accessed: 30 November 2019).

Arctic Council (2023) *Organization: Arctic Council Observers, Arctic Council.* Available at: https://arctic-council.org/about/observers/ (Accessed: 29 July 2023).

Arnold, S. (2010) '"The Men of the North" Redux: Nanook and Canadian National Unity', *American Review of Canadian Studies*, 40(4), pp. 452–463. Available at: https://doi.org/10.1080/02722011.2010.519 392.

Arnold, S. (2012) 'Constructing an Indigenous Nordicity: The "New Partnership" and Canada's Northern Agenda: Constructing an Indigenous Nordicity', *International Studies Perspectives*, 13(1), pp. 105–120. Available at: https://doi.org/10.1111/j.1528-3585.2011.00455.x.

Ashizawa, K. (2008) 'When Identity Matters: State Identity, Regional Institution-Building, and Japanese Foreign Policy', *International Studies Review*, 10(3), pp. 571–598.

Atkinson, D. and Dodds, K.J. (2000) 'Introduction to Geopolitical Traditions: A Century of Geopolitical Thought', in K.J. Dodds and D. Atkinson (eds) *Geopolitical Traditions: Critical Histories of Century of Geopolitical Thought.* London: Routledge, pp. 1–24. Available at: http://site.ebrary.com/id/10054082 (Accessed: 8 October 2013).

Atwood, M. (2004) *Strange Things: The Malevolent North in Canadian Literature.* London: Virago.

Axworthy, T.S., Koivurova, T. and Hasanat, W. (eds) (2012) *The Arctic Council: Its Place in the Future of Arctic Governance.* E-book: Munk-Gordon Arctic Security Program. Available at: http://gordonfoundation.ca/sites/default/files/publications/The%20Arctic%20Council_FULL_1.pdf.

Baird, J. (2013) *Address by Minister Baird to Media Concerning Canada's Continental Shelf Submissions, Foreign Affairs, Trade and Development Canada.* Available at: http://www.international.gc.ca/media/aff/speeches-discours/2013/12/09a.aspx?lang=eng (Accessed: 17 September 2015).

Baldwin, A., Cameron, L. and Kobayashi, A. (2012a) 'Introduction: Where Is the Great White North? Spatializing History, Historicizing Whiteness', in A. Baldwin, L. Cameron, and A. Kobayashi (eds) *Rethinking the Great White North: Race, Nature, and the Historical Geographies of Whiteness in Canada.* Vancouver: UBC Press, pp. 1–15.

Baldwin, A., Cameron, L. and Kobayashi, A. (eds) (2012b) *Rethinking the Great White North: Race, Nature, and the Historical Geographies of Whiteness in Canada.* Vancouver: UBC Press.

Barnes, T.J. (2007) 'The Geographical State: The Development of Canadian Geography', *Journal of Geography in Higher Education*, 31(1), pp. 161–177. Available at: https://doi.org/10.1080/03098260601033084.

Barraclough, E.R. (2012) 'Naming the Landscape in the Landnám Narratives of the Íslendingasögur and Landnámabók', *Saga-Book*, 36, pp. 79–101.

Bartenstein, K. (2011) 'The "Arctic Exception" in the Law of the Sea Convention: A Contribution to Safer Navigation in the Northwest Passage?', *Ocean Development & International Law*, 42(1–2), pp. 22–52. Available at: https://doi.org/10.1080/00908320.2011.542104.

Barth, F. (1969) *Ethnic Groups and Boundaries: The Social Organization of Culture Difference*. Boston: Little, Brown and Company.

Bélanger, L. and Doran, C.F. (2013) 'Quebec's Destiny', in M. Kasoff and P. James (eds) *Canadian Studies in the New Millennium*. 2nd edn. Toronto: University of Toronto Press, pp. 163–184.

Bennett, M.M. (2012) 'Iceland: Geopolitical Triangulation', *Foreign Policy Blog*, 10 July. Available at: http://foreignpolicyblogs.com/2012/10/07/iceland-geopolitical-triangulation/ (Accessed: 5 March 2014).

Bennett, M.M., Greaves, W., Riedlsperger, R., and Botella, A. (2016) 'Articulating the Arctic: Contrasting State and Inuit Maps of the Canadian North', *Polar Record*, 52(6), pp. 630–644. doi:10.1017/S0032247416000164.

Benwell, M.C. (2014) 'From the Banal to the Blatant: Expressions of Nationalism in Secondary Schools in Argentina and the Falkland Islands', *Geoforum*, 52, pp. 51–60. Available at: https://doi.org/10.1016/j.geoforum.2013.12.006.

Berdahl, L. and Raney, T. (2010) 'Being Canadian in the World: Mapping the Contours of National Identity and Public Opinion on International Issues in Canada', *International Journal*, 65(4), pp. 995–1010.

Bergmann, E. (2014) 'Iceland: A Postimperial Sovereignty Project', *Cooperation and Conflict*, 49(1), pp. 33–54. Available at: https://doi.org/10.1177/0010836713514152.

Berg-Nordlie, M. and Skogvang, S.F. (2022) 'Sametingets valgmanntall', in *Store norske leksikon*. Available at: https://snl.no/Sametingets_valgmanntall (Accessed: 3 July 2023).

Bhabha, H.K. (1994) *The Location of Culture*. Abingdon: Routledge.

Bialasiewicz, L., Campbell, D., Elden, S., Graham, S., Jeffrey, A., and Williams, A.J. (2007) 'Performing Security: The Imaginative Geographies of Current US Strategy', *Political Geography*, 26(4), pp. 405–422. Available at: https://doi.org/10.1016/j.polgeo.2006.12.002.

Biersteker, T.J. and Weber, C. (eds) (1996) *State Sovereignty as Social Construct*. Cambridge: Cambridge University Press.

Billig, M. (1995) *Banal Nationalism*. London: SAGE.

Biswas, S. (2002) 'W(h)ither the Nation-state? National and State Identity in the Face of Fragmentation and Globalisation', *Global Society*, 16(2), pp. 175–198. Available at: https://doi.org/10.1080/09537320220132910.

Bondi, L. (1993) 'Locating Identity Politics', in M. Keith and S. Pile (eds) *Place and the Politics of Identity*. London: Routledge, pp. 84–101.

Bone, R.M. (2009) *The Canadian North: Issues and challenges*. Toronto: Oxford University Press.

Bravo, M. (2019) *North Pole: Nature and Culture*. London: Reaktion Books.

Brenner, N., Jessop, B., Jones, M., and MacLeod, G. (eds) (2003) *State/Space: A Reader*. Malden, MA: Blackwell.

Brenner, N. (2004) *New State Spaces: Urban Governance and the Rescaling of Statehood*. New York: Oxford University Press, US.

Breuilly, J. (1996) 'Approaches to Nationalism', in G. Balakrishnan (ed.) *Mapping the Nation*. London: Verso, pp. 146–174.

Brown, W. (2008) *Regulating Aversion: Tolerance in the Age of Identity and Empire*. Princeton: Princeton University Press.

Brubaker, R. (2006) *Ethnicity without Groups*. Cambridge, MA: Harvard University Press.

Bruun, J.M. and Medby, I.A. (2014) 'Theorising the Thaw: Geopolitics in a Changing Arctic', *Geography Compass*, 8(12), pp. 915–929. Available at: https://doi.org/10.1111/gec3.12189.

Brydon, A. (1996) 'Whale-Siting: Spatiality in Icelandic Nationalism', in G. Pálsson and E.P. Durrenberger (eds) *Images of Contemporary Iceland: Everyday Lives and Global Contexts*. Iowa City: University of Iowa Press, pp. 25–45.

Burgess, J.P. (2001) 'Identitet og mangfald. Det norske, det skandinaviske, og det europeiske', in B. Stråth, J.P. Burgess, and S.I. Angell (eds) *Den europeiske identiteten og den skandinaviske*. Volda: Høgskulen i Volda, pp. 7–28.

Burke, D.C. (2017) 'Leading by example: Canada and its Arctic stewardship role', *International Journal of Public Policy*, 13(1–2), pp. 36–52. Available at: https://doi.org/10.1504/IJPP.2017.081050.

Burke, D.C. (2018) *International Disputes and Cultural Ideas in the Canadian Arctic: Arctic Sovereignty in the National Consciousness*. Cham, Switzerland: Palgrave Macmillan.

Burnasheva, D. (2019) 'Arctic Identity: Between Frontier and Homeland', *Anthropology & Archeology of Eurasia*, 58(4), pp. 271–307. Available at: https://doi.org/10.1080/10611959.2019.1786978.

Butler, J. (1999) *Gender Trouble: Feminism and the Subversion of Identity*. London: Routledge.

Butler, J. (2011) *Bodies That Matter*. 2nd edn. Abingdon: Routledge.

Byers, M. (2010) *Who Owns the Arctic?: Understanding Sovereignty Disputes in the North*. Vancouver: Douglas & McIntyre.

Byers, M. and Baker, J. (2013) *International Law and the Arctic*. Cambridge: Cambridge University Press.

Bykova, A. (2023) *Svalbard's Extractive Economy: Past, Present, Future*. The Arctic Institute. Available at: https://www.thearcticinstitute.org/wp-content/uploads/2023/06/Svalbards-Extractive-Economy-Report-2023.pdf (Accessed: 28 June 2023).

Byock, J. (2002) 'The Icelandic Althing: Dawn of Parliamentary Democracy', in J.M. Fladmark (ed.) *Heritage and Identity: Shaping the Nations of the North*. Donhead: The Heyerdahl Institute and Robert Gordon University, pp. 1–18.

Cairns, A.C., Courtney, J.C., MacKinnon, P., Michelmann, H.J., and Smith, D.E. (eds) (1999) *Citizenship, Diversity, and Pluralism: Canadian and Ccomparative Perspectives*. Montréal: McGill-Queen's University Press. Available at: http://site.ebrary.com/id/10135848 (Accessed: 15 September 2013).

Cameron, E. (2015) *Far Off Metal River: Inuit Lands, Settler Stories, and theMmakings of the Contemporary Arctic*. Vancouver: UBC Press.

Campbell, D. (1992) *Writing Security: United States Foreign Policy and the Politics of Identity*. Minneapolis: University of Minnesota Press.

Campbell, D. (2009) 'Discourse', in D. Gregory, R. Johnston, G. Pratt, M.J. Watts, and S. Whatmore (eds) *The Dictionary of Human Geography*. 5th edn. Malden, MA: Wiley-Blackwell, pp. 166–167.

Canada's Newest and Largest Marine Protected Area: Tallurutiup Imanga – Lancaster Sound (2017) IUCN. Available at: https://www.iucn.org/news/protected-areas/201708/canada%E2%80%99s-newest-and-largest-marine-protected-area-tallurutiup-imanga-%E2%80%93-lancaster-sound (Accessed: 22 February 2023).

Carvalho, B. de and Neumann, I.B. (eds) (2015) *Small State Status Seeking: Norway's Quest for International Standing*. Abingdon: Routledge.

Cavell, J. (2007) 'Comparing Mythologies: Twentieth-Century Canadian Constructions of Sir John Franklin', in N. Hillmer and A. Chapnick (eds) *Canadas of the Mind: The Making and Unmaking of Canadian Nationalisms in the Twentieth Century*. Montréal: McGill-Queens's University Press, pp. 15–45.

C.CIRNAC (2019) *Canada's Arctic and Northern Policy Framework*. Ottawa: Government of Canada: Crown-Indigenous Relations and Northern Affairs Canada. Available at: https://www.rcaanc-cirnac.gc.ca/eng/1560523306861/1560523330587 (Accessed: 12 January 2020).

C.DIAND (2009) *Canada's Northern Strategy: Our North, Our Heritage, Our Future*. Ottawa: Government of Canada, Department of Indian Affairs and Northern Development. Available at: http://www.northernstrategy.gc.ca/cns/cns-eng.asp (Accessed: 14 September 2016).

C.FATDC (2010) *Statement on Canada's Arctic Foreign Policy*. Ottawa: Government of Canada: Foreign Affairs, Trade and Development Canada. Available at: http://www.international.gc.ca/arctic-arctique/

arctic_policy-canada-politique_arctique.aspx?lang=eng (Accessed: 19 September 2015).

Chapnick, A. (2000) 'The Canadian Middle Power Myth', *International Journal*, 55(2), pp. 188–206. Available at: https://doi.org/10.2307/40 203476.

Chartier, D. (2006) 'The North and the Great Expanse: Representations of the North and Narrative Forms in French-Canadian Literature', *British Journal of Canadian Studies*, 19(1), pp. 33–46.

Chartier, D. (2007) 'Towards a Grammar of the Idea of North: Nordicity, Winterity', *Nordlit*, 22, pp. 35–47.

Chase, S. (2013) 'Canada Issues Santa Claus a Passport', *The Globe and Mail*, 20 December. Available at: http://www.theglobeandmail.com/ news/politics/canada-issues-santa-claus-a-passport/article16072973/ (Accessed: 8 July 2016).

Chung, A. (2007) 'The Peculiarity of Eracism: Mixed Race and Nonbelonging in the Multicultural Nation', in N. Hillmer and A. Chapnick (eds) *Canadas of the Mind: The Making and Unmaking of Canadian Nationalisms in the Twentieth Century*. Montréal: McGill-Queens's University Press, pp. 300–310.

Clark, J. and Jones, A. (2011) '"Telling Stories about Politics": Europeanization and the EU's Council Working Groups', *JCMS: Journal of Common Market Studies*, 49(2), pp. 341–366. Available at: https://doi. org/10.1111/j.1468-5965.2010.02143.x.

Closs Stephens, A. (2016) 'The Affective Atmospheres of Nationalism', *cultural geographies*, 23(2), pp. 181–198. Available at: https://doi. org/10.1177/1474474015569994.

Closs Stephens, A. (2022) *National Affects: The Everyday Atmospheres of Being Political*. London: Bloomsbury Academic.

Coates, K.S. and Morrison, B. (1992) *The Forgotten North: A History of Canada's Provincial Norths*. Toronto: Lorimer.

Cohen, A. (2008) *The Unfinished Canadian: The People We Are*. Toronto: McClelland & Stewart.

Connolly, W.E. (1991) *Identity/Difference: Democratic Negotiations of Political Paradox*. Minneapolis: University of Minnesota Press. Available at: https://www.jstor.org/stable/10.5749/j.ctttt4bf (Accessed: 12 July 2022).

Craciun, A. (2010) 'The Frozen Ocean', *PMLA*, 125(3), pp. 693–702.

Craciun, A. (2012) 'The Franklin Mystery', *Literary Review of Canada*. Available at: http://reviewcanada.ca/magazine/2012/05/the-franklin-mys tery/ (Accessed: 17 September 2015).

Crang, M. and Tolia-Kelly, D.P. (2010) 'Nation, Race, and Affect: Senses and Sensibilities at National Heritage Sites', *Environment and Planning A*, 42(10), pp. 2315–2331. Available at: https://doi.org/10.10 68/a4346.

Dalby, S. and Ó Tuathail, G. (eds) (1998) *Rethinking Geopolitics*. New York: Routledge.

Depledge, D. and Dodds, K. (2017) 'Bazaar Governance: Situating the Arctic Circle', in K. Keil and S. Knecht (eds) *Governing Arctic Change: Global Perspectives*. London: Palgrave Macmillan, pp. 141–160.

Dibben, N. (2009) 'Nature and Nation: National Identity and Environmentalism in Icelandic Popular Music Video and Music Documentary', *Ethnomusicology Forum*, 18(1), pp. 131–151. Available at: https://doi.org/10.1080/17411910902816542.

Dijink, G. (2002) *National Identity and Geopolitical Visions: Maps of Pride and Pain*. London: Routledge.

Dittmer, J. (2010) *Popular Culture, Geopolitics, and Identity*. Lanham: Rowman & Littlefield Publishers.

Dittmer, J., Moisio, S., Ingram, A., and Dodds, K. (2011) 'Have You Heard the One About the Disappearing Ice? Recasting Arctic Geopolitics', *Political Geography*, 30(4), pp. 202–214. Available at: https://doi.org/10.1016/j.polgeo.2011.04.002.

Dittmer, J. (2017) *Diplomatic Material: Affect, Assemblage, and Foreign Policy*. Durham, NC: Duke University Press.

Dittmer, J. and McConnell, F. (eds) (2015) *Diplomatic Cultures and International Politics: Translations, Spaces and Alternatives*. London: Routledge.

Dixon, D.P. and Marston, S.A. (2011) 'Introduction: Feminist Engagements with Geopolitics', *Gender, Place & Culture*, 18(4), pp. 445–453. Available at: https://doi.org/10.1080/0966369X.2011.583401.

Dodds, K. (2010a) 'A Polar Mediterranean? Accessibility, Resources and Sovereignty in the Arctic Ocean: A Polar Mediterranean?', *Global Policy*, 1(3), pp. 303–311. Available at: https://doi.org/10.1111/j.1758-5899.2010.00038.x.

Dodds, K. (2010b) 'Flag Planting and Finger Pointing: The Law of the Sea, the Arctic and the Political Geographies of the Outer Continental Shelf', *Political Geography*, 29(2), pp. 63–73. Available at: https://doi.org/10.1016/j.polgeo.2010.02.004.

Dodds, K. (2012) 'Graduated and Paternal Sovereignty: Stephen Harper, Operation Nanook 10, and the Canadian Arctic', *Environment and Planning D: Society and Space*, 30(6), pp. 989–1010. Available at: https://doi.org/10.1068/d17710.

Dodds, K. (2013a) 'Anticipating the Arctic and the Arctic Council: Pre-emption, Precaution and Preparedness', *Polar Record*, 49(02), pp. 193–203. Available at: https://doi.org/10.1017/S0032247412000198.

Dodds, K. (2013b) 'Commentary: Rendez-vous at Reykjavik', in L. Heininen, H. Exner-Pirot, and J. Plouffe (eds) *Arctic Yearbook 2013*.

Akureyri: Northern Research Forum, pp. 340–342. Available at: http://www.arcticyearbook.com (Accessed: 19 April 2014).

Dodds, K. (2018) *Ice: Nature and Culture*. London: Reaktion Books (Earth).

Dodds, K. and Ingimundarson, V. (2012) 'Territorial Nationalism and Arctic Geopolitics: Iceland as an Arctic Coastal State', *The Polar Journal*, 2(1), pp. 21–37. Available at: https://doi.org/10.1080/2154896X.2012.679557.

Dodds, K., Kuus, M., and Sharp, J.P. (eds) (2013) *The Ashgate Research Companion to Critical Geopolitics*. Farnham: Ashgate.

Dodds, K. and Nuttall, M. (2015) *The Scramble for the Poles: The Geopolitics of the Arctic and Antarctic*. Cambridge: Polity Press.

Doel, R.E., Friedman, R.M., Lajus, J., Sörlin, S., and Wråkberg, U. (2014) 'Strategic Arctic Science: National Interests in Building Natural Knowledge – Interwar Era through the Cold War', *Journal of Historical Geography*, 45, pp. 60–80. Available at: https://doi.org/10.1016/j.jhg.2013.12.004.

Doubleday, N.C. (2003) 'The Nexus of Identity, Inuit Autonomy and Arctic Sustainability: Learning from Nunavut, Community and Culture', *British Journal of Canadian Studies*, 16(2), pp. 297–308.

Dowler, L. and Sharp, J. (2001) 'A Feminist Geopolitics?', *Space and Polity*, 5(3), pp. 165–176. Available at: https://doi.org/10.1080/13562570120104382.

Drivenes, E.-A. and Jølle, H.D. (eds) (2004) *Norsk polarhistorie: Ekspedisjonene*. Oslo: Gyldendal (Norsk Polarhistorie).

Drivenes, E.-A. and Jølle, H.D. (eds) (2006) *Into the Ice: The History of Norway and the Polar Regions*. Oslo: Gyldendal.

Driver, F. (2001) *Geography Militant: Cultures of Exploration and Empire*. Oxford: Blackwell.

Dubow, J. (2009) 'Identity', in D. Gregory, R. Johnston, G. Pratt, M.J. Watts, and S. Whatmore, (eds) *The Dictionary of Human Geography*. 5th edn. Malden, MA: Wiley-Blackwell.

Dumas, D. (2023) 'Place Them on a Stamp: Inuit, Banal Colonialism, and the "Pioneer Experiment" of the High Arctic Relocations', *Political Geography*, 105, p. 102919. Available at: https://doi.org/10.1016/j.polgeo.2023.102919.

Dunn, K.C. (2010) 'There Is No Such Thing as the State: Discourse, Effect and Performativity', *Forum for Development Studies*, 37(1), pp. 79–92. Available at: https://doi.org/10.1080/08039410903558285.

Edensor, T. (2002) *National Identity, Popular Culture and Everyday Life*. Oxford: Berg Publishers.

Eggertsson, T. (1996) 'No Experiments, Monumental Disasters: Why it Took a Thousand Years to Develop a Specialized Fishing Industry in Iceland', *Journal of Economic Behavior & Organization*, 30(1), pp. 1–23. Available at: https://doi.org/10.1016/S0167-2681(96)00839-6.

Eglinger, H. (2010) '"Traces against Time's Erosion": The Polar Explorer between Documentation and Projection', in A. Ryall, J. Schimanski, and H.H. Wærp (eds) *Arctic Discourses*. Newcastle-upon-Tyne: Cambridge Scholars Publishing, pp. 2–18.

Einarsson, N. (1996a) 'A Sea of Images: Fishers, Whalers, and Environmentalists', in G. Pálsson and E.P. Durrenberger (eds) *Images of Contemporary Iceland: Everyday Lives and Global Contexts*. Iowa City: University of Iowa Press, pp. 46–59.

Einarsson, N. (1996b) 'The Wandering Semioticians: Tourism and the Image of Modern Iceland', in G. Pálsson and E.P. Durrenberger (eds) *Images of Contemporary Iceland: Everyday Lives and Global Contexts*. Iowa City: University of Iowa Press, pp. 215–236.

Einarsson, N., Larsen, J.N., Nilsson, A., and Young, O.R. (eds) (2004) *Arctic Human Development Report*. Copenhagen: Nordic Council of Ministers.

Elliot-Meisel, E. (2009) 'Politics, Pride, and Precedent: The United States and Canada in the Northwest Passage', *Ocean Development & International Law*, 40(2), pp. 204–232. Available at: https://doi.org/10.1080/00908320902864813.

Emmerson, C. (2010) *The Future History of the Arctic*. London: Vintage.

Everett-Heath, J. (2018) 'Arctic', in *The Concise Dictionary of World Place-Names*. 4th edn. Oxford: Oxford University Press. Available at: http://www.oxfordreference.com/view/10.1093/acref/9780191866326.001.0001/acref-9780191866326-e-365 (Accessed: 6 October 2019).

Exner-Pirot, H. (2016) 'Canada's Arctic Council Chairmanship (2013–2015): A Post-mortem', *Canadian Foreign Policy Journal*, 22(1), pp. 84–96. Available at: https://doi.org/10.1080/11926422.2015.1115772.

Fearon, J.D. (1999) 'What Is Identity (As We Now Use the Word)?' Department of Political Science, Stanford University.

Ferdoush, M.A. and Väätänen, V. (2022) 'Anticipatory State Identity: Understanding the Finnish State's Approach to the Arctic', *Area*, 54(4), pp. 618–626. Available at: https://doi.org/10.1111/area.12802.

Foucault, M. (1972) *Archaeology of Knowledge* [1969]. London: Tavistock.

Foucault, M. (1980) 'Questions on Geography', in C. Gordon (ed.) *Power/Knowledge. Selected Interviews and Other Writings 1972–1977*. New York: Pantheon.

Foucault, M. (1981) 'The Order of Discourse', in R. Young (ed.) *Untying the Text: A Post-Structuralist Reader*. London: Routledge and Kegan Paul, pp. 51–78.

Francis, D. (1997) *National Dreams: Myth, Memory and Canadian History*. Reprint edition. Vancouver, BC: Arsenal Pulp Press.

Friberg, J.H. (2021) 'Who Wants to Be Norwegian – Who Gets to Be Norwegian? Identificational Assimilation and Non-recognition among Immigrant Origin Youth in Norway', *Ethnic and Racial Studies*, 44(16), pp. 21–43. Available at: https://doi.org/10.1080/01419870.2020.1857813.

Frye, N. (1971) *The Bush Garden: Essays on the Canadian Imagination*. Toronto: Anansi.

Fulsås, N. (1997) 'Nordnorsk eigenart og nordnorsk identitet', in Ø. Thomassen and J. Lorås (eds) *Spenningenes land. Nord-Norge etter 1945*. Oslo: Ad Notam Gyldendal, pp. 207–222.

Gaski, H. (ed.) (1998) *Sami Culture in a New Era: The Norwegian Sami Experience*. Seattle: University of Washington Press.

Gautier, D.L., Bird, K.J., Charpentier, R.R., Grantz, A., Houseknecht, D.W., Klett, T.R., Moore, T.E., Pitman, J.K., Schenk, C.J., Schuenemeyer, J.H., Sørensen, K., Tennyson, M.E., Valin, Z.C., nd Wandrey, C.J. (2009) 'Assessment of Undiscovered Oil and Gas in the Arctic', *Science*, 324(5931), pp. 1175–1179. Available at: https://doi.org/10.1126/science.1169467.

Gellner, E. (1983) *Nations and Nationalism*. Oxford: Blackwell.

Gibbon, J.M. (1938) *Canadian Mosaic: The Making of a Northern Nation*. Toronto: McClelland & Stewart.

Giddens, A. (1991) *The Consequences of Modernity*. Cambridge: Polity Press.

Gimlette, J. (2009) 'Iceland: Beauty Born out of the Ashes', *Telegraph.co.uk*, 26 August. Available at: http://www.telegraph.co.uk/travel/destinations/europe/iceland/6089038/Iceland-Beauty-born-out-of-the-ashes.html (Accessed: 17 April 2014).

Gjerde, K.L. and Fjæstad, K. (2013) '"Det meste er nord": Støres største satsing', *Internasjonal Politikk*, 71(03), pp. 385–395.

Gorbachev, M. (1987) 'The Speech in Murmansk at the Ceremonial Meeting on the Occasion of the Presentation of the Order of Lenin and the Gold Star Medal to the City of Murmansk', *Novosti Press Agency*, 1 October, pp. 23–31.

Government of Canada (2010) *Difference between Canadian Provinces and Territories, Government of Canada: Intergovernmental Affairs*. Available at: http://www.pco-bcp.gc.ca/aia/index.asp?lang=eng&page=provterr&doc=difference-eng.htm (Accessed: 19 September 2015).

Government of Canada (2022) *Indigenous Peoples and Communities, Government of Canada: Crown-Indigenous Relations and Northern Affairs Canada*. Available at: https://www.rcaanc-cirnac.gc.ca/eng/1100100013785/1529102490303 (Accessed: 4 July 2023).

Government of Iceland (2013) *Platform of the Coalition Government Formed by the Progressive Party and the Independence Party | Government Offices, Government of Iceland*. Available at: http://www.government.is/government/coalition-platform/ (Accessed: 17 April 2014).

Government of Iceland (2014) *How Is Iceland governed? | Government Offices, Government of Iceland*. Available at: http://www.government.is/how-iceland-is-governed/ (Accessed: 17 April 2014).

Graburn, N. (2004) 'Inuksuk: Icon of the Inuit of Nunavut', *Études / Inuit / Studies*, 28(1), pp. 69–82. Available at: https://doi.org/10.7202/012640ar.

Grace, S.E. (2001) *Canada and the Idea of North*. Montréal: McGill-Queen's University Press.

Graczyk, P. and Koivurova, T. (2014) 'A New Era in the Arctic Council's External Relations? Broader Consequences of the Nuuk Observer Rules for Arctic Governance', *Polar Record*, 50(3), pp. 225–236. Available at: https://doi.org/10.1017/S0032247412000824.

Grant, S.D. (1988) *Sovereignty or Security? Government Policy in the Canadian North 1936–1950*. Vancouver: UBC Press.

Gregson, N. and Rose, G. (2000) 'Taking Butler Elsewhere: Performativities, Spatialities and Subjectivities', *Environment and Planning D: Society and Space*, 18(4), pp. 433–452. Available at: https://doi.org/10.1068/d232.

GRID-Arendal (2013) 'Boundaries of the Arctic Council Working Groups'. Arendal, Norway: GRID-Arendal. Available at: https://www.grida.no/resources/8387 (Accessed: 25 August 2023).

Griffiths, F., Huebert, R., and Lackenbauer, W.P. (eds) (2011) *Canada and the Changing Arctic: Sovereignty, Security, and Stewardship*. Waterloo: Wilfrid Laurier University Press.

Grímsson, Ó.R. (1978) *Icelandic Nationalism: A Dissolution of Force in the Danish Kingdom and Fundamental Cleavage in Icelandic Politics. A Draft Framework for Historical Analysis*. Reykjavik: University of Iceland.

Grímsson, Ó.R. (2014a) 'Opening speech at the Arctic Circle Second Assembly'. *Arctic Circle Assembly*, Reykjavik, 31 October. Available at: http://english.forseti.is/media/PDF/2014_10_31_Setning_AC.pdf (Accessed: 30 May 2015).

Grímsson, Ó.R. (2014b) 'People and Ice: The New Global Significance of the Arctic and the Himalayas - Speech at the World Affairs Council and the Commonwealth Club of California'. *World Affairs Council*, World Affairs Council and the Commonwealth Club of California, San Francisco, 22 April. Available at: http://english.forseti.is/media/PDF/2014_04_22_SanFrancisco.pdf (Accessed: 10 June 2016).

Guibernau, M. (2004) 'Anthony D. Smith on Nations and National Identity: A Critical Assessment', *Nations and Nationalism*, 10(1–2), pp. 125–141.

Guibernau, M. (2013) *Belonging: Solidarity and Division in Modern Societies*. Cambridge: Polity.

Hafstein, V.T. (2000) 'The Elves' Point of View: Cultural Identity in Contemporary Icelandic Elf-Tradition', *Fabula*, 41(1–2), pp. 87–104. Available at: https://doi.org/10.1515/fabl.2000.41.1-2.87.

Hálfdanarson, G. (2000) 'Þingvellir: An Icelandic "Lieu de Mémoire"', *History & Memory*, 12(1), pp. 4–29. Available at: https://doi.org/10.29 79/HIS.2000.12.1.4.

Halink, S. (2014) 'The Icelandic Mythscape: Sagas, Landscapes, and National Identity', *National Identities*, 16(3).

Hamelin, L.-E. (1978) *Canadian Nordicity: It's Your North Too*. Translated by W. Barr. Montréal: Harvest House.

Hansen, T.B. and Stepputat, F. (eds) (2001) *States of Imagination: Ethnographic Explorations of the Postcolonial State*. Durham, NC: Duke University Press.

Harding, P. and Bindloss, J. (2004) *Lonely Planet Iceland*. 5th edn. London: Lonely Planet Publications.

Harper, S. (2008) *Prime Minister Harper Delivers on Commitment to the 'New North'*, *Prime Minister of Canada*. Available at: http://pm.gc.ca/eng/news/2008/03/10/prime-minister-harper-delivers-commitment-new-north (Accessed: 30 August 2015).

Harper, S. (2014a) 'Franklin Discovery Strengthens Canada's Arctic Sovereignty', *The Globe and Mail*. Online, 12 September. Available at: http://www.theglobeandmail.com/news/politics/franklin-discovery-strengthens-canadas-arctic-sovereignty/article20590280/ (Accessed: 17 September 2015).

Harper, S. (2014b) *Statement by the Prime Minister of Canada Announcing the Discovery of One of the Ill-fated Franklin Expedition Ships Lost in 1846*, *Parks Canada*. Available at: http://www.pc.gc.ca/APPS/CP-NR/release_e.asp?id=2163&andor1=nr (Accessed: 18 October 2015).

Harris, R.C. (2001) 'Postmodern Patriotism: Canadian Reflections', *Canadian Geographer*, 45, pp. 193–207.

Harrison, T.W. (2014) 'Stephen Harper', *The Canadian Encyclopedia*. Online. Toronto: Historica Canada [web]. Available at: http://www.thecanadianencyclopedia.ca/en/article/stephen-joseph-harper/ (Accessed: 23 September 2014).

Hastrup, K. (1984) 'Defining a Society: The Icelandic Free State between Two Worlds', *Scandinavian Studies*, 56(3), pp. 235–255.

Hastrup, K. (2010) 'Emotional Topographies: The Sense of Place in the Far North', in J. Davies and D. Spencer (eds) *Emotions in the Field: The Psychology and Anthropology of Fieldwork Experience*. Stanford: Stanford University Press, pp. 191–211.

Hechter, M. (2000) *Containing Nationalism*. Oxford: Oxford University Press.

Heikkilä, M. (2019) *If We Lose the Arctic: Finland's Arctic Thinking from the 1980s to Present Day*. Rovaniemi, Finland: The Arctic Centre, University of Lapland.

Hermannsson, B. (2005) *Understanding Nationalism: Studies in Icelandic Nationalism 1800–2000*. Doctoral thesis. Stockholm University.

Herzfeld, M. (1992) *The Social Production of Indifference*. London: Berg.

Hillmer, N. and Chapnick, A. (eds) (2007a) *Canadas of the Mind: The Making and Unmaking of Canadian Nationalisms in the Twentieth Century*. Montréal: McGill-Queens's University Press.

Hillmer, N. and Chapnick, A. (2007b) 'Introduction: An Abundance of Nationalisms', in N. Hillmer and A. Chapnick (eds) *Canadas of the Mind: The Making and Unmaking of Canadian Nationalisms in the Twentieth Century*. Montréal: McGill-Queens's University Press, pp. 3–14.

Hobsbawm, E.J. and Ranger, T.O. (eds) (1983) *The Invention of Tradition*. Cambridge: Cambridge University Press.

Hønneland, G. (2011) *Arktiske utfordringer*. Oslo: Cappellen Damm.

Hønneland, G. (2017) *Arctic Euphoria and International High North Politics*. New York: Palgrave Macmillan.

Hønneland, G. and Jensen, L.C. (2008) *Den nye nordområdepolitikken: Barentsbilder etter årtusenskiftet ('The New Norwegian Politics in the High North: Barents Images after the Turn of the Millennium')*. Bergen: Fagbokforlaget (Nordområdepolitikk).

Howarth, D. (2000) *Discourse*. Milton Keynes: Open University Press.

Huebert, R., Exner-Pirot, H., Lajeunesse, A., and Gulledge, J. (2012) *Climate Change & International Security: The Arctic as a Bellwether*. Centre for Climate and Energy Solutions. Available at: http://www.c2es.org/document/climate-change-international-security-the-arctic-as-a-bellwether/ (Accessed: 28 February 2021).

Hulan, R. (2002) *Northern Experience and the Myths of Canadian Culture*. Montréal: McGill-Queen's University Press.

Humpert, M. (2013) *The Future of Arctic Shipping: A New Silk Road for China?* Washington, DC The Arctic Institute. Available at: http://issuu.com/thearcticinstitute/docs/the_future_of_arctic_shipping_-_a_n (Accessed: 27 May 2015).

Humpert, M. (2023) 'Norway Aims to Open Arctic Waters to Deep-Sea Mining', *High North News*, 13 June. Available at: https://www.high-northnews.com/en/norway-aims-open-arctic-waters-deep-sea-mining (Accessed: 20 June 2023).

Hylland Eriksen, T. and Neumann, I.B. (2011) 'Fra slektsgård til oljeplattform: Norsk identitet og Europa', *Internasjonal Politikk*, 69(3), pp. 413–436. Available at: https://doi.org/10.18261/ISSN1891-1757-2011-03-04.

Hyndman, J. (2004) 'Mind the Gap: Bridging Feminist and Political Geography through Geopolitics', *Political Geography*, 23(3), pp. 307–322. Available at: https://doi.org/10.1016/j.polgeo.2003.12.014.

Ilulissat Declaration (2008) *Arctic Portal*. Available at: https://arcticportal.org/images/stories/pdf/Ilulissat-declaration.pdf (Accessed: 13 July 2024).

I.MFA (2009) *Ísland á norðurslóðum* [*Iceland in the Arctic*]. Reykjavik: Icelandic Ministry of Foreign Affairs, Available at: http://www.utan rikisraduneyti.is/media/Skyrslur/Skyrslan_Island_a_nordurslodumm.pdf (Accessed: 1 June 2015).

I.MFA (2011) *A Parliamentary Resolution on Iceland's Arctic Policy*. Icelandic Ministry of Foreign Affairs. Available at: http://www.mfa.is/ media/nordurlandaskrifstofa/A-Parliamentary-Resolution-on-ICE-Arc tic-Policy-approved-by-Althingi.pdf (Accessed: 27 January 2013).

I.MFA (2021) *Iceland's Policy on Matters Concerning the Arctic Region*. Parliamentary Resolution 25/151. Reykjavík, Iceland: The Ministry of Foreign Affairs of Iceland. Available at: https://www.government.is/ library/01-Ministries/Ministry-for-Foreign-Affairs/PDF-skjol/Arctic%20 Policy_WEB.pdf (Accessed: 1 July 2023).

Ingimundarson, V. (2009) 'Iceland's Post-American Security Policy, Russian Geopolitics and the Arctic Question', *The RUSI Journal*, 154(4), pp. 74–80. Available at: https://doi.org/10.1080/03071840903216510.

Ingimundarson, V. (2011) 'Territorial Discourses and Identity Politics', in J. Kraska (ed.) *Arctic Security in an Age of Climate Change*. Cambridge: Cambridge University Press, pp. 174–190. Available at: http://ebooks.cambridge.org/ref/id/CBO9780511994784A020 (Acce ssed: 15 September 2013).

Jacobsen, J.K.S. (2015) 'North Cape: In the Land of the Midnight Sun', in N. Herrero and S.R. Roseman (eds) *The Tourism Imaginary and Pilgrimages to the Edges of the World*. Bristol: Channel View Publications Ltd, pp. 120–140.

Jensen, L.C. (2012) 'Norwegian Petroleum Extraction in Arctic Waters to Save the Environment: Introducing "Discourse Co-optation" as a New Analytical Term', *Critical Discourse Studies*, 9(1), pp. 29–38. Available at: https://doi.org/10.1080/17405904.2011.632138.

Jensen, Ø. (2011) 'Current Legal Developments The Barents Sea', *The International Journal of Marine and Coastal Law*, 26(1), pp. 151–168. Available at: https://doi.org/10.1163/157180811X541422.

Johnsen, I. (2015) 'Gifts Favour the Giver: Norway, Status and the Nobel Peace Prize', in B. de Carvalho and I.B. Neumann (eds) *Small State Status Seeking: Norway's Quest for International Standing*. Abingdon: Routledge, pp. 108–125.

Jones, A. (2024) '"Waging Word Wars": The "Emotionscape" of the United Nations Security Council and the Russian War in Ukraine',

Political Geography, 108. Available at: https://doi.org/10.1016/j.pol geo.2023.103032.

Jones, R. (2007) *People / States / Territories: The Political Geographies of British State Transformation*. Oxford: Wiley-Blackwell (RGS-IBG book series).

Jones, R. (2012) 'State Encounters', *Environment and Planning D: Society and Space*, 30(5), pp. 805–821. Available at: https://doi.org/10.1068/d9110.

Jones, R. and Merriman, P. (2009) 'Hot, Banal and Everyday Nationalism: Bilingual Road Signs in Wales', *Political Geography*, 28(3), pp. 164–173. Available at: https://doi.org/10.1016/j.polgeo.2009.03.002.

Jørgensen, M.W. and Phillips, L.J. (2002) *Discourse Analysis as Theory and Method*. London: SAGE.

Karlsson, G. (1994) 'When Did the Icelanders Become Icelanders?', in *Líf undir leiðarstjörnu (Man in the North-MAIN): ráðstefnurit*. Akureyri: Háskólinn á Akureyri, pp. 107–116.

Karlsson, G. (2000) *Iceland's 1100 Years: The History of a Marginal Society*. London: Hurst.

Karlsson, G. (2003) *The History of Iceland*. Minneapolis: University of Minnesota Press.

Kassianova, A. (2001) 'Russia: Still Open to the West? Evolution of the State Identity in the Foreign Policy and Security Discourse', *Europe-Asia Studies*, 53(6), pp. 821–839. Available at: https://doi.org/10.1080/09668130120078513.

Keskitalo, A. (2015) 'Velkommen til samisk nasjonaldag', *Nordlys*, 4 February.

Keskitalo, E.C.H. (2004) *Negotiating the Arctic: The Construction of an International Region*. London: Routledge.

Knecht, S. (2013) 'Arctic Regionalism in Theory and Practice: From Cooperation to Integration?', in L. Heininen, H. Exner-Pirot, and J. Plouffe (eds) *Arctic Yearbook 2013*. Akureyri: Northern Research Forum, pp. 164–183. Available at: http://www.arcticyear book.com/.

Knecht, S. and Keil, K. (2013) 'Arctic Geopolitics Revisited: Spatialising Governance in the Circumpolar North', *The Polar Journal*, 3(1), pp. 178–203. Available at: https://doi.org/10.1080/2154896X.2013.78 3276.

Koivurova, T. (2010) 'Limits and Possibilities of the Arctic Council in a Rapidly Changing Scene of Arctic Governance', *Polar Record*, 46(02), p. 146. Available at: https://doi.org/10.1017/S0032247409008365.

Koivurova, T. and VanderZwaag, D. (2007) 'The Arctic Council at 10 Years: Retrospect and Prospects', *University of British Columbia Law Review*, 40(1), pp. 121–194.

Konradsdóttir, U.B. and Nielsson, E.T. (2014) 'The West Nordic Council and the Arctic', in L. Heininen, H. Exner-Pirot, and J. Plouffe (eds) *Arctic Yearbook 2014*. Akureyri: Northern Research Forum, pp. 107–124. Available at: http://www.arcticyearbook.com (Accessed: 19 April 2014).

Kramvig, B. and Andersen, R.G. (2019) 'From Dreamland to Homeland: A Journey towards Futures Better than Pasts', in L. Kaganovsky, S. MacKenzie, and A.W. Stenport (eds) *Arctic Cinemas and the Documentary Ethos*. Bloomington: Indiana University Press, pp. 322–334.

Kraska, J. (2014) 'Governance of Ice-Covered Areas: Rule Construction in the Arctic Ocean', *Ocean Development & International Law*, 45(3), pp. 260–271. Available at: https://doi.org/10.1080/00908320.2014.929462.

Kristinsson, V. and Nordal, J. (eds) (1996) 'History and Culture', in *Iceland, the Republic*. Reykjavik: The Central Bank of Iceland, pp. 61–106.

Kristoffersen, B. (2015) 'Opportunistic Adaptation: New Discourses on Oil, Equity and Environmental Security', in K. O'Brien and E. Selboe (eds) *The Adaptive Challenge of Climate Change*. Cambridge: Cambridge University Press, pp. 140–159.

Kristoffersen, B. and Young, S. (2010) 'Geographies of Security and Statehood in Norway's "Battle of the North"', *Geoforum*, 41(4), pp. 577–584. Available at: https://doi.org/10.1016/j.geoforum.2009.11.006.

Krohn-Hansen, C. and Nustad, K.G. (eds) (2005) *State Formation: Anthropological Perspectives*. London and Ann Arbor, MI: Pluto Press (Anthropology, culture, and society).

Krupnik, I., Aporta, C., Gearheard, S., Laidler, G.J., and Kielsen Holm, L. (eds) (2010) *SIKU: Knowing Our Ice: Documenting Inuit Sea Ice Knowledge and Use*. New York: Springer.

Kuus, M. (2008) 'Professionals of Geopolitics: Agency in International Politics', *Geography Compass*, 2(6), pp. 2062–2079. Available at: https://doi.org/10.1111/j.1749-8198.2008.00172.x.

Kuus, M. (2013) 'Foreign Policy and Ethnography: A Sceptical Intervention', *Geopolitics*, 18(1), pp. 115–131. Available at: https://doi.org/10.1080/14650045.2012.706759.

Kuus, M. (2014) *Geopolitics and Expertise: Knowledge and Authority in European Diplomacy*. Chichester: Wiley-Blackwell.

Kuus, M. (2015) 'Symbolic Power in Diplomatic Practice: Matters of style in Brussels', *Cooperation and Conflict*, 50(3), pp. 368–384. Available at: https://doi.org/10.1177/0010836715574914.

Kymlicka, W. (2003) 'Being Canadian', *Government and Opposition*, 38(3), pp. 357–385. Available at: https://doi.org/10.1111/1477-7053.t01-1-00019.

Kymlicka, W. and Banting, K. (2006) 'Immigration, Multiculturalism, and the Welfare State', *Ethics & International Affairs*, 20(03), pp. 281–304. Available at: https://doi.org/10.1111/j.1747-7093.2006.00027.x.

Lackenbauer, P.W. (2011a) 'Conclusions: "Use It or Lose It," History, and the Fourth Surge', *The Calgary Papers in Military and Strategic Studies*. Edited by P.W. Lackenbauer, 4. Available at: http://cpmss.synergiesprairies.ca/cpmss/index.php/cpmss/article/view/20 (Accessed: 30 September 2014).

Lackenbauer, P.W. (2011b) 'Mixed Messages from an "Arctic Superpower"?: Sovereignty, Security, and Canada's Northern Strategy', *Atlantisch Perspectief*, 35(3), pp. 4–8.

Larsen, H. (2014) 'Discourses of State Identity and Post-Lisbon National Foreign Policy: The Case of Denmark', *Cooperation and Conflict*, 49(3), pp. 368–385. Available at: https://doi.org/10.1177/0010836713495000.

Larsen, J.N. and Fondahl, G. (eds) (2015) *Arctic Human Development Report: Regional Processes and Global Linkages*. Copenhagen: Nordic Council of Ministers. Available at: http://urn.kb.se/resolve?urn=urn:nbn:se:norden:org:diva-3809 (Accessed: 27 February 2015).

Larsen, K.S., Groberg, D.H., Krumov, K., Andrejeva, L., Kashlekeva, N., Russinova, Z., Csepeli, G., and Ommundsen, R. (1995) 'Ideology and Identity: A National Outlook', *Journal of Peace Research*, 32(2), pp. 165–179. Available at: https://doi.org/10.1177/0022343395032002004.

Larsson, C.-G. and Buljo, M.E. (2013) 'Unge om samisk identitet og valg', *NRK.no*, 9 April. Available at: http://www.nrk.no/sapmi/unge-om-samisk-identitet-og-valg-1.10978909 (Accessed: 24 July 2015).

Le Grand, J. (2003) *Motivation, Agency, and Public Policy: Of Knights and Knaves, Pawns and Queens*. Oxford: Oxford University Press.

Lempinen, H. (2016) *Arctic Bingo!*, *Arctic Centre: University of Lapland - Northern Political Economy Blog*. Available at: http://www.arcticcentre.org/blogs/Arctic-Bingo!/me32fvt0/39b6a050-6e85-46da-a64e-309027c601a3 (Accessed: 8 October 2017).

Lennox, P. (2012) 'Inuit Art and the Quest for Canadian Sovereignty', *The Calgary Papers in Military and Strategic Studies*, 5. Available at: http://cpmss.synergiesprairies.ca/cpmss/index.php/cpmss/article/view/39 (Accessed: 25 September 2014).

Livingstone, D.N. (1992) *The Geographical Tradition: Episodes in the History of a Contested Enterprise*. Oxford: Wiley-Blackwell.

Loftsdóttir, K. (2014) '"We Who Live in the Arctic Region": Iceland's Belonging in the Arctic', *Arctic Encounters: Researchers' Blog*, 27 February. Available at: http://www.arcticencounters.net/post.php?s=2014-02-27-we-who-live-in-the-arctic-region-icelands-belonging-in-the-arctic (Accessed: 3 May 2014).

Lomas, P. (2005) 'Anthropomorphism, Personification and Ethics: A Reply to Alexander Wendt', *Review of International Studies*, 31(02). Available at: https://doi.org/10.1017/S0260210505006480.

Mackey, E. (1999) *The House of Difference: Cultural Politics and National Identity in Canada*. London: Routledge.

Mann, M. (1984) 'The Autonomous Power of the State: Its Origins, Mechanisms and Results', *European Journal of Sociology*, 25(02), pp. 185–213. Available at: https://doi.org/10.1017/S000397560000 4239.

Mann, M. (1993) *The Sources of Social Power: Volume II The Rise of Classes and Nation-States, 1760–1914*. Cambridge: Cambridge University Press.

Manning, E. (2003) *Ephemeral Territories: Representing Nation, Home, and Identity in Canada*. Minneapolis: University of Minnesota Press.

Marcus, A.R. (1995) *Relocating Eden: The Images and Politics of Inuit Exile in the Canadian Arctic*. Hanover: University Press of New England (Arctic Visions). Available at: http://www.dartmouth. edu/~library/digital/publishing/books/marcus1995/ (Accessed: 10 October 2015).

Massaro, V.A. and Williams, J. (2013) 'Feminist Geopolitics', *Geography Compass*, 7(8), pp. 567–577. Available at: https://doi.org/10.1111/ gec3.12054.

Massey, D.B. (1993) 'Politics and Space/Time', in M. Keith and S. Pile (eds) *Place and the Politics of Identity*. London: Routledge, pp. 141–161.

Massey, D.B. (2005) *For Space*. London: SAGE.

Massey, D.B. (2006) 'Landscape as a Provocation: Reflections on Moving Mountains', *Journal of Material Culture*, 11(1–2), pp. 33–48. Available at: https://doi.org/10.1177/1359183506062991.

Mavroudi, E. and Holt, L. (2015) '(Re)constructing Nationalisms in Schools in the Context of Diverse Globalized Societies', in T. Matejskova and M. Antonsich (eds) *Governing through Diversity: Migration Societies in Post-Multiculturalist Times*. Houndsmills: Palgrave Macmillan (Global diversities), pp. 181–200.

Mayhew, S. (2015) 'Arctic', in *A Dictionary of Geography*. 5th edn. Oxford: Oxford University Press. Available at: http://www.oxfordref erence.com/view/10.1093/acref/9780199680856.001.0001/acref-9780199680856-e-174 (Accessed: 6 October 2019).

McCorristine, S. (2018) *The Spectral Arctic: A History of Ghosts and Dreams in Polar Exploration*. London: UCL Press.

Medby, I.A. (2014) 'Arctic State, Arctic Nation? Arctic National Identity among the Post-Cold War Generation in Norway', *Polar Geography*, 37(3), pp. 252–269. Available at: https://doi.org/10.1080/1088937X.20 14.962643.

Medby, I.A. (2015) 'Big Fish in a Small (Arctic) Pond: Regime Adherence as Status and Arctic State Identity in Norway', in L. Heininen, H. Exner-Pirot, and J. Plouffe (eds) *Arctic Yearbook 2015*. Akureyri: Northern Research Forum, pp. 313–326.

Medby, I.A. (2018) 'Sustaining the Arctic Nation-State: The Case of Norway, Iceland, and Canada', in U.P. Gad and J. Strandsbjerg (eds) *The Politics of Sustainability in the Arctic: Reconfiguring Identity, Time and Space*. Abingdon: Routledge (Routledge Studies in Sustainability).

Medby, I.A. (2019a) 'Language-games, Geography, and Making Sense of the Arctic', *Geoforum*, 107, pp. 124–133. Available at: https://doi.org/10.1016/j.geoforum.2019.10.003.

Medby, I.A. (2019b) 'State Discourses of Indigenous "Inclusion": Identity and Representation in the Arctic', *Antipode*, 4(51), pp. 1276–1295. Available at: https://doi.org/10.1111/anti.12542.

Medby, I.A. (2021) 'People, Politics, and Participation: What Can We Learn from the Barents Region?', *High North News*, 13 January. Available at: https://www.highnorthnews.com/en/people-politics-and-participation-what-can-we-learn-barents-region (Accessed: 6 March 2021).

Medby, I.A. (2023) 'An Articulation of Geopolitics Otherwise? Indigenous Language-use in Spaces of Arctic Geopolitics', *Area*, 55(1), pp. 18–25. Available at: https://doi.org/10.1111/area.12758.

Medby, I.A. and Barnes, J. (2022) 'Seasonal Geopolitics of the North Pole', *Arctic Relations*, 19 December. Available at: https://www.arctic-relations.info/seasonalgeopoliticsofthenorthpole (Accessed: 27 June 2023).

Medby, I.A. and Dittmer, J. (2021) 'From Death in the Ice to Life in the Museum: Absence, Affect and Mystery in the Arctic', *Environment and Planning D: Society and Space*, 39(1), pp. 176–193. Available at: https://doi.org/10.1177/0263775820953859.

Medby, I.A. and Thornton, P. (2023) 'More than Words: Geopolitics and Language', *Area*, 55(1), pp. 2–9. Available at: https://doi.org/10.1111/area.12817.

Mingels, G. (2014) 'Out of the Abyss: Looking for Lessons in Iceland's Recovery', *Spiegel Online*, 1 October. Available at: http://www.spiegel.de/international/europe/financial-recovery-of-iceland-a-case-worth-studying-a-942387.html (Accessed: 17 April 2014).

Mitchell, K. (2003) 'Educating the National Citizen in Neoliberal Times: From the Multicultural Self to the Strategic Cosmopolitan', *Transactions of the Institute of British Geographers*, 28(4), pp. 387–403. Available at: https://doi.org/10.1111/j.0020-2754.2003.00100.x.

Mitchell, T. (1991) 'The Limits of the State: Beyond Statist Approaches and Their Critics', *The American Political Science Review*, 85(1), pp. 77–96. Available at: https://doi.org/10.2307/1962879.

Mitchell, T. (2006) 'Society, Economy, and the State Effect [1999]', in A. Sharma and A. Gupta (eds) *The Anthropology of the State: A Reader.* Oxford: Wiley-Blackwell (9).

Mitzen, J. (2006) 'Ontological Security in World Politics: State Identity and the Security Dilemma', *European Journal of International Relations,* 12(3), pp. 341–370. Available at: https://doi.org/10.1177/1354066106 067346.

Moss, J.G. (1997) *Echoing Silence: Essays on Arctic Narrative.* Ottawa: University of Ottawa Press.

Mountz, A. (2004) 'Embodying the Nation-state: Canada's Response to Human Smuggling', *Political Geography,* 23(3), pp. 323–345. Available at: https://doi.org/10.1016/j.polgeo.2003.12.017.

Mountz, A. (2015) 'Political Geography II: Islands and Archipelagos', *Progress in Human Geography,* 39(5), pp. 636–646. Available at: https://doi.org/10.1177/0309132514560958.

Munton, D. and Keating, T. (2001) 'Internationalism and the Canadian Public', *Canadian Journal of Political Science / Revue canadienne de science politique,* 34(03), pp. 517–549. Available at: https://doi. org/10.1017/S0008423901777992.

Murphy, A.B., Bassin, M., Newman, D., Reuber, P., and Agnew, J. (2004) 'Is There a Politics to Geopolitics?', *Progress in Human Geography,* 28(5), pp. 619–640. Available at: https://doi.org/10.1191/0309132504 ph508oa.

Murray, M. (2018) 'The Struggle for Recognition: State Identity and the Problem of Social Uncertainty in International Politics', in M. Murray (ed.) *The Struggle for Recognition in International Relations: Status, Revisionism, and Rising Powers.* Oxford: Oxford University Press, pp. 29–52. Available at: https://doi.org/10.1093/oso/9780190 878900.003.0002.

Nansen, F. (1897) *Farthest North: Being the Record of a Voyage of Exploration of the Ship Fram 1893–1896 and of Fifteen Months' Sleigh Journey by Dr. Nansen and Lieut. Johansen with an Appendix by Otto Sverdrup, Captain of the Fram.* Westminster: Constable. Available at: https://www.gutenberg.org/files/30197/30197-h/30197-h.htm.

Neumann, I.B. (2001) *Mening, materialitet, makt: en innføring i diskur-sanalyse.* Bergen: Fakbokforlaget.

Neumann, I.B. (2005) 'To Be a Diplomat', *International Studies Perspectives,* 6(1), pp. 72–93. Available at: https://doi.org/10.1111/j.15 28-3577.2005.00194.x.

Neumann, I.B. (2007) '"A Speech that the Entire Ministry May Stand for," or: Why Diplomats Never Produce Anything New', *International Political Sociology,* 1(2), pp. 183–200. Available at: https://doi.org/10.11 11/j.1749-5687.2007.00012.x.

Niemi, E. (1993) 'Regionalism in the North: The Creation of "North Norway"', *Acta Borealia*, 10(2), pp. 33–45. Available at: https://doi.org/10.1080/08003839308580428.

N.MFA (2011) *The High North: Visions and Strategies*. Oslo: Norwegian Ministry of Foreign Affairs. Available at: http://www.regjeringen.no/upload/UD/Vedlegg/Nordomr%c3%a5dene/UD_nordomrodene_EN_web.pdf (Accessed: 28 March 2014).

N.MFA (2014a) *Norway's Arctic Policy*. Oslo: Norwegian Ministry of Foreign Affairs. Available at: https://www.regjeringen.no/globalassets/departementene/ud/vedlegg/nord/nordkloden_en.pdf (Accessed: 20 July 2015).

N.MFA (2014b) *The High North, Norwegian Ministry of Foreign Affairs Online*. Available at: http://www.regjeringen.no/en/dep/ud/campaigns/the-high-north.html?id=450629 (Accessed: 10 June 2014).

N.MFA (2021) *The Norwegian Government's Arctic Policy*. Oslo: Norwegian Ministry of Foreign Affairs. Available at: https://www.regjeringen.no/en/dokumenter/arctic_policy/id2830120/ (Accessed: 13 March 2021).

N.MTIF (2015) *Future North: Final Report from 'Knowledge Gathering – Value Creation in the North'*. Oslo: Norwegian Ministry of Trade, Industry and Fisheries. Available at: https://www.regjeringen.no/contentassets/8aa6fc353593499ea9e1a343fcb19600/final-report_future-north.pdf (Accessed: 20 July 2015).

Ó Tuathail, G. (1996) *Critical Geopolitics: The Politics of Writing Global Space*. Minneapolis: University of Minnesota Press.

Ó Tuathail, G. and Agnew, J. (1992) 'Geopolitics and Discourse: Practical Geopolitical Reasoning in American Foreign Policy', *Political Geography*, 11(2), pp. 190–204.

OED Online (2019) 'Arctic, adj. and n.', *OED Online*. 2019 edn. Oxford: Oxford University Press. Available at: http://www.oed.com/view/Entry/10461 (Accessed: 6 October 2019).

O'Farrell, C. (2005) *Michel Foucault*. London: SAGE Publications.

Offerdal, K. (2014) 'Interstate Relations: The Complexities of Arctic Politics', in R. Tamnes and K. Offerdal (eds) *Geopolitics and Security in the Arctic: Regional Dynamics in a Global World*. Abingdon: Routledge, pp. 73–96.

Osherenko, G. and Young, O.R. (2005) *The Age of the Arctic: Hot Conflicts and Cold Realities*. Cambridge: Cambridge University Press (Studies in Polar Research).

Oslund, K. (2011) *Iceland Imagined: Nature, Culture, and Storytelling in the North Atlantic*. Seattle: University of Washington Press.

Østhagen, A. (ed.) (2023) *Norway's Arctic Policy: Geopolitics, Security and Identity in the High North*. Cheltenham: Edward Elgar.

Özkirimli, U. (2000) *Theories of Nationalism: A Critical Introduction.* New York: Palgrave Macmillan.

Painter, J. (2006) 'Prosaic Geographies of Stateness', *Political Geography*, 25(7), pp. 752–774. Available at: https://doi.org/10.1016/j.polgeo.200 6.07.004.

Painter, J. (2010) 'Rethinking Territory', *Antipode*, 42(5), pp. 1090–1118. Available at: https://doi.org/10.1111/j.1467-8330.2010.00795.x.

Painter, J. and Jeffrey, A. (2009) *Political Geography: An Introduction to Space and Power.* Los Angeles, LA: SAGE.

Pálsson, G. (2000) *The Legacy of Vilhjalmur Stefansson, TheArctic.is.* Available at: http://www.thearctic.is/PDF/G%C3%ADsli%20um%20Vilj%C3%A1lm.pdf (Accessed: 25 May 2015).

Pálsson, G. (2004) 'Race and the Intimate in Arctic Exploration', *Ethnos*, 69(3), pp. 363–386. Available at: https://doi.org/10.1080/00141840420 00260053.

Pálsson, G. and Durrenberger, E.P. (1992) 'Icelandic Dialogues: Individual Differences in Indigenous Discourse', *Journal of Anthropological Research*, 48(4), pp. 301–316.

Pálsson, G. and Durrenberger, E.P. (1996) *Images of Contemporary Iceland: Everyday Lives and Global Contexts.* Iowa City: University of Iowa Press.

Pálsson, G. and Helgason, A. (1996) 'The Politics of Production: Enclosure, Equity, and Efficiency', in G. Pálsson and E.P. Durrenberger (eds) *Images of Contemporary Iceland: Everyday Lives and Global Contexts.* Iowa City: University of Iowa Press, pp. 60–86.

Peck, J. (2001) 'Neoliberalizing States: Thin Policies / Hard Outcomes', *Progress in Human Geography*, 25(3), pp. 445–455.

Pedersen, T. (2017) 'The Politics of Presence: The Longyearbyen Dilemma', *Arctic Review on Law and Politics*, 8, pp. 95–108.

Penrose, J. (2002) 'Nations, States and Homelands: Territory and Territoriality in Nationalist Thought', *Nations and Nationalism*, 8(3), pp. 277–297. Available at: https://doi.org/10.1111/1469-82 19.00051.

Pharand, D. (2007) 'The Arctic Waters and the Northwest Passage: A Final Revisit', *Ocean Development & International Law*, 38(1–2), pp. 3–69. Available at: https://doi.org/10.1080/00908320601071314.

Pierson, C. (2011) *The Modern State.* 3rd edn. London: Routledge.

Pile, S. and Thrift, N. (eds) (1995) *Mapping the Subject: Geographies of Cultural Transformation.* London: Routledge.

Pompeo, M.R. (2019) 'Looking North: Sharpening America's Arctic Focus'. *11th Arctic Council Ministerial*, Rovaniemi, Finland, 6 May. Available at: https://www.youtube.com/watch?v=6Bk8PeRBYcg (Accessed: 5 March 2024).

Potter, J. and Wetherell, M. (1994) 'Analyzing Discourse', in A. Bryman and R.G. Burgess (eds) *Analyzing Qualitative Data*. London: Routledge, pp. 47–66.

Powell, R.C. (2008) 'Configuring an "Arctic Commons"?', *Political Geography*, 27(8), pp. 827–832.

Powell, R.C. and Dodds, K. (eds) (2014) *Polar Geopolitics?: Knowledges, Resources and Legal Regimes*. Cheltenham: Edward Elgar.

PRC (2018) *Full text: China's Arctic Policy*. The State Council Information Office of the People's Republic of China. Available at: https://english.www. gov.cn/archive/white_paper/2018/01/26/content_281476026660336. htm (Accessed: 29 September 2024).

Pupchek, L.S. (2001) 'True North: Inuit Art and the Canadian Imagination', *American Review of Canadian Studies*, 31(1–2), pp. 191–208. Available at: https://doi.org/10.1080/02722010109481590.

Quinn, E. (2019) 'U.S. Stuns Audience by Tongue-lashing China, Russia on Eve of Arctic Council Ministerial', *The Independent Barents Observer*, 6 May. Available at: https://thebarentsobserver.com/en/arctic/2019/05/ us-stuns-audience-tongue-lashing-china-russia-eve-arctic-council-minis terial (Accessed: 5 March 2024).

Quinn, E. (2022) 'Canada Extends Continental Shelf Claim, Increasing Overlaps with Russia in Arctic', *The Independent Barents Observer*, 23 December. Available at: https://thebarentsobserver.com/en/arctic/2 022/12/canada-extends-continental-shelf-claim-increasing-overlaps-rus sia-arctic (Accessed: 30 July 2023).

Reuters (2023) 'Putin Discusses Russia's Claim to Giant Chunk of Arctic Ocean Seabed', 27 January. Available at: https://www.reuters.com/ world/europe/putin-discusses-russias-claim-giant-chunk-arctic-ocean-seabed-2023-01-27/ (Accessed: 5 March 2024).

Rimmer, M. (2016) 'Investing in the Future: Norway, Climate Change and Fossil Fuel Divestment', in G. Sosa-Nunez and E. Atkins (eds) *Environment, Climate Change and International Relations*. Bristol: E-International Relations Publishing, pp. 206–225.

Robert, Z. (2014) *Iceland Left out of EU Mackerel Deal, Iceland Review*. Available at: http://icelandreview.com/news/2014/03/13/iceland-left-out-eu-mackerel-deal (Accessed: 17 April 2014).

Robertson, A. (2023) 'Arctic Connections – Scotland's Growing Links with the Arctic: Ministerial Speech'. Scottish Parliament, Edinburgh, 2 March. Available at: http://www.gov.scot/publications/arctic-con nections-scotlands-growing-links-arctic/ (Accessed: 6 March 2024).

Rottem, S.V. (2020) *The Arctic Council: Between Environmental Protection and Geopolitics*. Singapore: Springer.

Sæþórsdóttir, A.D., Hall, C.M. and Saarinen, J. (2011) 'Making Wilderness: Tourism and the History of the Wilderness Idea in Iceland', *Polar*

Geography, 34(4), pp. 249–273. Available at: https://doi.org/10.1080/1 088937X.2011.643928.

Said, E.W. (1979) *Orientalism*. New York: Vintage Books.

Said, E.W. (2000) 'Invention, Memory, and Place', *Critical Inquiry*, 26(2), pp. 175–192.

Sannhet- og forsoningskommisjonen (2023) *Sannhet og forsoning*. Oslo: Sannhet- og forsoningskommisjonen. Available at: https://www. stortinget.no/globalassets/pdf/sannhets--og-forsoningskommisjonen/ rapport-til-stortinget-fra-sannhets--og-forsoningskommisjonen.pdf (Accessed: 5 June 2023).

Schiffrin, D., Tannen, D. and Hamilton, H.E. (2003) *Handbook of Discourse Analysis*. Oxford: Blackwell.

Scottish Government (2019) *Arctic Connections: Scotland's Arctic Policy Framework*. Edinburgh: Scottish Government: External Affairs.

Sharma, A. and Gupta, A. (eds) (2006) *The Anthropology of the State: A Reader*. Oxford: Blackwell (Blackwell readers in anthropology, 9).

Sharp, J.P. (1993) 'Publishing American Identity: Popular Geopolitics, Myth and the Reader's Digest', *Political Geography*, 12(6), pp. 491–503.

Shields, R. (1991) *Places on the Margin: Alternative Geographies of Modernity*. New York: Routledge.

Sizemore, B.A. and Walker, C.H. (1996) 'Literacy Identity and Literacy Practice', in G. Pálsson and E.P. Durrenberger (eds) *Images of Contemporary Iceland: Everyday Lives and Global Contexts*. Iowa City: University of Iowa Press, pp. 191–214.

Skagestad, O.G. (2010) *The 'High North': An Elastic Concept in Norwegian Arctic Policy*. FNI Report 10. Lysaker: Fridtjof Nansen Institute. Available at: https://www.fni.no/getfile.php/131978-1469869945/Filer/ Publikasjoner/FNI-R1010.pdf (Accessed: 10 June 2014).

Smith, K.E. (2006) 'Problematising Power Relations in "Elite" Interviews', *Geoforum*, 37(4), pp. 643–653. Available at: https://doi.org/10.1016/j. geoforum.2005.11.002.

Smith, S. (2020) *Intimate Geopolitics: Love, Territory, and the Future on India's Northern Threshold*. New Brunswick: Rutgers University Press.

Solli, P.E., Wilson Rowe, E. and Lindgren, W.Y. (2013) 'Coming into the Cold: Asia's Arctic Interests', *Polar Geography*, 36(4), pp. 253–270. Available at: https://doi.org/10.1080/1088937X.2013.825345.

Sörlin, S. (2013) 'Introduction: Polar Extensions - Nordic States and Their Polar Strategies', in S. Sörlin (ed.) *Science, Geopolitics and Culture in the Polar Region: Norden beyond Borders*. Farnham: Ashgate (The Nordic experience), pp. 1–19.

Sparke, M. (2005) *In the Space of Theory: Postfoundational Geographies of the Nation-state*. Minneapolis: University of Minnesota Press.

Sparke, M. (2009) 'Geopolitics', in D. Gregory, R. Johnston, G. Pratt, M.J. Watts, and S. Whatmore (eds) *The Dictionary of Human Geography*. 5th edn. Malden, MA: Wiley-Blackwell, pp. 300–302.

Squire, R. (2016) 'Rock, Water, Air and Fire: Foregrounding the Elements in the Gibraltar-Spain Dispute', *Environment and Planning D: Society and Space*, 34(3), pp. 545–563. Available at: https://doi.org/10.1177/0263775815623277.

Statistics Norway (2022) *Sami, Statistisk Sentralbyrå (SSB) / Statistics Norway*. Available at: https://www.ssb.no/en/befolkning/folketall/statistikk/samiske-forhold (Accessed: 3 July 2023).

Statistics Norway (2023) *Fakta om Svalbard - Statistisk sentralbyrå, SSB*. Available at: https://www.ssb.no/svalbard/faktaside/svalbard (Accessed: 30 July 2023).

Steele, B.J. (2008) *Ontological Security in International Relations: Self-identity and the IR State*. New York: Routledge.

Steinberg, P.E. (2014) 'Steering between Scylla and Charybdis: The Northwest Passage as Territorial Sea', *Ocean Development & International Law*, 45(1), pp. 84–106. Available at: https://doi.org/10.1080/00908320.2014.867193.

Steinberg, P.E. (2016) 'Europe's "Others" in the Polar Mediterranean', *Tijdschrift voor economische en sociale geografie*, 107(2), pp. 177–188. Available at: https://doi.org/10.1111/tesg.12176.

Steinberg, P.E., Bruun, J.M. and Medby, I.A. (2014) 'Covering Kiruna: A Natural Experiment in Arctic Awareness', *Polar Geography*, 37(4), pp. 273–297. Available at: https://doi.org/10.1080/1088937X.2014.978409.

Steinberg, P.E., Tasch, J. and Gerhardt, H. (2015) *Contesting the Arctic: Politics and Imaginaries in the Circumpolar North*. London: I.B. Tauris.

Steinveg, B. (2021a) 'The Role of Conferences within Arctic Governance', *Polar Geography* [Preprint], 44(1), pp. 37–54. Available at: https://doi.org/10.1080/1088937X.2020.1798540.

Steinveg, B. (2021b) 'Exponential Growth and New Agendas – a Comprehensive Review of the Arctic Conference Sphere', *Arctic Review*, 12, pp. 134–160. Available at: https://doi.org/10.23865/arctic.v12.3049.

Steinveg, B. (2023) *Arctic Governance through Conferencing: Actors, Agendas and Arenas*. Cham, Switzerland: Springer.

Steinveg, B. (2024) 'Small States in World Politics: Norwegian Interests and Foreign Policy Challenges in the Arctic', *Arctic Review on Law and Politics*, 15, pp. 3–24. Available at: https://doi.org/10.23865/arctic.v15.5125.

Steinveg, B. and Medby, I.A. (2023) 'Norwegian High North Narratives and Identity Construction in the North', in Andreas Østhagen (ed.)

Norway's Arctic Policy: Geopolitics, Security, and Identity in the High North. Cheltenham: Edward Elgar, pp. 109–120.

Stokke, O.S. and Hønneland, G. (eds) (2007) *International Cooperation and Arctic Governance: Regime Effectiveness and Northern Region Building.* Abingdon: Routledge.

Storey, D. (2001) *Territory: The Claiming of Space.* Harlow: Prentice Hall.

Strandsbjerg, J. (2012) 'Cartopolitics, Geopolitics and Boundaries in the Arctic', *Geopolitics*, 17(4), pp. 818–842. Available at: https://doi.org/10.1080/14650045.2012.660581.

Sumarliðason, E.Í. (2021) *Imagining an Arctic State: An Analysis of the Performance of the Icelandic State's Arctic Identity.* Master's thesis. Lund University. Available at: http://lup.lub.lu.se/student-papers/record/9065493 (Accessed: 15 June 2022).

Tajfel, H. (1978) *Differentiation between Social Groups: Studies in the Social Psychology of Intergroup Relations.* London: Academic Press.

Tjelmeland, H. (1996) 'Kva tid oppstod Nord-Norge. Regional-iseringsprosessar i Nord-Norge fram til ca. 1950', in B.-P. Finstad, L.I. Hansen, H. Minde, E. Niemi, and H. Tjelmeland (eds) *Stat, religion, etnisitet.* Tromsø: University of Tromsø (Skriftserie 4, Centre for Sami Studies).

Tønnesson, S. (2009) 'The Class Route to Nationhood: China, Vietnam, Norway, Cyprus – and France', *Nations and Nationalism*, 15(3), pp. 375–395. Available at: https://doi.org/10.1111/j.1469-8129.2009.00398.x.

UN (1987) *Our Common Future.* United Nations World Commission on Environment and Development. Available at: http://www.un-documents.net/wced-ocf.htm.

Valdimarsson, O.R. (2013) 'Iceland Pushes to Become Arctic Hub After Scrapping EU Accession', *Bloomberg*, 29 October. Available at: http://www.bloomberg.com/news/2013-10-29/iceland-pushes-to-become-arctic-hub-after-scrapping-eu-accession.html (Accessed: 17 April 2014).

Vannini, P., Baldacchino, G., Guay, L., Royle, S.A., and Steinberg, P.E. (2009) 'Recontinentalizing Canada: Arctic Ice's Liquid Modernity and the Imagining of a Canadian Archipelago', *Island Studies Journal*, 4(2), pp. 121–138.

Vasey, D. (1996) 'Premodern and Modern Constructions of Population Regimes', in G. Pálsson and E.P. Durrenberger (eds) *Images of Contemporary Iceland: Everyday Lives and Global Contexts.* Iowa City: University of Iowa Press, pp. 149–190.

Vassenden, A. (2010) 'Untangling the Different Components of Norw-egianness', *Nations and Nationalism*, 16(4), pp. 734–752. Available at: https://doi.org/10.1111/j.1469-8129.2009.00438.x.

Waage, E.R.H. and Benediktsson, K. (2010) 'Performing Expertise: Landscape, Governmentality and Conservation Planning in Iceland', *Journal of Environmental Policy & Planning*, 12(1), pp. 1–22. Available at: https://doi.org/10.1080/15239080903220112.

Wærp, H.H. (2010) 'Fridtjof Nansen, First Crossing of Greenland (1890): Bestseller and Scientific Report', in A. Ryall, J. Schimanski, and H.H. Wærp (eds) *Arctic Discourses*. Newcastle-upon-Tyne: Cambridge Scholars Publishing, pp. 43–58.

Wærp, H.H. (2014) 'Arktiske diskurser – mennesket i Arktis', *Nordlit*, 32, pp. 147–159.

Watt-Cloutier, S. (2015) *The Right to Be Cold: One Woman's Story of Protecting Her Culture, the Arctic and the Whole Planet*. Toronto: Allen Lane.

Weber, C. (1998) 'Performative States', *Millennium*, 27(1), pp. 77–95. Available at: https://doi.org/10.1177/03058298980270011101.

Weber, M. (1946) *Essays from Max Weber*. London: Routledge and Kegan Paul.

Wendt, A. (1992) 'Anarchy Is What States Make of It', *International Organization*, 46, pp. 391–426.

Wendt, A. (1994) 'Collective Identity Formation and the International State', *American Political Science Review*, 88, pp. 384–396.

Wendt, A. (1999) *Social Theory of International Politics*. New York: Cambridge University Press.

Wendt, A. (2004) 'The State as Person in International Theory', *Review of International Studies*, 30(02). Available at: https://doi.org/10.1017/S0260210504006084.

Wilson, P. (2016) 'Society, Steward or Security Actor? Three Visions of the Arctic Council', *Cooperation and Conflict*, 51(1), pp. 55–74. Available at: https://doi.org/10.1177/0010836715591711.

Wilson Rowe, E. (2018) *Arctic Governance: Power in Cross-border Cooperation*. Manchester: Manchester University Press.

Winter, E. (2007) 'Neither "America" nor "Québec": Constructing the Canadian Multicultural Nation', *Nations and Nationalism*, 13(3), pp. 481–503. Available at: https://doi.org/10.1111/j.1469-8129.2007.00295.x.

Wood-Donnelly, C. (2018) *Performing Arctic Sovereignty: Policy and Visual Narratives*. Abingdon: Routledge.

Woods, M. (1998) 'Rethinking Elites: Networks, Space, and Local Politics', *Environment and Planning A*, 30(12), pp. 2101–2119. Available at: https://doi.org/10.1068/a302101.

Woon, C.Y. (2015) '"Peopling" Geographies of Peace: The Role of the Military in Peacebuilding in the Philippines', *Transactions of the Institute of British Geographers*, 40(1), pp. 14–27. Available at: https://doi.org/10.1111/tran.12059.

Woon, C.Y. and Dodds, K. (eds) (2020) *'Observing' the Arctic: Asia in the Arctic Council and Beyond*. Cheltenham: Edward Elgar.

World Bank Open Data (2021) *Surface Area (sq. km)*, World Bank Open Data. Available at: https://data.worldbank.org (Accessed: 5 March 2024).

World Bank Open Data (2022) *World Bank Open Data: Population, total*, World Bank Open Data. Available at: https://data.worldbank.org (Accessed: 9 August 2023).

Wormbs, N. (ed.) (2018) *Competing Arctic Futures: Historical and Contemporary Perspectives*. London: Palgrave Macmillan.

Yaeger, P. (ed.) (1996) *The Geography of Identity*. Ann Arbor: University of Michigan Press (Ratio).

Young, O.R. (1985) 'The Age of the Arctic', *Foreign Policy*, 61, pp. 160–179. Available at: https://doi.org/10.2307/1148707.

Young, O.R. (2005) 'Governing the Arctic: From Cold War Theater to Mosaic of Cooperation', *Global Governance: A Review of Multilateralism and International Organizations*, 11(1), pp. 9–15. Available at: https://doi.org/10.5555/ggov.2005.11.1.9.

Young, O.R. (2009) 'Arctic in Play: Governance in a Time of Rapid Change', *The International Journal of Marine and Coastal Law*, 24, pp. 423–442.

Young, O.R. (2010) 'Arctic Governance – Pathways to the Future', *Arctic Review on Law and Politics*, 1(2), pp. 164–185.

Young, O.R. (2011) 'If an Arctic Ocean Treaty Is Not the Solution, What Is the Alternative?', *Polar Record*, 47(04), pp. 327–334. Available at: https://doi.org/10.1017/S0032247410000677.

Young, O.R. (2012) 'Building an International Regime Complex for the Arctic: Current Status and Next Steps', *Polar Journal*, 2(2), pp. 391–407.

Index

EU authorised representative for GPSR:
Easy Access System Europe, Mustamäe tee 50,
10621 Tallinn, Estonia
gpsr.requests@easproject.com